WITHDRAWN
From the
Dean B. Ellis Library
Arkansas State University

The Institute of Mathematics
and its Applications
Conference Series

The Institute of Mathematics
and its Applications
Conference Series

Previous volumes in this series were published by
Academic Press to whom all enquiries should be addressed.
Forthcoming volumes will be published by
Oxford University Press throughout the world.

NEW SERIES
1. *Supercomputers and parallel computation* Edited by D. J. Paddon
2. *The mathematical basis of finite element methods*
   Edited by David F. Griffiths
3. *Multigrid methods for integral and differential equations*
   Edited by D. J. Paddon and H. Holstein
4. *Turbulence and diffusion in stable environments* Edited by J. C. R. Hunt
5. *Wave propagation and scattering* Edited by B. J. Uscinski
6. *The mathematics of surfaces* Edited by J. A. Gregory
7. *Numerical methods for fluid dynamics II*
   Edited by K. W. Morton and M. J. Baines
8. *Analysing conflict and its resolution* Edited by P. G. Bennett
9. *The state of the art in numerical analysis*
   Edited by A. Iserles and M. J. D. Powell
10. *Algorithms for approximation* Edited by J. C. Mason and M. G. Cox
11. *The mathematics of surfaces II* Edited by R. R. Martin
12. *Mathematics in signal processing*
    Edited by T. S. Durrani, J. B. Abbiss, J. E. Hudson, R. N. Madan,
    J. G. McWhirter, and T. A. Moore
13. *Simulation and optimization of large systems*
    Edited by Andrzej J. Osiadacz
14. *Computers in mathematical research*
    Edited by N. M. Stephens and M. P. Thorne
15. *Stably stratified flow and dense gas dispersion*
    Edited by J. S. Puttock
16. *Mathematical modelling in non-destructive testing*
    Edited by Michael Blakemore and George A. Georgiou
17. *Numerical methods for fluid dynamics III*
    Edited by K. W. Morton and M. J. Baines
18. *Mathematics in oil production*
    Edited by Sir Sam Edwards and P. King
19. *Mathematics in major accident risk assessment*
    Edited by R. A. Cox
20. *Cryptography and coding*
    Edited by Henry J. Beker and F. C. Piper

Cryptography and coding

Based on the proceedings of a conference organized by The Institute of Mathematics and its Applications on Cryptography and Coding, held at the Royal Agricultural College, Cirencester on 15th–17th December 1986.

Edited by

HENRY J. BEKER
Zergo Consultants Ltd.

and

F. C. PIPER
Royal Holloway and Bedford New College

CLARENDON PRESS · OXFORD · 1989

Oxford University Press, Walton Street, Oxford OX2 6DP
Oxford New York Toronto
Delhi Bombay Calcutta Madras Karachi
Petaling Jaya Singapore Hong Kong Tokyo
Nairobi Dar es Salaam Cape Town
Melbourne Auckland

and associated companies in
Berlin Ibadan

Oxford is a trademark of Oxford University Press

Published in the United States
by Oxford University Press, New York

© *The Institute of Mathematics and its Applications 1989*

All rights reserved. No part of this publication may be reproduced,
stored in a retrieval system, or transmitted, in any form or by any means,
electronic, mechanical, photocopying, recording, or otherwise, without
the prior permission of Oxford University Press

British Library Cataloguing in Publication Data
Data available

Library of Congress Cataloging in Publication Data
Data available

ISBN 0-19-853623-2

Printed in Great Britain by St. Edmundsbury Press
Bury St. Edmunds, Suffolk

PREFACE

The Conference on Cryptography and Coding was held at the Royal Agricultural College, Cirencester, Gloucester on 15th - 17th December, 1986. It was sponsored and organised by the Institute of Mathematics and its Applications.

Both topics, Cryptography and Coding, are areas of mathematics that have developed with increasing momentum since their formalization by C. Shannon in the 1940s. The Communications Revolution, in particular, has made these disciplines of vital importance to modern day electronic computer networks.

Coding of information is predominantly concerned with ensuring that the data is in a form suitable for transmission and that the information can be protected from any errors that occur during its transmission. Cryptography, on the other hand, is a technique for ensuring the security of that information by ensuring its privacy, authenticity and its protection from deliberate alteration.

The aim of the Conference was to bring together mathematicians working in both cryptography and coding theory. The mathematical tools and techniques required for these two applications are similar. Yet, they tend to be treated as distinct disciplines and for many communications systems are applied as transformations to the data, in series. Within many of these applications there may be advantages in combining these processes. The result may produce both efficient and secure communications and storage of information with considerable cost benefits. This conference has begun the process of a better understanding between the cryptographers and coding theorists.

H.J. Beker
Zergo Consultants Ltd.

F.C. Piper
Royal Holloway and
Bedford New College.

ACKNOWLEDGEMENTS

The Institute thanks the authors of the papers, the editors, Professor H.J. Beker, AFIMA (Zergo Consultants Limited, Hampshire) and Professor F.C. Piper, FIMA (Royal Holloway and Bedford New College, Surrey) and also Miss Pamela Irving for typing the papers.

CONTENTS

Contributors

Coding for disparity and spectral control by J.J. O'Reilly	1
Mealy machines as coding devices by V.J. Rayward-Smith	13
The theory and generation of sets of uncorrelated digital sequences by M. Darnell	23
Information theory without the finiteness assumption, III: data compression and codes whose rates exceed unity by G.R. Blakley and C. Meadows	67
Adaptive product codes with soft/hard decision decoding by P.G. Farrell, B.K. Honary and S.D. Bate	95
Minimum weight decoding for cyclic codes by P.G. Farrell, M. Rice and F. Taleb	113
Embedded array coding for HF channels, theoretical and practical studies by M. Darnell, B.K. Honary and F. Zolghadr	135
Optimum binary words for frame synchronisation by M. Beale and R.T.C. Kwok	153
An overview of computer security by R.A. Kemmerer	163
An algebraic construction of sonar sequences using M-sequences by R.A. Games	175
Public-key cryptography and re-usable shared secrets by R.A. Croft and S.P. Harris	189
The GEC ic card: a reliable and secure token by N.A. McDonald and S.J. Sylvester	203
Encryption using random Boolean functions by M. Beale and M.F. Monaghan	219
Speech security and permanents of $(0,1)$ matrices by C. Mitchell	231

Digital multisignatures by C. Boyd   241

Smart cards for POS-banking by A.G. Kersten   247

Geometric structures as threshold schemes by   255
A. Beutelspacher and K. Vedder

Fast multiplicative inverse in modular arithmetic by   269
J. Gordon

Standards for data security by W.L. Price   281

Correlation analysis of cascaded sequences by D. Gollmann   289

CONTRIBUTORS

S.D. BATE; Department of Electrical Engineering, Coventry
    Polytechnic, Priory Street, Coventry, CV1 5FB.

M. BEALE; Department of Electrical Engineering, University of
    Manchester, Manchester, M13 9PL.

A. BEUTELSPACHER; Mathematics Institute, University of Giessen,
    Arndtstr 2, D6300, Giessen, West Germany.

G.R BLAKLEY; Department of Mathematics, Texas A&M University,
    College Station, Tx 77843-3368, U.S.A.

C.A. BOYD; British Telecom, Data Security Laboratory,
    St. Vincent House, 1 Cutler Street, Ipswich, IP1 1UX.

R.A. CROFT; Plessey Electronic Systems Research Limited,
    Roke Manor, Romsey, Hampshire, SO51 O2N.

M. DARNELL; Department of Electronic Engineering, University
    of Hull, Hull, HU6 7RX.

P.G. FARRELL; Department of Electrical Engineering,
    University of Manchester, Manchester, M13 9PL.

R.A. GAMES; The MITRE Corporation, Bedford, Massachusetts,
    01730, U.S.A.

D. GOLLMANN; University of Karlsruhe, Institut fur Informatik,
    Technologie-Fabrik, Haid-und-Neu-Str., 7, D-7500 Karlsruhe 1,
    West Germany.

J. GORDON; Cybermation, 144 Ashley Road, St. Albans,
    Hertfordshire, AL1 5JR.

S.P. HARRIS; Plessey Electronic Systems Research Limited,
    Roke Manor, Romsey, Hampshire, SO51 O2N.

B.K. HONARY; Department of Engineering, University of Warwick,
    Coventry, CV4 7AL.

R.A. KEMMERER; Department of Computer Science, University of
    California, Santa Barbara, California 93106, U.S.A.

A.G. KERSTEN; Siemens AG, Postfach 830953, D-8000 Munchen 83, Germany.

R.T.C. KWOK; Department of Electrical Engineering, University of Manchester, Manchester, M13 9PL.

N.A. McDONALD; GEC Card Technology, West Hanningfield Road, Great Baddow, Chelmsford, Essex, CM2 8HN.

C. MEADOWS; Information Technology Division, Naval Research Laboratory, Washington, D.C. 20375, U.S.A.

C. MITCHELL; Hewlett-Packard Laboratories, Filton Road, Stoke Gifford, Bristol, BS12 6QZ.

M.F. MONOGHAN; Department of Electrical Engineering, University of Manchester, Manchester, M13 9PL.

J.J. O'REILLY; School of Electronic Engineering Science, University College of North Wales, Dean Street, Bangor, Gwynedd, LL57 1UT.

W.L. PRICE; Division of Information Technology and Computing, National Physical Laboratory, Teddington, Middlesex, TW11 0LW.

V.J. RAYWARD-SMITH; School of Information Systems, University of East Anglia, Norwich, NR4 7TJ.

M. RICE; Department of Electrical Engineering, University of Manchester, Manchester, M13 9PL.

S.J. SYLVESTER; GEC Card Technology, West Hanningfield Road, Great Baddow, Chelmsford, Essex, CM12 8HN.

F. TALEB; Department of Electrical Engineering, University of Manchester, Manchester, M13 9PL.

K. VEDDER; GAO, Gessellschaft für Automation und Organisation, Euckenstr. 12, 8000 Munchen 70, Federal Republic of Germany.

F. ZOLGHADR; Department of Engineering, University of Warwick, Coventry, CV4 7AL.

CODING FOR DISPARITY AND SPECTRAL CONTROL

J.J. O'Reilly
*(School of Electronic Engineering Science,
University College of North Wales, Gwynedd)*

ABSTRACT

Line coding techniques which enable the disparity and spectrum of a digital line signal to be controlled by way of the introduction of redundancy into the transmitted signal are examined. An indication is provided of the problem of spectral analysis of line coded signal processes and it is noted that line codes may contain sufficient structure to enable a modest degree of error control to be achieved. This leads to the suggestion that the development of combined error control and line coding strategies may offer advantages compared with the cascade implementation of the two disparate functions and this is identified as an area well deserving of further research.

1. INTRODUCTION

Digital communication generally involves the transformation of a sequence of message vectors produced by the source into a waveform representation which is compatible with the available communication channel, as shown in Figure 1. In this paper we shall concern ourselves primarily with the lowest level of this coding hierarchy - line coding - placing particular emphasis on disparity and power spectral density considerations. Towards the end of the paper we examine briefly the prospects for combining the bottom two layers of our coding hierarchy to effect combined error control and line coding.

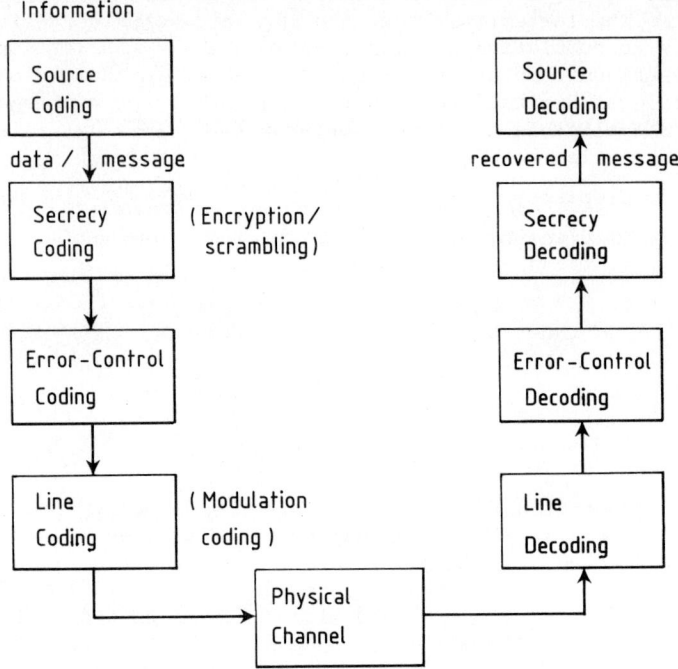

Fig. 1 Coding in Digital Communications

2. LINE CODING OBJECTIVES

The primary purpose of a line code is to render the signal compatible with the physical channel taking account, for example, of its frequency response. In particular, it is frequently required that the d.c. and low frequency content of the transmitted signal be suppressed and that there should be a sufficient density of signal transitions to facilitate recovery of symbol timing information. Further attributes may be desirable for specific applications. The main objectives may be summarised as [1]:

* d.c. suppression/disparity control.

* run-length limitation.

* introduction of in-band spectral nulls.

* adequate transition density for synchronisation.

* provision of error monitoring.

* provision of auxiliary signalling channel.

DISPARITY AND SPECTRAL CONTROL   3

In the above, we have linked d.c. suppression with disparity control. The latter involves ensuring that for binary signalling there is no cumulative imbalance between the number of 'ones' and 'zeros' transmitted and the idea is extended in the obvious way to multilevel digital transmission. A definition of disparity which is applicable to signals of arbitrary radix, r, is as follows [1]: let a_i be the ith digit with complement $\bar{a}_i = r-1-a_i$. The <u>digit</u> disparity is then $d_i = a_i - \bar{a}_i$. For a K-bit word the disparity is given by:

$$d = \sum_{i=1}^{K} d_i = 2 \sum_{i=1}^{K} a_i - K(r-1) \qquad (2.1)$$

It is readily shown that if the disparity is constrained such that the accumulated digital sum is strictly bounded then the line process exhibits a spectral null at d.c. and low frequency content is suppressed.

3. CODES WITH SPECTRAL NULLS

A spectral null at d.c. is achieved if and only if the running digital sum, RDS_o, is bounded.

$$RDS_o (\underline{a}) \triangleq \sum_{n=0}^{N} a_n \leq B_o, \quad \forall \underline{a} \equiv \{a_n\} \qquad (3.1)$$

A null at some other frequency $f=kf_s/m$, a rational submultiple of the signalling rate f_s, occurs if and only if:

$$|RDS_f (\underline{a})| \triangleq \left| \sum_{n=0}^{N} a_n \exp\{i2\pi kn/m\} \right| \leq B_f \qquad (3.2)$$

such that RDS_f has a finite range of values [3]. Codes with spectral nulls at specific frequencies lying between d.c. and the signalling rate find application in digital magnetic recording for which 'buried servo signals' for speed control are often encountered.

4. LOW DISPERSITY BLOCK CODES: REPRESENTATION AND ANALYSIS

Codes of this class, widely used for digital telecommunications transmission, involve a block of m p-ary digits being mapped into a block of L K-ary digits in accordance with an encoding rule which, in the general case, takes account of previous data. The potential information capacity of the input and output data blocks depends on the number of digits in the blocks and the size of the digit alphabets (the <u>radix</u>). For an (m,p) input and (L,K) output we have of necessity:

$$p^m \geq K^L \qquad (4.1)$$

if the mapping is to be information preserving.

5. REDUNDANCY AND EFFICIENCY

Generally the code design is based on a strict inequality for (4.1) and the possible number of output words exceeds the possible number of input words so that output word sequences can be constrained. Considering a general case, efficiency, E, may be defined in terms of input and output statistics:

$$E = \frac{H_K(S)}{<L>}$$

where $\qquad (4.2)$

$$H_K(S) = - \sum_i p(s_i) \log_K p(s_i)$$

is the entropy of the information source expressed in the K-ary (output) units.

$<L>$ = Average length of K-ary output codewords; $<L> = L$ for codewords of fixed length,

and S represents a source with Q distinct words $\{s_1, s_2, \ldots s_Q\}$.

The redundancy allows us to control RDS_o.

5. REDUNDANCY AND EFFICIENCY

Consider a binary sequence in which the 'ones' are designated as marks and the 'zeros' as spaces. We may render such a signal d.c. free by the simple expedient of inverting alternate marks, representing them as +1 and -1. Illustrative waveforms are presented in Figure 2 together with state transition diagram (STD). The STD indicates the disparity state - the net imbalance of the transmitted signal - we note that this code has just two states.

DISPARITY AND SPECTRAL CONTROL

Binary Data:

A M I Signal:

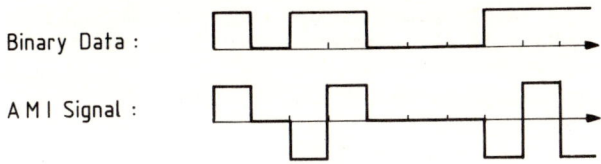

+1 increments the disparity
−1 decrements the disparity
0 does not alter disparity
+1s and −1s alternate ∴ 2 disparity states.

State Transition Diagram (STD)

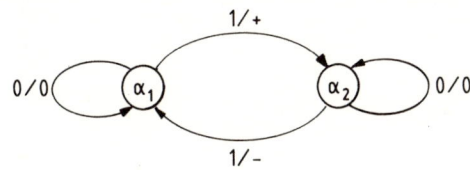

Note: Disparity is controlled but arbitrarily long runs of 0s can occur giving synchronisation difficulties. HDB_n inserts AMI 'violations' after n consecutive 0s.

Fig. 2 Alternate Mark Inversion (AMI) Line Code

While the disparity is very tightly controlled with AMI, so that d.c. and low frequency content is suppressed, arbitrarily long runs of zeros can occur. This can give rise to synchronization difficulties since it is effected by observing data transitions. To circumvent this difficulty a class of codes known as HDB_n, has been devised in which 'violations' of the alternative mark inversion rules are introduced after n consecutive zeros: Spurious marks of incorrect polarity are introduced in such a way that they can be recognised and removed in the receiver decoding process. The most common realisation uses n=3, the HDB_3 linecode.

4B3T Codes

Both AMI and HDB_3 are rather inefficient since individual binary input digits are mapped into individual ternary output digits. A class of binary-to-ternary codes known as 4B3T - in which blocks of 4 binary input digits are mapped into blocks of 3 ternary output digits - offers improved efficiency. A particular illustrative code table and STD is shown in Figure 3.

Input binary word	Output ternary word		
	RDS = -2	RDS = -1,0	RDS = +1
0000	+ + +	- + -	- + -
0001	+ + 0	0 0 -	0 0 -
0010	+ 0 +	0 - 0	0 - 0
0100	0 + +	- 0 0	- 0 0
1000	+ - +	+ - +	- - -
0011	0 - +	0 - +	0 - +
0101	- 0 +	- 0 +	- 0 +
1001	0 0 +	0 0 +	- - +
1010	0 + 0	0 + 0	- 0 -
1100	+ 0 0	+ 0 0	0 - -
0110	- + 0	- + 0	- + 0
1110	+ - 0	+ - 0	+ - 0
1101	+ 0 -	+ 0 -	+ 0 -
1011	0 + -	0 + -	0 + -
0111	- + +	- + +	- - +
1111	+ + -	+ - -	+ - -

STD:

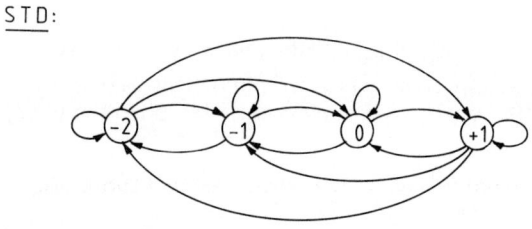

Fig. 3 MS43, An Illustrative 4B3T Line Code

6. DESIGN OF A PPM LINE CODE

Recently there has been some interest in the use of digital pulse position modulation for optical communications [4] and to facilitate synchronisation special PPM line codes have been devised [4]. The digital PPM signal format is illustrated in Figure 4. The primary objective of PPM line coding is to ensure that the short term running average position of pulses within the PPM frames is centralized. This facilitates synchronisation if a simple phase locked loop (PLL) circuit is used to extract the frequency and phase of the frame clock. Redundancy is introduced to ensure that pulses are not on average unduly biased early or late within a sequence of frames. Investigation has shown that on both efficiency and coder/decoder complexity grounds, there is little to be gained by choosing output block sizes of more than two frames. In particular, a

(9B 2-32) PPM line code - in which 9 bit binary words are mapped onto 2 PPM frames, each comprising 32 slots or possible positions for a single pulse per frame - has been shown to be close to optimum for wideband optical fibre transmission [3], whilst achieving an efficiency of 90% [4]

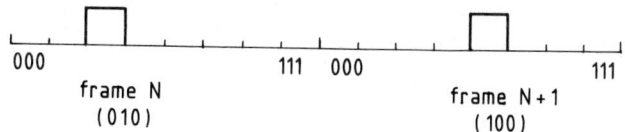

Fig. 4 Illustrative Digital PPM Signal Format

7. SPECTRAL CONSIDERATIONS FOR LINE CODES

Since codeword sequences are constrained by the linecoding process, correlations are introduced into the transmitted symbol sequence which gives rise in part to the structure of the spectrum - the other major factor being the form of the individual output words allowed for the code. While it is quite straightforward to show that a constrained disparity signal has zero d.c. and suppressed low frequency content, detailed evaluation of the code spectrum is rather less straightforward. For codes of the type described here, this may be effected via the Carriolaro and Tronca algorithm; we shall not give the details here but refer the reader to the literature [e.g. 6,7]. By way of illustration Figure 5 shows the code spectrum for the 9B2-32 line code mentioned previously. It should be noted that these spectra relate not to the PPM line <u>signal</u> but to the <u>line code</u> - that is to the effective modulation signal process, this being of critical importance for synchronisation purposes.

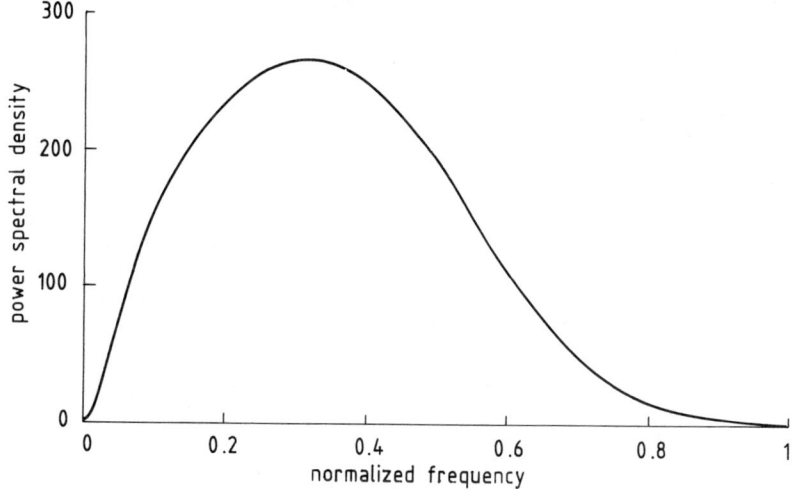

Fig. 5 Power spectral Density (PSD) for the 9B2-32 Line Code

8. COMBINED ERROR CONTROL AND LINE CODING

Up to this point, we have considered only the problem of line coding directed towards effecting disparity and spectral control. To achieve this it is necessary to introduce into the transmitted signal redundancy at a level which varies with the code selected, efficiency typically ranging from perhaps as low as 50% to 90%.

An entirely different form of coding which involves the deliberate introduction of redundancy is aimed at combating transmission errors: error control coding. Furthermore, in some instances it is appropriate to employ both error control and line coding so that the overall code rate or efficiency can be quite low. However, it is possible in principle to make use of the redundancy in a line code to achieve some modest degree of error control. Most commonly this is employed to achieve error monitoring [1] but use of soft decision techniques can allow a useful amount of error detection and correction to be effected for certain low rate (high redundancy) line codes such as AMI and HDB_3 [e.g. 8]. This naturally brings into question the possibility of combining error control and line coding with a view to achieving improvements in overall code rate. This is a research topic of current interest. Here we shall restrict ourselves to consideration of a very simple illustrative example, based on PPM transmission.

Consider analogue PPM transmission in which a signal is sampled and the value of each sample is conveyed over the channel as the position of the pulse in the corresponding PPM frame. Synchronization of this PPM sequence can be difficult since, as noted previously for the digital case, d.c. and low frequency information in the message will give rise to PPM pulses biased towards one or other extreme end of each of a potentially long sequence of frames. There is the likelihood that the synchronisation circuits employed at the receiver - often a phase locked loop - will drift towards this short term mean pulse location and result in loss of d.c. and low frequency information. This can be avoided by the simple transform coding arrangement shown in Figure 6. A set of (N-1) signal samples is viewed as the element vector of a discrete Fourier spectrum $X(1) .. X(N-1)$. This is augmented by the addition of a 'zero' in the $X(0)$ position to produce an N-element spectral vector $\underline{X}$ with a zero d.c. term, the message information being embedded in $X(1)$ to $X(N-1)$. If we now take the inverse discrete Fourier transform (DFT) we obtain a new vector $\underline{x}$. This, of course, contains zero d.c. content and can be transmitted over the PPM channel without fear of synchronisation problems: any sequence of such $\underline{x}$ vectors will be d.c. free. At the receiver the information may be recovered by taking the DFT of the received vector $\underline{x}$ to obtain $\underline{X}$, the message being $X(1)$ to $X(N-1)$.

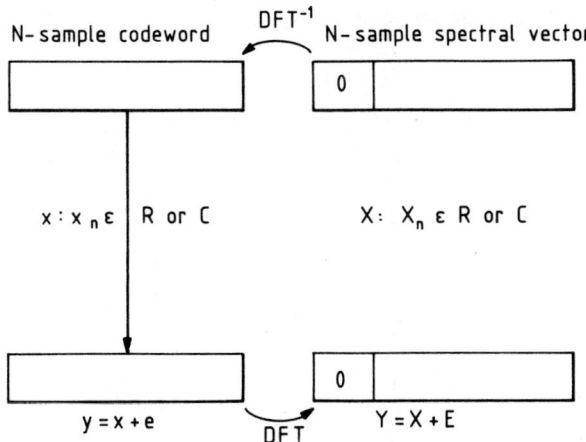

Fig. 6 Analogue Line Coding and Erasure Control Based on the DFT

Up to this point, what has been described is essentially an analogue PPM <u>line code</u>. It provides, though, a degree of error control in that if a PPM frame is recognised as erroneous - for example by having within it either no pulse, or more than one pulse - the correct signal sample can be deduced. We term such an erroneous PPM frame an <u>erasure</u> and the code provides for erasure correction. This may be achieved for this simple case in the time domain by simply setting the erased frame sample to the value required to render <u>x</u> to be d.c. free. Alternatively it may be effected by operating on the spectral vector and indeed, examination of $X(0) \neq 0$ is a means of detecting that a transmission error has occurred.

We have, in the above, glossed over many attributes of this coding scheme and also a number of practical difficulties with its implementation. Further details and useful extensions to provide error detection and correction based on use of the discrete Hartley transform are available elsewhere. Nevertheless, the outline given here provides an illustration of the general idea of combining error control and line coding - albeit for a perhaps somewhat idiosyncratic case. Other rather more practical examples have been devised and are now appearing in the literature [e.g. 10]. The power spectrum for a simple illustrative example of a binary-binary error correcting line code based on the Hamming [7,4] error control code, with relative rate 0.75, is shown in Figure 7.

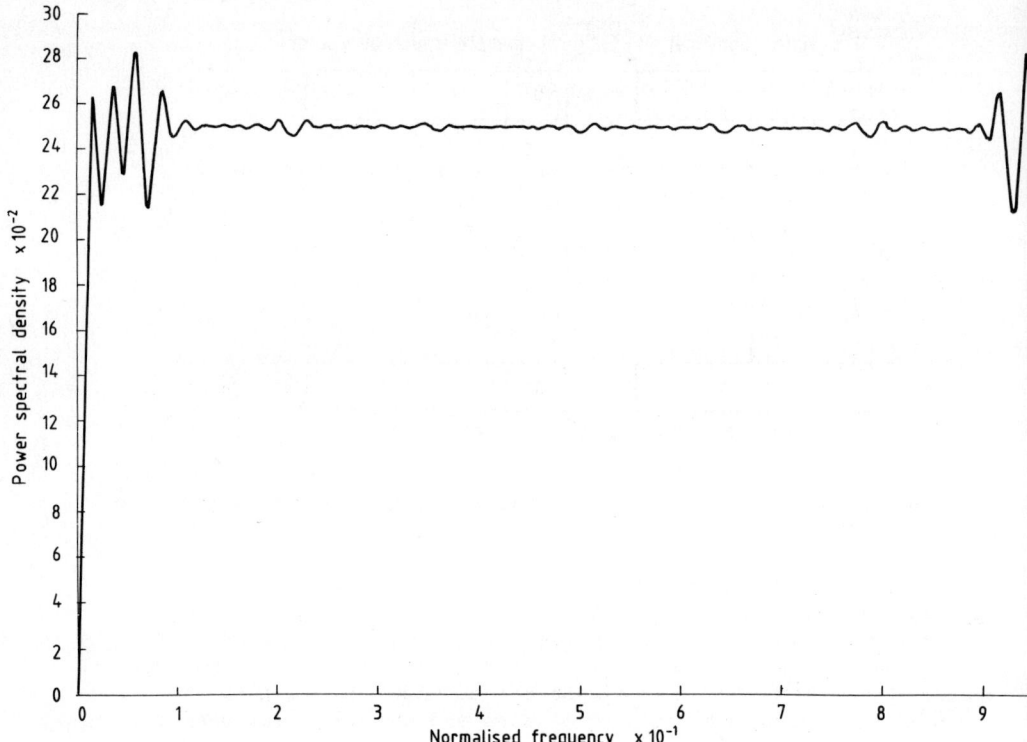

Fig. 7 Illustrative spectrum of an error-correcting line code based on the Hamming (7.4) error control code.

9. CONCLUDING REMARKS

This contribution has provided an introduction to some of the basic principles of line coding, emphasising disparity and spectral control. Since this involves the introduction of redundancy - much as does error control coding - the possibility of combining error control and line coding has been briefly considered. A simple analogue PPM coding scheme which achieves this desired combination has been presented essentially as an 'existence proof' indicating this as an appropriate topic for further research and reference to recent literature reporting progress has been provided.

REFERENCES

[1] Bylanski, P. and Ingram, D.G.W., (1976) Digital Transmission Systems, (Peter Peregrinus).

[2] Cattermole, K.W., (1983) Principles of Line Coding, *Int. J. Electronics,* Vol. 55, 3-33.

[3] Seigel, P., (1985) Code Design for Storage Channels, IBM Workshop on Signal Processing and Coding for Storage Channels, Paris.

[4] Garrett, I., (1983) Pulse Position Modulation for Transmission over Optical Fibres with Direct or Heterodyne Detection, IEEE Trans. Commun., COM-31, 518-527.

[5] O'Reilly, J.J. and Wang, Y., (1985) Line Code Design for Digital Pulse Position Modulation, Proc. IEE, Pt. F, 132, 441-446.

[6] Carriolaro, G.L. and Tronca, G.P., (1974) Spectra of Block Coded Digital Signals, IEEE Trans. Commun., COM-22, 1555-1564.

[7] Cattermole, K.W. and O'Reilly, J.J., (1984) Problems of Randomness in Communications Engineering, (Pentech, London/Wiley, New York).

[8] Hodges, M.R.L. and Jones, E.V., (1978) Soft Decision Decoding of Transmission Codes, Electron Lett., Vol. 14, 582-584.

[9] O'Reilly, J.J. and Monteiro. M., (1988) Further Links Between Signal Processing and Channel Coding with Special Reference to Optical Communications, in: Moscardini, A.O., and Robson, E.H., Mathematical Modelling for Information Technology. (Ellis Horwood).

[10] O'Reilly, J.J. and Popplewell, A., (1988) Design and Spectral Characterisation of Error Correcting Line Codes, Digest IEEE International Symposium on Information Theory, Japan.

MEALY MACHINES AS CODING DEVICES

V.J. Rayward-Smith
*(School of Information Systems,
University of East Anglia, Norwich)*

ABSTRACT

If a Mealy Machine satisfies a property which we define called the decodable property it computes an injective function and hence provides a sinple coding device. We show that a class of coding devices based on shift registers are all Mealy Machines satisfying this property. We also establish that, in general, the task of "cracking" a Mealy machine with the decodable property is NP-hard.

1. FINITE STATE AUTOMATA

A deterministic finite state automaton, A, is a 5-tuple (K, T, δ, k_1, F) where

(1) K is a finite state of <u>states</u>,

(2) T is a finite <u>input alphabet</u>,

(3) $\delta: K \times T \to K$ is a <u>transition function</u>,

(4) $k_1 \in K$ is a designated <u>start state</u>,

(5) $F \subseteq K$ is a set of <u>final states</u>.

By introducing a new (dummy) state, if necessary, the transition function can be made into a total function and, in this paper, we will thus assume that δ is total. The function δ is extended to a function $\delta: K \times T^* \to K$ by defining

$$\delta(k,\varepsilon) = k,$$

$$\delta(k,ax) = \delta(\delta(k,a),x), \quad a \in T, \; x \in T^*.$$

The set of strings accepted by a deterministic finite state automaton (DFSA), $A = (K,T,\delta,k_1,F)$, is then defined to be the language

$$L_A = \{x \in T^* | \delta(k_1,x) \in F\}.$$

The class of <u>regular</u> languages in T^* are precisely those languages accepted by some DFSA with input alphabet T. Regular languages have been well studied and their properties are well known [see, e.g. 2, 4]. In particular, there is an algorithm which given any regular language $L \subseteq T^*$ constructs a DFSA which accepts L with a minimum number of states.

DFSAs are generally represented as labelled digraphs. Each node represents a state and there is an arc from node k to node k' labelled with a $\in$ T iff $\delta(k,a) = k'$. The start state is distinguished by an arrow ↓ and the final state(s) by being in square boxes rather than circles. Figure 1 gives a simple example which accepts the regular language $\{01\}^* \{00\} \{0\}^*$. Note how k_4 is the dummy state acting as a "dead end" and is only necessary to make the transition function total.

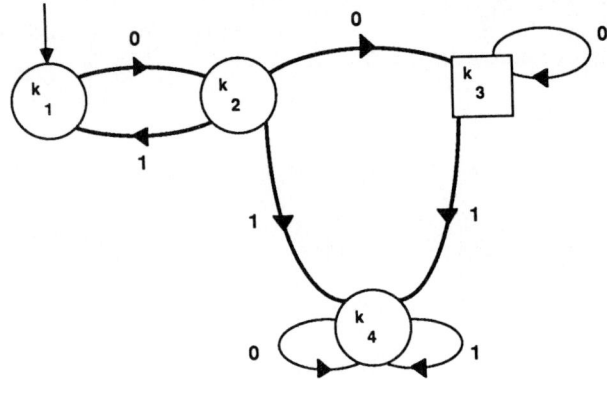

Fig. 1

Assuming the states of a DFSA are $K = \{k_1, k_2, \ldots, k_m\}$ and the input alphabet is $T = \{a_1, a_2, \ldots, a_n\}$, the transition function can be represented using an m x n integer array, Δ, with

$$\Delta[p,q] = r \text{ iff } \delta(k_p, a_q) = k_r.$$

This is the usual way of representing DFSAs in a computer.

There are two ways of extending DFSAs to include the concept of an output. Mealy machines are essentially DFSAs with outputs

MEALY MACHINES

associated with the transitions. Moore machines have outputs associated with the states. These two classes of machine are equivalent in the sense that any function computable by a Mealy machine is computable by some Moore machine and vice versa [2]. In this paper we concentrate on the Mealy machine.

2. MEALY MACHINES

A (deterministic) Mealy machine is a 5-tuple, $M = (K, T_1, T_2, \delta, k_1)$ where

(1) K is a finite set of <u>states</u>,

(2) T_1 is a finite <u>input alphabet</u>,

(3) T_2 is a finite <u>output alphabet</u>,

(4) $\delta: K \times T_1 \to K \times T_2$ is a (total) <u>transition function</u>,

(5) $k_1 \in K$ is a designated <u>start state</u>.

We will denote the first projection of δ by $\delta_1: K \times T_1 \to K$ and the second by $\delta_2: K \times T_1 \to T_2$. The function δ_1 is then extended to a function $K \times T_1^* \to K$ defining

$$\delta_1(k,\varepsilon) = k,$$

and

$$\delta_1(k,ax) = \delta_1(\delta_1(k,a),x), \quad a \in T_1, \quad x \in T_1^*.$$

δ_2 is extended to a function $K \times T_1^* \to T_2^*$ by defining

$$\delta_2(k,\varepsilon) = \varepsilon,$$

and

$$\delta_2(k,ax) = concat(\delta_2(k,a), \delta_2(\delta_1(k,a),x)), \quad a \in T_1, \quad x \in T_1^*.$$

It is then a routine exercise to show that

$$\delta_2(k,xy) = concat(\delta_2(k,x), \delta_2(\delta_1(k,x),y)) \text{ for any } x,y \in T_1^*.$$

Given an input of $x \in T_1^*$, the Mealy machine $M = (K, T_1, T_2, \delta, k_1)$ will result in an output of $f_M(x) = \delta_2(k_1, x)$. Note that $|x| = |f_M(x)|$ follows immediately from the definitions. Providing f_M is injective, Mealy machines provide a simple model of a coding device.

As with DFSAs, Mealy machines can be represented as labelled digraphs with nodes representing states and labelled edges representing transitions. Each such label is of the form i/o with $i \in T_1$, $o \in T_2$. We have an edge labelled i/o from a node representing k to node representing k' iff $\delta(k,i) = (k',o)$.

For example, consider the Mealy machine with $T_1 = T_2 = \{0,1\}$, $K = \{a,b,c\}$ with start state, a, and δ_1, δ_2 defined as in the tables below.

state transition table

δ_1	0	1
a	a	b
b	c	a
c	a	c

output table

δ_2	0	1
a	1	0
b	0	1
c	0	1

This is represented in the labelled digraph of Figure 2. For an input sequence of x = 0110, this Mealy machine will compute an output of $y = f_M(x) = 1011$.

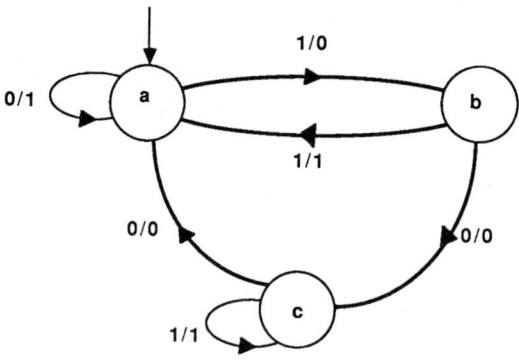

Fig. 2

In order to guarantee that the function f_M computed by M is injective we constrain M to satisfy the

<u>Decodable Property</u>: $\delta_2(k,i) = \delta_2(k,i') \Rightarrow i = i'$ for all $k \in K$.

The fact that δ is a function ensures that for each node k in the digraph representing M there are no two arcs leaving k with the same input label. We are now insisting that there are no two arcs leaving with the same output label. Figure 2 satisfies this property.

Providing a Mealy machine, M, satisfies the decodable property, we can easily construct the inverse machine, M^{-1}. We simply define $M^{-1} = (K, T_2, T_1, \delta^{-1}, k_1)$ where

$$\delta^{-1}(k,o) = (k',i) \text{ iff } \delta(k,i) = (k',o).$$

The decodable property ensures that δ^{-1} is a well defined (but possibly partial) function. As with DFSAs, it is always possible to ensure δ^{-1} is total by the addition of a new dummy state.

<u>Theorem 1</u>. $f_M(x) = z \Rightarrow f_M^{-1}(z) = x$

Proof: A simple induction argument on $|x|=|z|$ can be used to show that $\delta_2(k,x) = z \Rightarrow \delta_2^{-1}(k,z) = x$ for any $k \in K$. The result then follows.

We call a Mealy machine that satisfies the decodable property a <u>Mealy Coding Machine</u>. Theorem 1 has established that the corresponding decoding machine is simple to construct. Diagrammatically, it simply involves changing each arc label from i/o to o/i. For example, the decoder for the Mealy coding machine of Figure 2 is given in Figure 3. If the input sequence is 1011, the output sequence will be 0110.

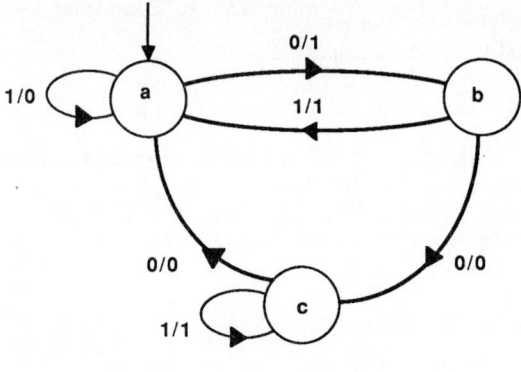

Fig. 3

It should be noted that the Decodable property is a sufficient condition for f_M to be injective but it is not a necessary condition. For example, the Mealy machine of Figure 4 computes an injective function but does not satisfy the decodable property.

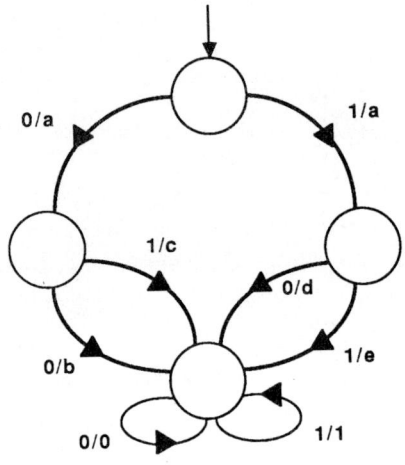

Fig. 4

3. SHIFT REGISTERS

A shift register used as an encoding device can be represented as in Figure 5. Each of $S_0, S_1, \ldots, S_{n-1}$ is a binary storage element called a <u>stage</u> of the shift register. At any given time their content is a vector in $\{0,1\}^n$ and this vector is called the <u>state</u> of the register. Thus, an n-stage shift register has 2^n possible states.

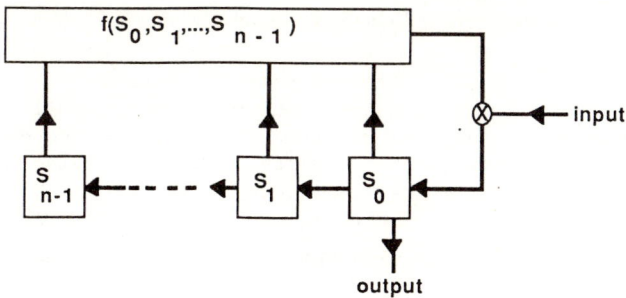

Fig. 5

At each time interval, the value of the feedback function $S = f(S_0, S_1, \ldots, S_{n-1})$ is calculated. Then the content is transferred to S_{i+1} for $i = 0, 1, \ldots, n-2$. The new value for S_0 is computed as a combination (usually exclusive or) of S and the input symbol, i. The new value of S_0 is also the output value. If the feedback function $f(S_0, S_1, \ldots, S_{n-1})$ is computed as the exclusive or of a selection of its parameters, the shift register is called <u>linear</u>.

As an example, consider the case where n = 3 and $f(S_0, S_1, S_2)$ = S_1 XOR S_2. Say $S_0 S_1 S_2$ = 011 and a 1 is input. The value of $f(S_0, S_1, S_2)$ = 1 XOR 1 = 0 which when exclusively ored with the input 1 results in a new value of S_0 = 1. Hence the output is 1 and the new state is $S_0 S_1 S_2$ = 101. This shift register is represented as a Mealy machine in Figure 6.

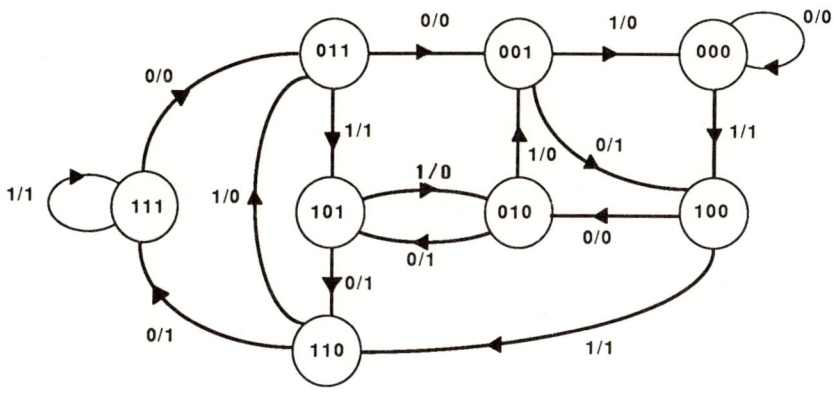

Fig. 6

Providing S is exclusively ored with the input symbol, the Mealy machine representing the shift register will satisfy the decodable property since $\delta_2(k,i) = \delta_2(k,i') \Rightarrow f(k)$ XOR i = $f(k)$ XOR $i' \Rightarrow i = i'$.

The decoder for such a shift register is thus easily constructed. We simply reverse the i/o labels in the Mealy machine. This corresponds to a shift register machine which behaves slightly differently from that of Figure 5. At each time interval, the value of $S = f(S_0, S_1, \ldots, S_{n-1})$ is calculated. The content of each S_i is then transferred to S_{i+1} for $i = 0,1,\ldots,n-2$ and S_0 is the given input. The resulting output is the exclusive or of S and this input. Although this result is well known [1], it is easier to understand if approached via the Mealy coding machine.

4. THE NP-COMPLETENESS RESULT

In this section, we establish the NP-completeness of the following problem.

MINIMUM INFERRED MEALY CODING MACHINE (MIMCM)

INSTANCE: Finite alphabets T_1 and T_2, finite set $S \subset T_1^* \times T_2^*$, positive integer, n.

QUESTION: Is there a Mealy coding machine, M, with n states such that for all $(x,y) \in S$, $y = f_M(x)$?

<u>Theorem 2</u>   MIMCM is NP-complete.

Proof: MIMCM $\in$ NP since, if $n \leq \Sigma \{\text{length } (x) \mid (x,y) \in S\}$, we can simply guess the structure of a Mealy machine with n states, input alphabet, T_1, output alphabet, T_2, and, in polynomial time, check that each $(x,y) \in S$ satisfies $y = f_M(x)$. If $n > \Sigma \{\text{length } (x) \mid (x,y) \in S\}$, then the problem instance can be solved in polynomial time on a deterministic machine.

To show MIMCM is NP-complete, we exhibit a polynomial transformation from the following problem already known to be NP-complete [3].

MINIMUM INFERRED FINITE STATE AUTOMATON (MIFSA).

INSTANCE: A finite alphabet, T, and two subsets $L_1, L_2 \subset T^*$, a positive intger, m.

QUESTION: Is there an m-state deterministic finite state automaton, A, which accepts a language $L \subset T^*$ such that $L_1 \subset L$ and $L_2 \subset T^* - L$?

To show MIFSA $\propto$ MIMCM, we construct an instance $f(I) \in D_{MIMCM}$ from an instance $I \in D_{MIFSA}$ as follows.

If I comprises T, L_1, L_2 and m then $f(I)$ has:

alphabets $T_1 = T \cup \{\$\}$ and $T_2 = T \cup \{\bar{0},\bar{1}\}$ where $\$,\bar{0},\bar{1}$ are new symbols $\notin T$;

a finite set $S \subset T_1^* \times T_2^*$ where

(x,y) $\in$ S iff either $x = w\$$ and $y = w\bar{1}$ where $w \in L_1$

or $x = w\$$ and $y = w\bar{0}$ where $w \in L_2$;

and

a positive integer $n = m$.

f can clearly be computed in polynomial time so all we need to do to complete the proof is show that $I \in Y_{MIFSA} \Leftrightarrow f(I) \in Y_{MIMCM}$.

$\Rightarrow$: Say $A = (K,T,\delta,F,k_1)$ is a DFSA with n states that accepts strings in L_1 and rejects strings in L_2. From A, construct the Mealy machine $M = (K,T_1,T_2,\delta',k_1)$

where $\delta'(k,a) = (\delta(k,a),a)$ if $a \in T$

and $\delta'(k,\$) = \begin{cases} (k,\bar{1}) & \text{if } k \in F, \\ (k,\bar{0}) & \text{if } k \notin F. \end{cases}$

M is an n state Mealy coding machine where for all (x,y) $\in$ S, $y = f_M(x)$. Thus $f(I) \in Y_{MIMCM}$.

$\Leftarrow$: Let $M = (K,T_1,T_2,\delta,k_1)$ be a Mealy coding machine with n states such that $y = f_M(x)$ for all (x,y) $\in$ S. Construct an n state DFSA, A, as follows. $A = (K,T,\delta',k_1,F)$ where $\delta'(k,a) = \delta_1(k,a)$ for all $a \in T$ and $F = \{k' \in K | \exists k \in K \text{ s.t. } \delta(k',\$) = (k,\bar{1})\}$. It is easy to verify that A accept L_1 but rejects L_2.

The fact that MIMCM is NP-complete shows that it is, in general, a hard problem to "crack" a Mealy coding machine, i.e. given a sample set of inputs and corresponding outputs, the problem of correctly inferring the transition function is hard. This does not, of course, mean that every Mealy coding machine is unbreakable. It just implies that there is no universally applicable, polynomial time algorithm for the task.

REFERENCES

[1] Beker, H. and Piper, F., (1982) "Cipher Systems: the Protection of Communication", Northwood, London.

[2] Eilenberg, S., (1974) "Automata, Languages and Machines," Academic Press, New York.

[3] Pfleeger, C.F., (1973) State reduction in incompletely specified finite-state machines, *IEEE Trans. Computers*. C-22, 1099-1102.

[4] Rayward-Smith, V.J., (1983) "A First Course in Formal Language Theory", Blackwell Scientific, Oxford.

THE THEORY AND GENERATION OF SETS OF UNCORRELATED DIGITAL SEQUENCES

M. Darnell
(Department of Electronic Engineering, University of Hull)

ABSTRACT

In many communications applications, requirements exist for limited sets of uncorrelated digital sequences with defined characteristics. Examples of such applications include data transmission, synchronisation and code division multiple access (CDMA) systems. The paper attempts to provide a comprehensive discussion of the theory and generation of sets of such sequences.

A distinction is made initially between "orthogonal" and "uncorrelated" sets of sequences. The necessary time and frequency domain conditions for uncorrelatedness are then developed and illustrated by means of specific examples.

In many applications, it is also important that the members of the set, in addition to having low or zero crosscorrelation, should also have approximately 2-valued (impulsive) autocorrelation functions. This latter property facilitates the detection of each member of the set by means of matched filtering. Sequences of various types, eg. maximum-length (m) sequences, and inverse - repeat sequences, having appropriate autocorrelation functions are considered.

Four methods of producing limited sets of uncorrelated sequences, all with approximately impulsive autocorrelation functions, are then discussed:

(i) the use of binary m-sequences in conjunction with Hadamard matrices;

(ii) the use of phase - locked loops (PLL's) to synchronise sequence periods in predetermined ratios:

(iii) the use of a sequence expansion technique;

(iv) selection of specific sequences with appropriate properties from a library of binary and multi-level sequences, and combining methods (i), (ii) and (iii) above.

Consideration is given to the form of the equivalent sequence generators and synchronisation schemes for the various synthesis methods with a view to minimisation of complexity.

Whereas the techniques discussed initially relate essentially to sets of periodic sequences, it is also possible to synthesize completely uncorrelated sets of aperiodic sequences. The most useful types of aperiodic sequences, from the viewpoint of their autocorrelation properties, are Golay's complementary sequences. Non-periodic sequence sets of this type have certain advantages over periodic sets: specifically, they can be employed as the basis of pulse compression waveforms. The principles and properties of sets cf complementary sequences will be outlined and methods of generation indicated.

Finally, the attention is turned to a discussion of the applications of uncorrelated sequence sets - both periodic and aperiodic. These applications include system identification and multiple-access techniques in communication systems.

1. INTRODUCTION

Over the past three decades, pseudorandom (PR) sequences of various types have found wide practical application, particularly in the fields of communication and control engineering [1],[2]. In the former, they are used for data encoding, synchronisation and spectrum - spreading purposes whilst, in the latter area, they have tended to be used primarily as test signals for the identification of the parameters of unknown linear systems by means of correlation processing. The majority of applications in both fields require that the autocorrelation functions (ACF's) of the PR sequences are approximately impulsive in nature.

In this paper, attention is concentrated upon the problem of synthesising sets of uncorrelated PR sequences, ie. the crosscorrelation functions (CCF's) between all members of the set are zero. In addition, a requirement is imposed whereby the ACF of each member of the set should be approximately 2 - valued (impulsive) - at least for a specified range of delay.

2. DEFINITIONS

A number of definitions, required in the subsequent discussion, will now be presented.

2.1 Randomness and Pseudorandomness

The three major characteristics of truly random binary sequences of 1's and 0's may be summarised as follows [3]:

(a) that the numbers of 1's and 0's in group of N digits (N very large) are approximately equal, i.e.

$$\underset{N\to\infty}{\text{Limit}} \left[\frac{\Sigma\ 1's}{\Sigma\ 0's} \right] = 1 \qquad (1)$$

(b) that in a group of N digits (N very large), the probability of finding a "run" of i digits of the same type is approximately twice that of finding a run of (i + 1) digits, ie.

$$\underset{N\to\infty}{\text{Limit}} \left[\frac{\Sigma\ \text{Run}(i)}{\Sigma\ \text{Run}(i+1)} \right] = 2 \qquad (2)$$

(c) that if '1' is transformed to '-1' and '0' to '+1', then the ACF, $\phi(r)$, of a transformed sequence, x_k, of (2j+1) digits ((2j+1) very large) is approximately 2-valued, ie.

$$\phi(r) = \underset{j\to\infty}{\text{Limit}} \frac{1}{(2j+1)} \sum_{k=-j}^{+j} x_k x_{k+r} \qquad (3)$$

$$= \left. \begin{array}{l} 0;\ r \neq 0 \\ +1;\ r = 0 \end{array} \right\} \qquad (4)$$

where r is a discrete shift, variable in units of one digit position. In the above N, i, j, k and r are all integers.

Pseudorandom binary sequences have properties which, to a large extent, replicate those of truly random binary sequences given above.

2.2 Ideal & Quasi - Ideal Autocorrelation Functions

For the purposes of this discussion, an "ideal" ACF for a periodic PR sequence, $\phi_{ii}(r)$, is defined as [4]

$$\phi_{ii}(r) = \left. \begin{array}{l} + P_N;\ r = 0 (\text{modulo-N}) \\ 0;\ \text{otherwise} \end{array} \right\} \qquad (5)$$

where N is the number of digits in one sequence period (N can be odd or even) and P_N is the peak value of the ACF.

The term "ideal" will also be applied to ACF's of M - digit sequences (M even) having the form:

$$\phi_{ii}(r) = \begin{cases} +P_M; & r = 0\,(\text{modulo-}M) \\ -P_M; & r = M/2\,(\text{modulo-}M) \\ 0; & \text{otherwise} \end{cases} \qquad (6)$$

where P_M is the peak value of the ACF. The ACF's of expressions (5) and (6) correspond to the best possible approximations to the ACF of truly random sequences which can be obtained with deterministic periodic signals.

With practical transformed sequences - as opposed to the original number sequences - it is appropriate to use a continuous ACF delay variable τ; the function $\phi_{ii}(\tau)$, defined at all values of τ, is derived simply by joining the discrete values of $\phi_{ii}(r)$ by straight lines. The delay interval between the points of $\phi_{ii}(r)$ is taken to be Δt, the clock interval of the transformed PR sequence.

Figs. 1(a) and (b) show the ideal ACF's of expressions (5) & (6) respectively, as functions of the continuous delay variable τ.

Figs 2(a) and (b) illustrate what will be termed "quasi-ideal" ACF's, described respectively by the expressions

$$\begin{cases} \phi_{qq}(r) = +Q_N; & r = 0\,(\text{modulo-}N) \\ |\phi_{qq}(r)| \leq \alpha; & \text{otherwise } (\alpha << Q_N) \end{cases} \qquad (7)$$

where N can be odd or even, and

$$\begin{cases} \phi_{qq}(r) = +Q_M; & r = 0\,(\text{modulo-}M) \\ \phantom{\phi_{qq}(r) =} -Q_M; & r = M/2\,(\text{modulo-}M) \\ |\phi_{qq}(r)| \leq \beta; & \text{otherwise } (\beta << Q_M) \end{cases} \qquad (8)$$

where M is even.

α and β are practical bounds on the off-peak ACF which can be specified to match the requirements of a particular application. The off-peak ACF need not be uniform, providing that it always lies within the ±α, ±β limits.

In the following sections of this paper, only PR sequences with ideal, or quasi-ideal, ACF's will be considered.

2.3 Level Transformations

Basic PR sequences comprise sequences of all - positive integer numbers. However, in the applications mentioned in Section 1, sequences of both positive and negative numbers, with appropriate ACF properties, are required. In order to produce these latter sequences, it is necessary to apply a level transformation to the all-positive integer sequences [5]. Both integer and non-integer transformations have been developed: Table 1 below defines the most widely - used integer transformation.

Table 1

Integer Level Transformation

ALL - POSITIVE SEQUENCE ELEMENTS	TRANSFORMED SEQUENCE LEVELS					
	P = 2	p = 3	p = 5	p = 7	. . . . .	p
0	+1	0	0	0		0
1	-1	+1	+2	+3		+(p-1)/2
2		-1	+1	+2		+(p-3)/2
3			-1	+1		+(p-5)/2
4			-2	-1		.
5				-2		.
6				-3		.
7						.
.						.
.						.
.						.
.						.
p-3						-(p-5)/2
p-2						-(p-3)/2
p-1						-(p-1)/2

The above enables p-level maximum-length (m) integer sequences to be transformed into p-level sequences of positive and negative integers (p prime ≥ 2).

An example of a non-integer transformation, also applicable to p-level m-sequences, is one in which an integer, q, in the range 0, 1, 2,....(p-1) is transformed sinusoidally, i.e.

$$q \rightarrow \sin\left(\frac{2\pi q}{p}\right) \qquad (9)$$

2.4 Orthogonality and Uncorrelatedness

The distinction between the terms "orthogonal" and "uncorrelated" will be illustrated by means of a specific example. Consider a set of Walsh functions [6] (a) to (h) below:

$$\begin{array}{lrrrrrrrr}
(a) & +1 & +1 & +1 & +1 & +1 & +1 & +1 & +1 \\
(b) & +1 & -1 & +1 & -1 & +1 & -1 & +1 & -1 \\
(c) & +1 & +1 & -1 & -1 & +1 & +1 & -1 & -1 \\
(d) & +1 & -1 & -1 & +1 & +1 & -1 & -1 & +1 \\
(e) & +1 & +1 & +1 & +1 & -1 & -1 & -1 & -1 \\
(f) & +1 & -1 & +1 & -1 & -1 & +1 & -1 & +1 \\
(g) & +1 & +1 & -1 & -1 & -1 & -1 & +1 & +1 \\
(h) & +1 & -1 & -1 & +1 & -1 & +1 & +1 & -1
\end{array} \qquad (10)$$

Taking the product between corresponding digits in any two rows and summing the result over 8 digits always produces a zero sum; thus, all rows are orthogonal.

Crosscorrelation involves introducing a variable delay between the two functions being correlated. Rows (c) and (d), rows (e) and (g), and rows (f) and (h) are simple phase-shifts of each other; therefore, these pairs of rows cannot be uncorrelated over all relative shifts. Row (a) is uncorrelated with all other rows; similarly, rows (b) and (c) rows (c) and (e), and rows (b) and (e) are also completely uncorrelated.

Hence, it is important to appreciate that orthogonality does not necessarily imply uncorrelatedness.

3. CONDITIONS FOR SEQUENCES TO BE UNCORRELATED

Any periodic function of time can be specified in the frequency domain by means of a Fourier series. Such a series describes a discrete spectrum in which energy is concentrated only at frequencies which are harmonics of the fundamental repetition frequency of the periodic function [7].

A periodic PR sequence with no embedded symmetry will in general have discrete, or "line", components at the following frequencies:

$$0, \ 1/_{N\Delta t}, \ 2/_{N\Delta t}, \ 3/_{N\Delta t}, \ \ldots \ldots, \ 1/_{\Delta t}, \ (N+1)/_{N\Delta t}, \ \ldots \quad (11)$$

The ACF for such a sequence would be of the form illustrated in Figs 1(a) and 2(a), where N is odd or even and Δt is the clock interval.

For periodic sequences with ACF's of the form shown in Figs. 1(b) and 2(b) and M even, the spectral components are:

$$1/_{M\Delta t}, \ 3/_{M\Delta t}, \ 5/_{M\Delta t}, \ \ldots (M-1)/M_{\Delta t}, \ (M+1)/M_{\Delta t} \ \ldots \quad (12)$$

i.e. only odd harmonic components of the fundamental repetition frequency are present. This arises from the fact that time domain waveform has half-wave, or rotational, symmetry - as exemplified in Fig. 3, where in the second - half period is the inverse of the first - half period; this is also referred to as "inverse-repeat" symmetry [5].

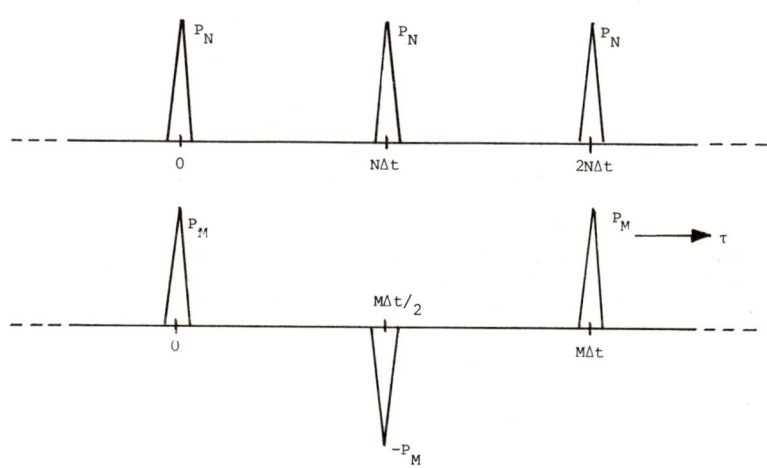

Fig. 1 Examples of "ideal" acf's

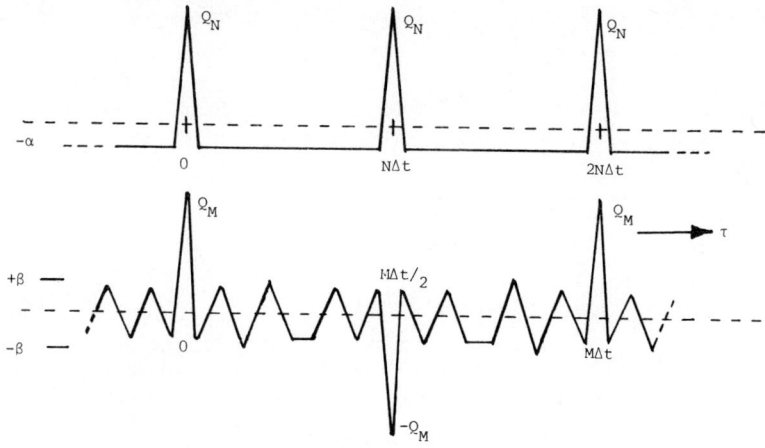

Fig. 2 Examples of "quasi-ideal" acf's

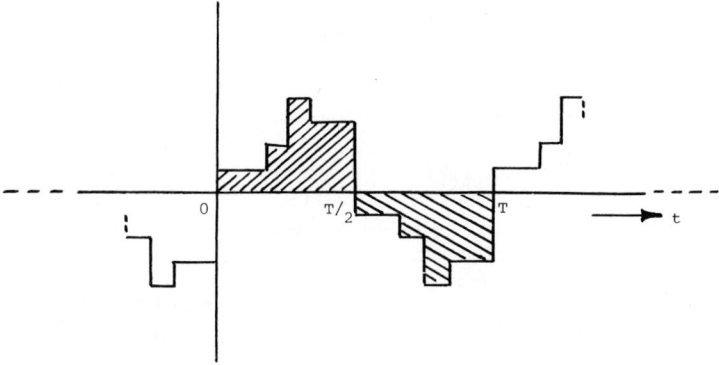

Fig. 3 Example of "inverse-repeat (IR)" symmetry

Considering now two sequences having line spectra with components of the type described by expressions (11) and (12): these are illustrated respectively in Figs. 4(a) and (b). If these two sequences are to be uncorrelated, their discrete cross power spectra should be zero over their least common period, within the bandwidth of interest. (Normally, this bandwidth will be somewhat less than the clock frequency of the sequence.)

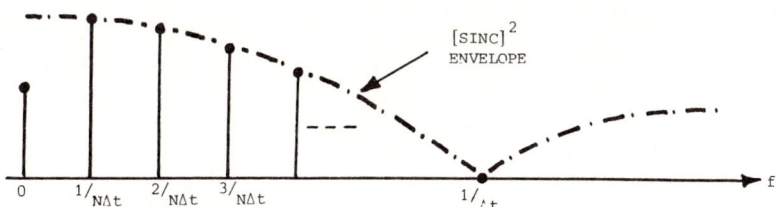

(a) Spectrum of sequence with no symmetry

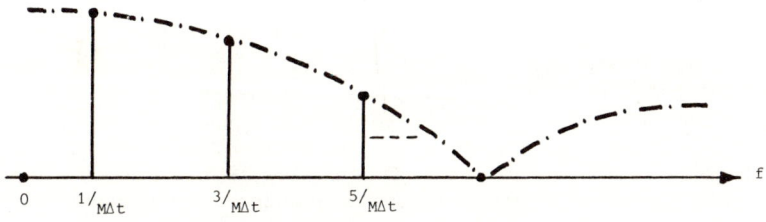

(b) Spectrum of sequence with inverse-repeat symmetry

Fig. 4   Sequence spectra

Thus, the simplest way to ensure that two sequences are uncorrelated is to prevent any coincidence of their line spectral components. For the two sequences of expressions (11) and (12), this is achieved by letting them have the same clock interval Δt, subject to the constraint that

$$M = 2N \tag{13}$$

The least common period of the two sequences is then $2N\Delta t$ and the two sets of spectral lines will interleave as shown in Fig. 5.

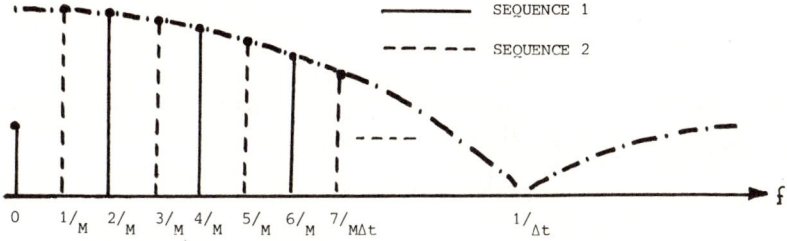

Fig. 5   Interleaved spectra of uncorrelated sequences

A further periodic sequence of length L digits (L even), with inverse-repeat symmetry, and having the spectral components

$$1/_{L\Delta t},\ 3/_{L\Delta t},\ 5/_{L\Delta t},\ \ldots (L-1)/_{L\Delta t},\ (L+1)/_{L\Delta t},\ \ldots \qquad (14)$$

will also be uncorrelated with the sequences of expressions (11) and (12) over their least common period if

$$L = 2M = 4N \qquad (15)$$

In general, the three sequences will also be uncorrelated if

$$L = 2^y M$$
$$\& \ M = 2^z N \qquad (16)$$

where y and z are positive integers (≥ 1). The procedure can be extended indefinitely by adding extra sequences to the set, each having a length twice that of the previous longest sequence, together with an inverse - repeat format. It now becomes apparent that the major practical problem is not one of synthesising sets of uncorrelated sequences: the above procedure allows this to be accomplished; difficulty arises in ensuring that each sequence has a useful (ideal or quasi-ideal) ACF.

Examination of expressions (11), (12) and (14) would appear to eliminate the possibility of sequences being uncorrelated if they have the same period, since this would imply a common frequency component at

$$\frac{1}{\text{Sequence period}} \qquad (17)$$

However, considering two sequences of the same length: if, for example, one sequence has cosine frequency components only and the other sequence has sine components only, the integral

$$\int_{\substack{\text{common} \\ \text{period}}} \sin nw_1 t \cos mw_1 t \, dt \qquad (18)$$

(where w_1 is the fundamental angular repetition frequency) is zero for all n and m. Thus, the sequences will still be uncorrelated over the common period. Appendix 1 gives an example of a construction to generate two uncorrelated sequences of exactly the same length [8]. Unfortunately, these sequences do not have useful ACF's.

In summary, the necessary requirements for a set of uncorrelated PR sequences are:

(i) that each member of the set should have an ideal, or quasi-ideal, ACF;

(ii) that the clock rate, and hence bandwidth of each member of the set should be approximately the same;

(iii) that the periods of the members of a set of n sequences should be in the ratio

$$1:2:4: \ldots :2^{n-1}$$

for most efficient synthesis;

(iv) that all members of the set should be even - length inverse - repeat (IR) sequences, with the possible exception of the first member which can be a sequence of any length (e.g. derived from a binary m sequence).

4. THE SYNTHESIS OF UNCORRELATED SETS OF PR SEQUENCES: METHOD I

A "composite" sequence may be defined as a sequence generated by the term - by - term multiplication of two component sequences. When the lengths and ACF properties of the component sequences are selected according to specified criteria, the composite sequence itself will have PR properties.

Consider two sequences of lengths J and K digits, expressed as

$$[a_i]_{i=1}^{J} \text{ and } [b_i]_{i=1}^{K} \qquad (19)$$

respectively, where J and K are selected to be relatively prime so that their least common multiple, i.e. the period of the composite sequence, is JK. It can be shown that [5] the ACF of the composite sequence $\phi_{cc}(r)$, is given by:

$$\phi_{cc}(r) = \phi_{aa}(r) \cdot \phi_{bb}(r) \qquad (20)$$

where $\phi_{aa}(r)$ and $\phi_{bb}(r)$ are the individual ACF's of component sequences $[a_i]$ and $[b_i]$ respectively.

If the two component sequences are selected to be:

(i) a binary m-sequence
(ii) a sequence derived from the rows or columns of a Hadamard matrix

then the resulting composite sequence will take an IR form and may have a quasi-ideal ACF [9]. Hadamard matrices of orders

2, 4 and 8 are shown below:

```
Row             Row                   Row
 1   +1+1        1   +1+1 +1+1         1   +1+1+1+1 +1+1+1+1
 2   +1-1        2   +1-1 +1-1         2   +1-1+1-1 +1-1+1-1
                 3   +1+1 -1-1         3   +1+1-1-1 +1+1-1-1
                 4   +1-1 -1+1         4   +1-1-1+1 +1-1-1+1
                                       5   +1+1+1+1 -1-1-1-1
                                       6   +1-1+1-1 -1+1-1+1
                                       7   +1+1-1-1 -1-1+1+1
                                       8   +1-1-1+1 -1+1+1-1
```

(21)

It is seen that the matrix of order 4 can be synthesised recursively from the matrix of order 2, and the matrix of order 8 from that of order 4, etc. Note that the rows and columns of the Hadamard matrix are identical to the Walsh functions of expression (10), and are therefore orthogonal; also all rows and columns of the matrix, except the first, have an IR format over their least repetition intervals.

The composite sequences formed by multiplying a binary m-sequence by rows 1, 2, 3 and 5 of the 8th - order Hadamard matrix make up a set of four uncorrelated sequences with quasi-ideal ACF's. From the expression (20), the ACF of the composite sequence generated by multiplication of the m-sequence by x^{th} row of the Hadamard matrix, $\phi_{ccx}(r)$, is given by:

$$\phi_{ccx}(r) = \phi_{mm}(r) \cdot \phi_{hhx}(r) \qquad (22)$$

where $\phi_{mm}(r)$ is the m-sequence ACF and $\phi_{hhx}(r)$ the ACF of the xth row of the matrix. The periods of the m-sequence and the rows of the matrix are relatively prime.

Fig. 6 shows the ACF's of the set of four composite sequences generated by multiplying a 7-bit binary m-sequence by rows 1, 2, 3 and 5 of an 8th - order Hadamard matrix. The first three members of the set satisfy all the four requirements for a set of uncorrelated PR sequences listed in Section 3. However, the ACF of the 4th sequence, $\phi_{cc5}(r)$, may or may not fulfil requirement (i), depending upon the particular application, because the subsidiary ACF peaks are clearly not negligible in comparison with the major peaks.

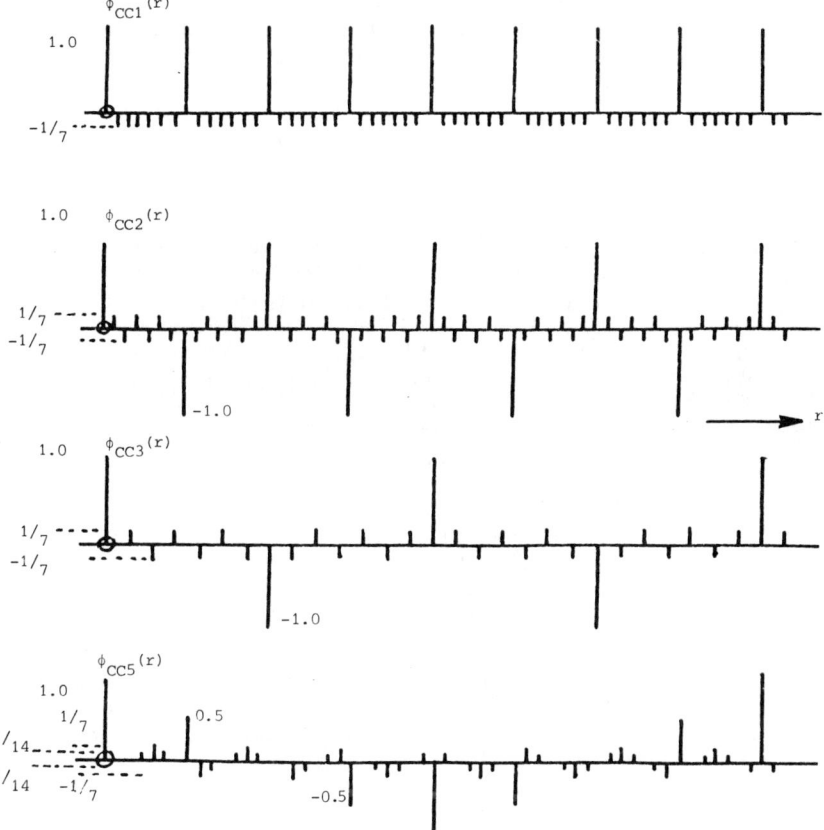

Fig. 6 Acf's of set of 4 composite sequences generated using Hadamard Matrix

The composite sequences produced by this method have the form:

```
Row
(1) +1+1+1-1-1+1-1  +1+1+1-1-1+1-1  +1+1+1-1-1+1-1  +1+1+1-1-1+1-1
    +1+1+1-1-1+1-1  +1+1+1-1-1+1-1  +1+1+1-1-1+1-1  +1+1+1-1-1+1-1
(2) +1-1+1+1-1-1-1  -1+1-1-1+1+1+1  +1-1+1+1-1-1-1  -1+1-1-1+1+1+1
    +1-1+1+1-1-1-1  -1+1-1-1+1+1+1  +1-1+1+1-1-1-1  -1+1-1-1+1+1+1
(3) +1+1-1-1+1-1+1+1  -1+1+1+1+1+1-1  -1-1+1-1+1-1-1  +1-1-1-1-1-1+1
    +1+1-1-1+1-1+1+1  -1+1+1+1+1+1-1  -1-1+1-1+1-1-1  +1-1-1-1-1-1+1
(5) +1+1+1-1+1-1+1  -1+1+1-1-1-1+1  -1-1+1-1-1+1+1  -1-1-1-1-1+1-1
    -1-1-1+1-1+1-1  +1-1-1+1+1+1-1  +1+1-1+1+1-1-1  +1+1+1+1-1+1
```

(23)

It is seen that the latter three sequences all have an IR format.

Generally, the particular application for an uncorrelated set of PR sequences will determine how rigorously the four requirements listed in Section 3 should be applied. Further uncorrelated members of the set can be synthesised using Hadamard matrices of order > 8, and these may have acceptable ACF's in a given situation.

5. THE SYNTHESIS OF UNCORRELATED SETS OF PR SEQUENCES: METHOD II

5.1 Principle of the method

Method II relaxes the requirements for the sequences in the uncorrelated set to have numbers of digits in their cycles exactly in the ratios 1:2:4:8:.. etc, and to be run at the same clock rate. Instead, a set of sequences with numbers of digits per cycle <u>approximately</u> in the ratios 1:2:4:8:.. etc ($N_1:N_2:N_3:N_4:..$ etc) is selected; the corresponding clock intervals Δt_1, Δt_2, Δt_3, Δt_4, ... etc are allowed to vary slightly so that the real-time period ratios

$$N_1 \Delta t_1 : N_2 \Delta t_2 : N_3 \Delta t_3 : N_4 \Delta t_4 : \ldots \text{etc} \tag{24}$$

are <u>exactly</u> in the ratio 1:2:4:8: ...etc

If driven at the same clock frequency, these sequences would have some degree of cross-correlation; however, when the periods of expression (24) are constrained to be in the required ratios, the set is completely uncorrelated since the sequences do not infringe any of the requirements stated in Section 3. The sequence N_1 can be an m-sequence or an IR sequence, but sequences N_2, N_3, N_4, etc must all have an IR format if their spectral lines are to interleave as in Method 1.

The vehicle for constraining the period ratios is a phase-locked loop (PLL), a schematic diagram of which is given in Fig. 7. The "mark" output shown is produced once per PR sequence generator cycle by gating one particular sequence state: hence the &-gate output is a pulse of width Δt once every cycle, or every N clock pulses, where Δt is the clock interval and N is the number of digits per sequence period. Essentially, this process divides the generator clock frequency by a factor of N times. If the loop reference is derived from the mark pulse of a separate PR sequence generator, with N' digits per cycle and clock interval $\Delta t'$, the PLL will automatically synchronise the two periods such that

$$N\Delta t = N'\Delta t' \tag{25}$$

by feedback control action.

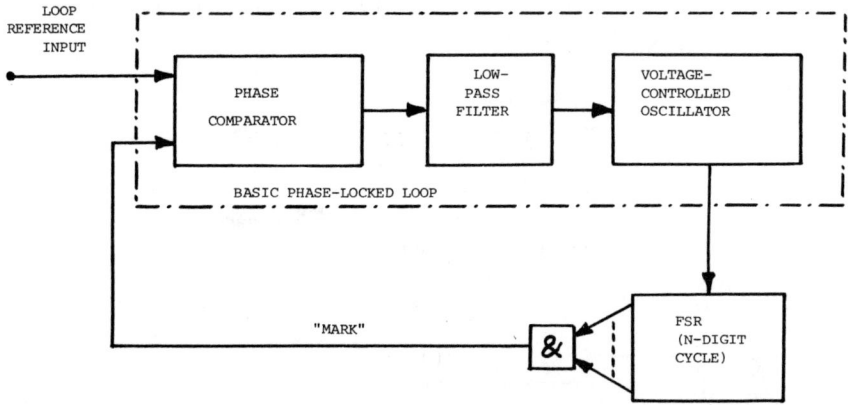

Fig. 7 Schematic diagram of phase-locked loop

5.2 Synchronisation of Inverse-Repeat Sequence Periods

Considering a set of binary IR_2 sequences derived from binary m-sequences and row 2 of a Hadamard matrix: in general, these will have a length of

$$[2^{n+1} - 2] \text{ digits (n integer)} \tag{26}$$

The m-sequences from which they are derived will have length

$$[2^n - 1] \text{ digits} \tag{27}$$

Such a set of IR sequences might have lengths 30, 62, 126, 254, 510 .... digits; to this set can be appended a 15-bit m-sequence, as described in Sections 3 and 4 of this paper. This group of sequences has lengths approximately in the ratio 1 : 2: 4: ... etc. Fig. 8 shows a schematic arrangement by which the real-time periods of the sequences can be locked exactly in the required ratios; all sequences in the set have quasi-ideal ACF's.

It was shown in Section 4 and Fig. 6 that the ACF's of the IR_3 sequences derived from m-sequences and row 3 of a Hadamard matrix also have quasi-ideal ACF's. This class of sequences will in general have length of

$$[2^{n+2} - 4] \text{ digits} \tag{28}$$

assuming the original m-sequence to have a length given by expression (27). They can be incorporated into the PLL arrangement, as shown in Fig. 9.

Appendix B gives methods of generating binary IR sequences indirectly and directly.

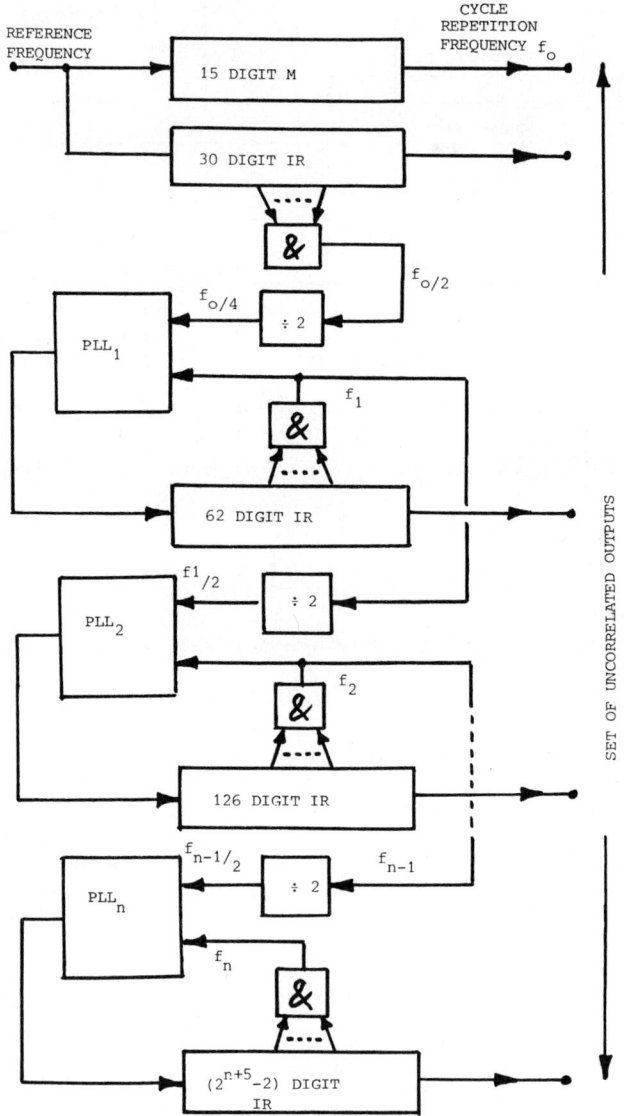

Fig. 8 Use of PLL's to synchronise PR sequence periods

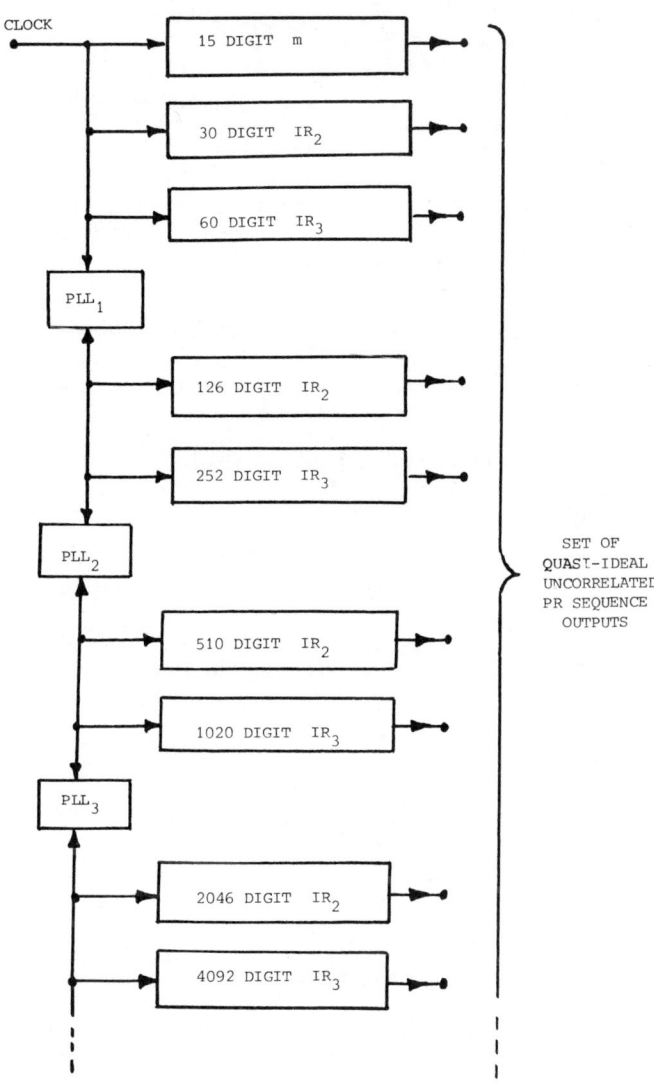

Fig. 9 PLL synchronisation of a set of uncorrelated PR sequences including IR_3 sequences

6. THE SYNTHESIS OF UNCORRELATED SETS OF PR SEQUENCES: METHOD III

6.1 Interleaved Sequences

Further sets of uncorrelated PR sequences may be synthesised with the aid of the simple procedure described below. If two sequences, each of length N digits, are interleaved digit - by - digit to form a composite sequence of length 2N, then that interleaved sequence may have certain PR correlation properties if the two N-digit component sequences are appropriately chosen. An analysis of this procedure in which digits are selected alternately from the two component sequences is presented in Appendix C. The expression for the ACF of the interleaved sequence, $\phi_{33}(r)$, in terms of the ACF's of the two component sequences, $\phi_{11}(r)$ and $\phi_{22}(r)$, is shown to be:

$$\phi_{33}(r) = \begin{cases} \phi_{11}(r/2) + \phi_{22}(r/2); & r \text{ even or zero (modulo-N)} \\ \phi_{12}((r+1)/2) + \phi_{12}(N - (r-1)/2); & r \text{ odd (modulo-N)} \end{cases}$$

(29)

where $\phi_{12}(r)$ is the CCF between the two component sequences.

If it is required that the ACF $\phi_{33}(r)$ should be ideal or quasi-ideal, the simplest synthesis technique is to make the ACF $\phi_{11}(r)$ ideal or quasi-ideal, e.g. from a p-level m-sequence ($p \geq 2$), and to constrain $\phi_{22}(r)$ and $\phi_{12}(r)$ to be zero for all r by choosing an "all zero" sequence as the second component. In this case

$$\phi_{33}(r) = \begin{cases} \phi_{11}(r/2); & r \text{ even or zero (modulo-N)} \\ 0; & r \text{ odd (modulo-N)} \end{cases}$$

(30)

In practice, this implies that the length of the original sequence is doubled by simply inserting a zero after each of the digits of component sequence 1; the ACF of this double-length sequence will be ideal or quasi-ideal if $\phi_{11}(r)$ is ideal or quasi-ideal. Note that the peak and sidelobe values of the double length sequence will still have the same maximum magnitudes as for sequence 1; the normalised ACF values will be halved however.

If the sequence 1 is binary, then the interleaved sequence will be 3-level (ternary); if sequence 1, has p levels, then the interleaved sequence will also have p levels.

6.2 *The Expansion Operator*

In a similar manner, it can be shown that a quadruple-length sequence, with an ideal or quasi-ideal ACF, can be synthesised by inserting three zeros after each digit of sequence 1. In general, if it is required to lengthen the sequence 1 by 2^n times, then (2^n-1) zeros must be inserted after each digit of sequence 1. This operation will be denoted by

$$E(2^n-1) \text{ for } n = 1, 2, 3 \ldots \quad (31)$$

where $E( )$ denotes expansion of the original sequence. In principle, there is no limit to the value of n, apart from that which may be imposed by the reduction of the normalised ACF peak value. If a systematic technique could be developed to allow two non-zero sequences to be interleaved, this would overcome the above problem.

Fig. 10 is a schematic diagram showing one method whereby an $E(1)$ sequence can be generated. Sequence 1 is generated at half the desired clock rate; half of each clock interval is made to yield zero by means of an inhibit gate, thus producing an interleaved sequence at an effective clock rate which is twice that of sequence 1. Similar methods can be employed to generate $E(3)$, $E(7)$, ... etc. sequences, all with ideal or quasi-ideal ACF's.

When the original non-zero component sequence is IR in form, a set of sequences comprising the original and $E(1)$, $E(3)$, ... $E(2^n-1)$ derived sequences satisfies all the four requirements for an uncorrelated set listed in Section 3.

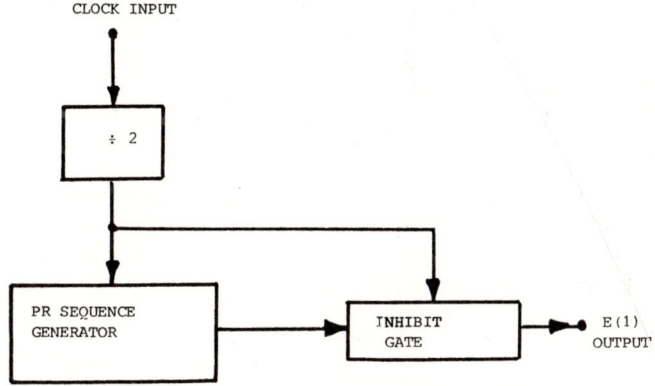

Fig. 10 Implementation of $E(1)$ operation

7. THE SYNTHESIS OF UNCORRELATED SETS OF PR SEQUENCES: METHOD IV

Methods I and II, described in Sections 4 and 5, produce sets of binary uncorrelated PR sequences comprising a binary m-sequence (optional) and multiple binary IR sequences, the latter being derived by multiplying binary m-sequences by various rows of a Hadamard matrix. Method III extends the range of uncorrelated sets available by employing the E( ) expansion operator.

Method IV uses a combination of Methods I, II and III, and incorporates other non-binary PR sequences, eg p-level m-sequences, in a systematic manner.

7.1 Multi-Level Sequences

A p-level m-sequence (p prime >2) in general will have length

$$N = (p^n - 1) \text{ digits} \qquad (32)$$

where n is an integer (≥ 2). Table 2 lists the feedback connections for equivalent shift register generators for p-level m-sequences.

These basic integer sequences may then be modified by the integer or sinusoidal level transformations given in Section 2.3 to produce sequences of positive and negative numbers which are more useful in practice.

For p>2, all p-level m-sequences have a structure whereby:

(a) the number of digits in one period is always even;
(b) the latter half of the sequence is always the modulo -p complement of the first half.

This structure, when the level transformations of Table 1 or expression (9) are applied, always leads to a transformed-level sequence having an IR format. Such transformed sequences are thus potentially useful in uncorrelated sets. Thus, Method II could also be employed to synchronise the real-time periods of p-level sequences in the ratios 1: 2: 4: ...etc to provide an uncorrelated set, or to synchronise the periods of hybrid sets of both binary and mult-level sequences.

A major disadvantage of the Hadamard matrix synthesis technique (Method I) is that the first sequence of the set must be of odd-length. The only sequences discussed so far which fulfil this requirement are binary m-sequences. However, other types of binary PR sequences [10] are also of odd-length with a quasi-ideal ACF.

Table 2

Feedback Connections for Equivalent p-level m-sequence Shift-register

p	n	$(p^n - 1)$	a_1	a_2	a_3	a_4	a_5	a_6	a_7	a_8	a_9	a_{10}
2	2	3	1	1								
	3	7	0	1	1							
	4	15	0	0	1	1						
	5	31	0	0	1	0	1					
	6	63	0	0	0	0	1	1				
	7	127	0	0	0	1	0	0	1			
	8	255	0	1	1	1	0	0	0	1		
	9	511	0	0	0	0	1	0	0	0	1	
	10	1023	0	0	1	0	0	0	0	0	0	1
3	2	8	2	1								
	3	26	0	1	2							
	4	80	0	0	2	1						
	5	242	0	0	0	1	2					
	6	728	0	0	0	0	2	1				
	7	2186	0	0	0	0	1	0	2			
5	2	24	2	2								
	3	124	0	2	3							
	4	624	0	4	3	3						
7	2	48	2	2								
	3	342	0	4	5							
11	2	120	1	3								
	3	1330	0	10	7							
13	2	168	2	7								
	3	2196	0	12	7							
17	2	288	16	7								
	3	4912	0	16	14							
19	2	360	18	16								
	3	6858	0	18	15							
23	3	12166	0	22	20							
29	3	24388	0	28	18							
31	2	960	30	19								
	3	29790	0	30	17							

7.2 Modified Matrix Approach

p-level m-sequences (p>2) are always of even length. If a set of multi-level uncorrelated sequences is required, this can be achieved either via PLL synchronisation (Method II) or via the expansion operation (Method III). It is also possible to derive an odd-length sequence with an ideal ACF from say a ternary m-sequence as follows.

Considering the 26-digit sequence obtained via the level transformation of Table 1, and using the feedback connections of Table 2:

$$0 \ +1 \ +1 \ +1 \ 0 \ 0 \ -1 \ 0 \ -1 \ +1 \ -1 \ -1 \ +1$$
$$0 \ -1 \ -1 \ -1 \ 0 \ 0 \ +1 \ 0 \ +1 \ -1 \ +1 \ +1 \ -1 \quad (33)$$

If one period of this sequence is now multiplied by row 2 of the Hadamard matrix, +1 -1 +1 -1 ...., two repetitions of the same 13-digit sequence result, ie the inverse procedure to that adopted in Method I to obtain an IR sequence from an odd-length m-sequence. The resulting 13-digit sequence is:

$$0 \ -1 \ +1 \ -1 \ 0 \ 0 \ -1 \ 0 \ -1 \ -1 \ -1 \ +1 \ +1 \quad (34)$$

This is of odd length and has the ACF illustrated in Fig. 11. The ACF is ideal and therefore the sequence can be used to produce a set of ideal uncorrelated sequences using rows 1, 2 and 3 of the Hadamard matrix via Method I.

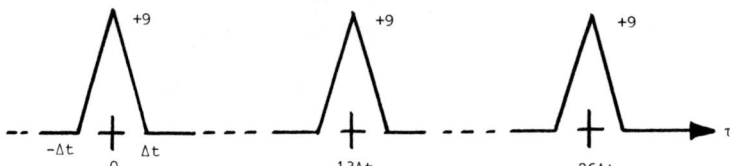

Fig. 11 Acf of 13-digit ternary sequence

If more than three uncorrelated sequences are required, multiplying sequences of lengths 8, 16, 32, ... etc, all with ideal or quasi-ideal ACF's, must be provided. These can be produced from an 8-digit ternary IR signal, derived from an 8-digit ternary m-sequence via the level transformation of Table 1, ie

$$+1 \ +1 \ 0 \ +1 \ -1 \ -1 \ 0 \ -1 \quad (35)$$

The sequence length may then be doubled, quadrupled, etc by the use of $E(1)$, $E(3)$, etc operations (Method III).

For example, a set of five uncorrelated sequences, all with ideal ACF's, can be derived by using as multiplying sequences the rows of the non-binary matrix shown below:

```
Row
1    + + + + + + + + + + + + + + +
2    + - + - + - + - + - + - + - +
3    + + - - + + - - + + - - + + -           (36)
4    + + 0 + - - + - + + 0 + - - 0 -
5    + 0 + 0 0 0 + 0 - 0 - 0 0 0 - 0
```

The only requirement is for the shortest member of the set to be of odd length, and to have an ideal ACF. The rows of the matrix can be increased in number by E(3), E(7), etc operations. Again, the sequence of expression (34) would be an appropriate first member of the set.

The modified matrix (36) may also be used in conjunction with the PLL synchronisation technique (Method II) to yield an extended set of uncorrelated sequences all with ideal or quasi-ideal ACF's. Assume a block of five sequences, all having the same clock frequency f_1 and produced by the use of modified matrix (36), is synchronised with a second block of four uncorrelated sequences, all with the same clock frequency f_2, such that the real-time period of the longest member of the first block is exactly half the period of the shortest member of the second block: all the sequences in both blocks will be uncorrelated if the second block is derived from rows 2 to 5 of matrix (36), using an appropriate odd-length initial sequence. The procedure can be extended to more that two blocks by the use of more PLL's, as shown in Fig. 12. Note, however, that not all the sequences will be binary due to some of the rows of matrix (36) being ternary.

The number of sequences in an uncorrelated set can also be increased by simply doubling, quadrupling, etc the clock interval of the last IR member of the set. However, this will increase the width of the ACF peak and may limit the practical usefulness (see section 9).

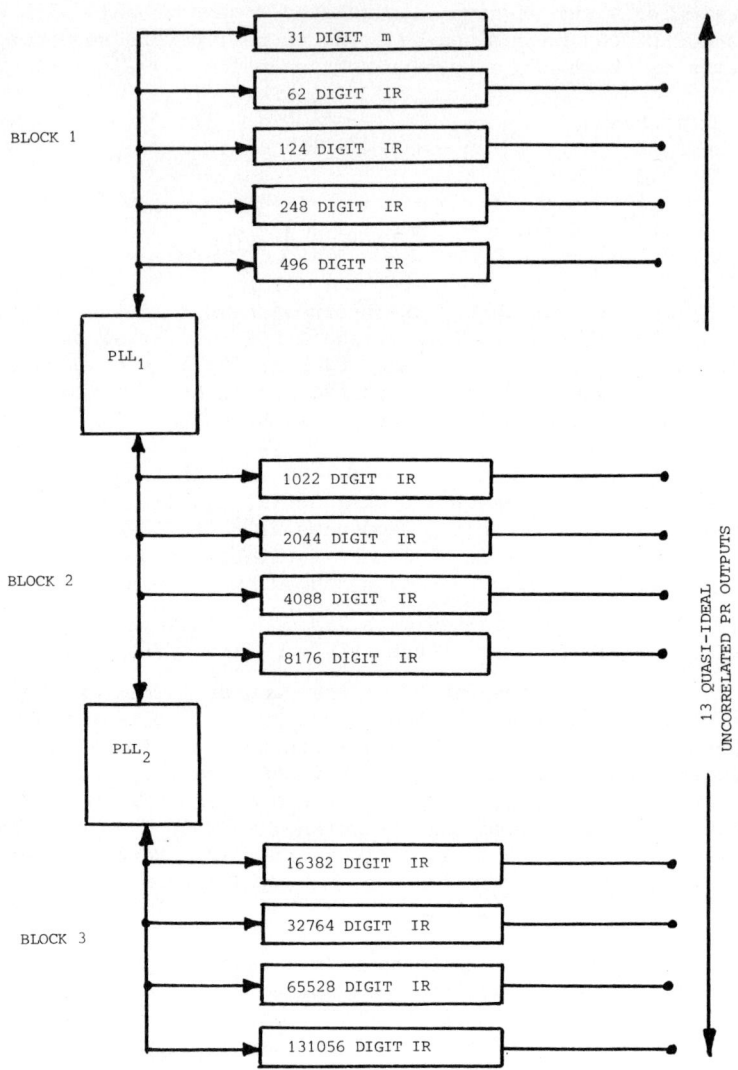

Fig. 12 Uncorrelated sequence set produced using modified matrix method and PLL's

7.3 Sequence Concatenation

It is also possible to use matrix (36), in conjunction with an odd-length ideal or quasi-ideal sequence, to produce a set of uncorrelated sequences by concatenation. This is accomplished by simply replacing each digit of matrix (36) by a complete period of the odd-length sequence, with a positive, negative or zero weighting determined by the individual digits of the matrix.

For example, if 'm' represents the complete period of a transformed binary m-sequence, and $\bar{m}$ the inverse of that same sequence, then the set of sequences

$$
\begin{array}{l}
\text{m m m m m m m m m m m m m m m} \\
\text{m } \bar{m} \text{ m } \bar{m} \text{ m } \bar{m} \text{ m } \bar{m} \text{ m } \bar{m} \text{ m } \bar{m} \text{ m } \bar{m} \text{ m} \\
\text{m m } \bar{m} \text{ } \bar{m} \text{ m m } \bar{m} \text{ } \bar{m} \text{ m m } \bar{m} \text{ } \bar{m} \text{ m m } \bar{m} \text{ } \bar{m} \\
\text{m m o m } \bar{m} \text{ } \bar{m} \text{ o } \bar{m} \text{ m m o m } \bar{m} \text{ } \bar{m} \text{ o } \bar{m} \\
\text{m o m o o o m o } \bar{m} \text{ o } \bar{m} \text{ o o o } \bar{m} \text{ o}
\end{array}
\quad (37)
$$

will be uncorrelated.

8. SETS OF NON-PERIODIC UNCORRELATED PR SEQUENCES

8.1 *Complementary Sequences* [11]

A pair of binary complementary sequences can be defined as two, equal-length sequences having the property that the number of pairs of like elements with any given spacing in one sequence is exactly equal to the number of pairs of unlike elements with the same spacing in the other sequence. The sum of the individual non-periodic (aperiodic) ACF's at corresponding shifts for the two sequences is zero, except at the zero-shift (in-phase) position where it takes the value 2N, N being the number of digits in each sequence. Thus, if the two sequences are expressed as

$$[x_i]_{i=1}^{N} \text{ and } [y_i]_{i=1}^{N} \qquad (38)$$

and their respective aperiodic ACF's are $\phi_{xx}(r)$ and $\phi_{yy}(r)$, then

$$\phi_{xx}(r) + \phi_{yy}(r) = \sum_{\ell=1}^{n-r} x_\ell x_{\ell+r} + \sum_{\ell=1}^{n-r} y_\ell y_{\ell+r} \qquad (39)$$

$$= \begin{cases} 2N \; ; \; r = 0 \\ 0 \; ; \; \text{otherwise} \end{cases} \qquad (40)$$

Note that the individual ACF's, $\phi_{xx}(r)$ and $\phi_{yy}(r)$, will not normally be of the form of expression (40), but will have significant sidelobes. Also, the aperiodic CCF between the two sequences will not be zero at all shifts. Fig. 13 illustrates typical ACF's for a pair of complementary sequences. (Appendix D discussed the fundamental differences between the evaluation of periodic and non-periodic correlation functions).

In general, N can be expressed as

$$N = 2^n \tag{41}$$

where n is an integer ≥ 1.

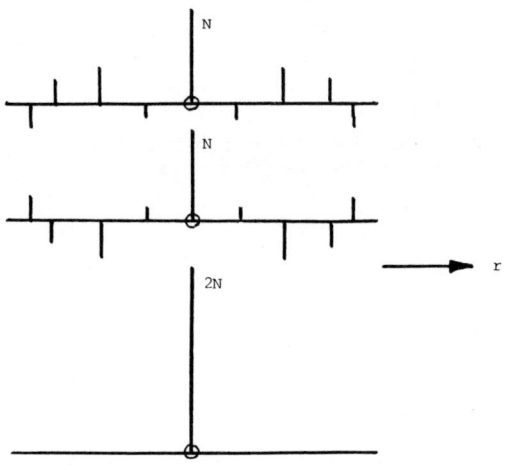

Fig. 13 Individual and summed acf's for a pair of complementary sequences

8.2 Synthesis of Pairs of Complementary Sequences

Complementary sequences have a fundamental "block" structure illustrated below

$$\begin{array}{c|c|c} \text{Sequence 1} & \xrightarrow{+A} & \xrightarrow{+B} \\ \hline \text{Sequence 2} & \xleftarrow{+B} & \xleftarrow{-A} \end{array} \tag{42}$$

where A and B denote blocks of length 2^{n-1} digits, the arrows indicate the orientation of the blocks, and the signs specify the relative polarity of all digits in a given block. This structure allows complementary sequences to be synthesised by the recursive procedure indicated below:

Initial elements: $\left.\begin{matrix} +1 \\ -1 \end{matrix}\right\}$ Selected arbitrarily (43)

1st recursion: $\left.\begin{matrix} +1 & | & +1 \\ \hline +1 & | & -1 \end{matrix}\right\}$ Using expression (42) (44)

UNCORRELATED DIGITAL SEQUENCES   49

$$\text{2nd recursion:} \quad \begin{matrix} +1+1 & -1+1 \\ \hline +1-1 & -1-1 \end{matrix} \Bigg\} \quad (45)$$

$$\text{3rd recursion:} \quad \begin{matrix} +1+1-1+1 & -1-1-1+1 \\ \hline +1-1-1-1 & -1+1-1-1 \end{matrix} \Bigg\} \quad (46)$$

etc

Note that the first 2^{n-1} digits of each pair of 2^n-length sequences are identical to the sequences from the previous recursion.

8.3 Uncorrelated Sets of Complementary Sequences

It is also possible to synthesise uncorrelated sets of complementary sequences in a systematic manner [12]. The two pairs of sequences with block structures

$$\text{1st sequence} \quad \begin{array}{|c|c|} \hline \rightarrow & \rightarrow \\ +A & +B \\ \hline \leftarrow & \leftarrow \\ +B & -A \\ \hline \end{array} \quad \text{and} \quad \begin{array}{|c|c|} \hline \rightarrow & \rightarrow \\ +A & -B \\ \hline \leftarrow & \leftarrow \\ +B & +A \\ \hline \end{array} \quad (47)$$

are uncorrelated in the sense that the CCF's between corresponding sequences sum to zero for all shifts. The ACF and CCF calculations for complementary sequence pairs can be simplified by employing the block structures as exemplified in expressions (42) and (47).

Since A and B themselves form a complete pair of complementary sequences for $n \geq 2$ (see expressions (43) to (46)), by definition they will only have a non-zero summed ACF when they are in phase. Thus, it is only necessary to consider correlation function values at integral block shifts, because elsewhere the values will be zero. For example, the summed ACF of a pair of sequences having the form of expression (42) may be computed as follows:

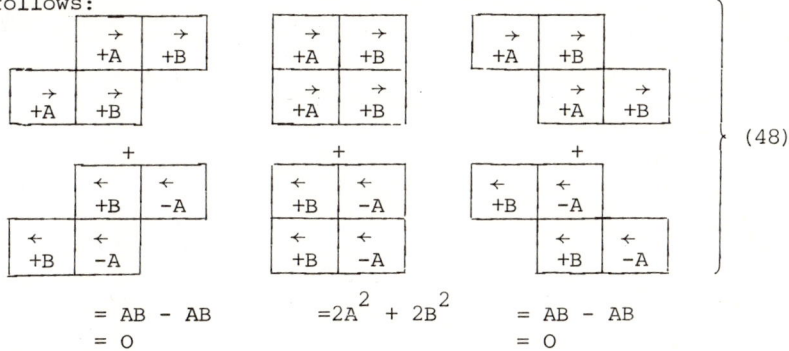

(48)

Similarly, the CCF between the pairs given in expression (47) can be evaluated by

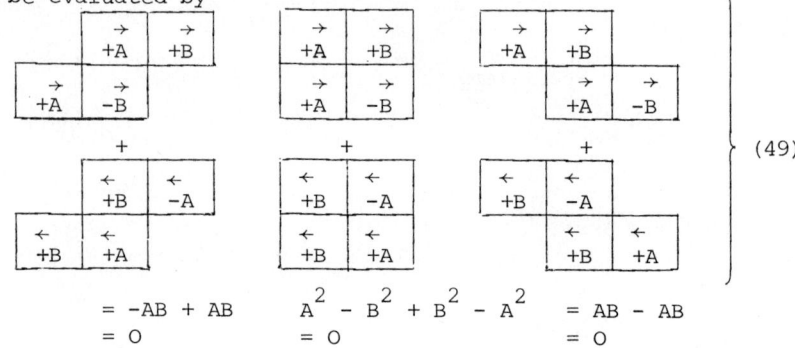

$$\left.\begin{array}{ccc} = -AB + AB & A^2 - B^2 + B^2 - A^2 & = AB - AB \\ = 0 & = 0 & = 0 \end{array}\right\} \quad (49)$$

ie zero for all shifts.

The complementary sequence concept can be further extended to include sets of sequences with more than two members [13]. Here, a set of equal-length binary sequences is defined as a complementary set if the sum of the ACF's of the individual sequences is zero everywhere except at zero shift. Two sets of such sequences are uncorrelated if the sum of the CCF's between corresponding sequences is zero at all shifts.

The synthesis techniques for generalised complementary sets make use of matrices with orthogonal rows of elements. For example, the 2 - digit sequences

$$\begin{array}{cc} +1\ +1 & +1\ -1 \\ +1\ -1 \quad\text{and}\quad +1\ +1 \end{array} \quad (50)$$

are specific versions of the generalised structure given in expression (47); they have already been shown to be uncorrelated in a complementary sense. Thus a composite matrix, Δ, can be defined as

$$\Delta = \begin{bmatrix} +1 & +1 & +1 & -1 \\ +1 & -1 & +1 & +1 \end{bmatrix} \quad (51)$$

in which the columns represent pairs of uncorrelated 2-digit complementary sequences. A matrix Δ', can be defined as [13]

$$\Delta' = \left[\begin{array}{c|c} \Delta/\Delta & -\Delta/\Delta \\ \hline -\Delta/\Delta & \Delta/\Delta \end{array}\right] \quad (52)$$

where the / symbol indicates an interleaving of the corresponding columns of Δ and $-\Delta$, and the minus sign denotes the fact that all elements of Δ are inverted. It can then be shown that all the columns of Δ' are uncorrelated in a complementary sense. Hence, applying this procedure to the matrix (51) yields

$$\Delta' = \begin{bmatrix} +1+1+1+1 & +1+1-1-1 & -1+1-1+1 & -1+1+1-1 \\ +1+1-1-1 & +1+1+1+1 & -1+1+1-1 & -1+1-1+1 \\ -1+1-1+1 & -1+1+1-1 & +1+1+1+1 & +1+1-1-1 \\ -1+1+1-1 & -1+1-1+1 & +1+1-1-1 & +1+1+1+1 \end{bmatrix} \quad (53)$$

Each of the four sets (columns) of 4-bit sequences in matrix (53) is uncorrelated in a complementary sense with the other three sets. Clearly, if the length of the original sequences is N digits, k recursions of this synthesis procedure will give

$$[2^{k+1}] \text{ mutually uncorrelated sets} \quad (54)$$

with each set comprising

$$[2^{k+1}] \text{ sequences} \quad (55)$$

each of length

$$[2^k N] \text{ digits} \quad (56)$$

Other methods of synthesising uncorrelated sets are also described in References [12] and [13].

9. APPLICATION AREAS FOR UNCORRELATED SETS OF PR SEQUENCES

9.1 System Identification

The technique of identifying the unit impulse response function, h(t), of a linear time-invariant (LTI) system is well established [14]. Applications have been mainly in the fields of automatic control and radio communications [15] [16]. Extension of the basic technique to the identification of multi-input system responses has also been investigated [17].

Taking the LTI system shown schematically in Fig. 14, with m periodic input signals and n output ports: the periodic CCF between the ith input port and the jth output port ($1 \leqslant i \leqslant m$; $1 \leqslant j \leqslant n$) has the form [14]:

$$\phi_{ij}(\tau) = \int_0^T x_i(t) \, y_j(t + \tau) \, dt \quad (57)$$

$$= \int_{-\infty}^{\infty} h_{ij}(u) \, \phi_{ii}(\tau - u) \, du$$

$$+ \sum_{k \neq i} \int_{-\infty}^{\infty} h_{kj}(u) \, \phi_{ki}(\tau - u) \, du \quad (58)$$

where $h_{kj}(t)$ is the unit impulse response function of the LTI path between k^{th} input port and j^{th} output port, and u is a dummy time variable. If the input CCF terms $\phi_{ki}(\tau)$ can be made zero, and the input ACF term $\phi_{ii}(\tau)$ can be made ideal or or quasi-ideal, the input - output CCF $\phi_{ij}(\tau)$ will be directly proportional to the impulse response function $h_{ij}(\tau)$; in addition, there will be no contribution to that CCF from the other inputs ($k \neq i$), if correlation is carried out over the least common period.

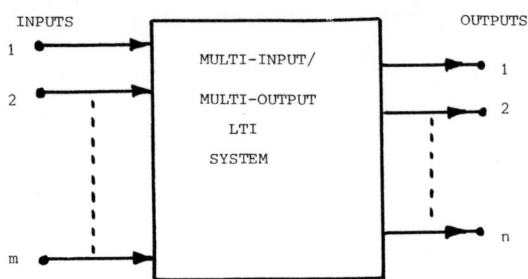

Fig. 14 Multi-input/multi-output LTI system

The sets of sequences described in previous sections fulfil these requirements and can thus be used as system identification stimuli for multi-input LTI systems, e.g. see Refs. [9] and [17].

An alternative approach which has been employed for the identification of multi-input systems is to constrain $\phi_{ki}(\tau)$ values to be negligible for all τ less than the maximum response time of the system, without the inputs necessarily being completely uncorrelated for all τ. The "phase-separation" technique [18] allows the inputs to be conditionally uncorrelated over a limited range of delay; here, phase-shifted versions of the same long PR sequence are used as test inputs for the multiple - input system.

Fig. 15 shows three impulse responses obtained simultaneously using Method I, ie employing a 127 - bit m-sequence, a 254 - bit IR_2 sequence and a 508 - bit IR_3 sequence as test inputs. It is seen that there is no discernable interaction between the oscillatory responses.

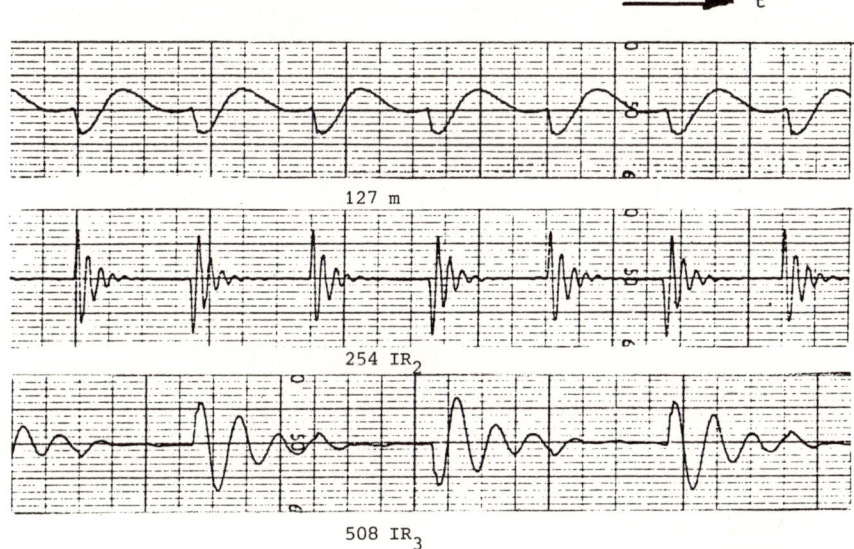

Fig. 15 Simultaneous impulse-response obtained using Method I

Fig. 16 shows two impulse responses obtained simultaneously using Method II. Here, the periods of a 62 - bit IR_2 signal and a 126 - bit IR_2 signal were constrained to be exactly the ratio 1: 2 by means of a PLL. Again, it is seen that there is negligible interaction between the responses.

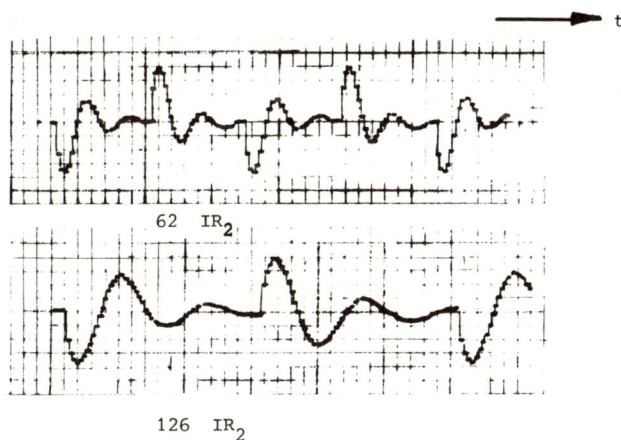

Fig. 16 Simultaneous impulse responses obtained using Method II

In a similar manner, uncorrelated sets of aperiodic PR sequences, eg complementary sequences, can be used for multi-input system identification. Once more considering an LTI system with unit impulse response function h(t); if two complementary sequences, a(t) and b(t), are applied in turn to the system input, outputs y(t) and z(t) respectively result. Assuming that all cross-correlation between the two outputs has been eliminated, as before, the input - output CCF's will be given by the convolutions:

$$\phi_{ay}(\tau) = \int_{-\infty}^{\infty} h(u)\, \phi_{aa}(\tau - u)\, du \quad (59)$$

and

$$\phi_{bz}(\tau) = \int_{-\infty}^{\infty} h(u)\, \phi_{bb}(\tau - u)\, du \quad (60)$$

Summing equations (59) and (60) gives:

$$\phi_{ay}(\tau) + \phi_{bz}(\tau) = \int_{-\infty}^{\infty} h(u)\, \left[\phi_{aa}(\tau - u) + \phi_{bb}(\tau - u)\right] du \quad (61)$$

Equation (61) shows that the sum of the two separate input - output CCF's at corresponding values of τ is equal to the convolution of h(t) and the sum of the two individual input ACF's. By definition, for complementary sequences, this summed ACF is ideal.

As indicated previously, the above result assumes that the two input sequences are applied in such a way that there are no cross-correlation effects. The simplest way of ensuring this is to apply the sequences one after the other with an interval between them longer than the longest time constant of the system being identified. This situation is illustrated in Fig. 17. The system output response to the first sequence is then stored and processed in delay synchronism with the output response to the second sequence, with the two CCF's being summed to give the required response.

UNCORRELATED DIGITAL SEQUENCES   55

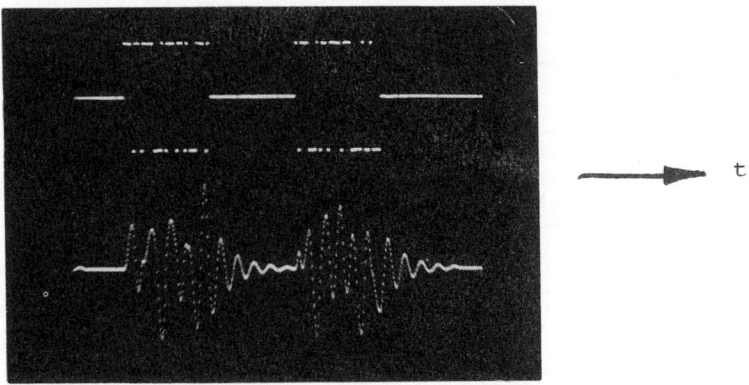

Fig. 17 Serial application of complementary sequence test
        signal

9.2 *Multiple-Access Communications*

Sets of uncorrelated PR sequences of the types described in
this paper can be employed as the basis of a code - division
multiple - access (CDMA) communication system. Such a system
is illustrated schematically in Fig. 18. Here, m message
originators require to be able to communicate with n message
recipients, without interaction. Assume that each of the
originators is assigned one member of a set of uncorrelated
PR sequences as a "carrier" signal, and each of the n possible
recipients has a bank of m matched filters, one for each
of the m possible transmitted sequences. Matched filtering is
equivalent to correlation processing, and thus the bank of
matched filters at each receiver can be viewed as being
functionally equivalent to a cross-correlator with m alternative
reference signals.

Originator sequences are then encoded with the data to be
transmitted, e.g. via sequence inversion, and transmitted over
the channel. Only those filters matched to the particular
sequences transmitted at any time will respond; all other
filters will only respond to an extent determined by the noise
present, because of the uncorrelated properties of the
sequence set.

A selective -addressing facility can be incorporated into
the system by assigning sub -sets of the overall set of
uncorrelated sequences for use by different originator/
recipient combinations.

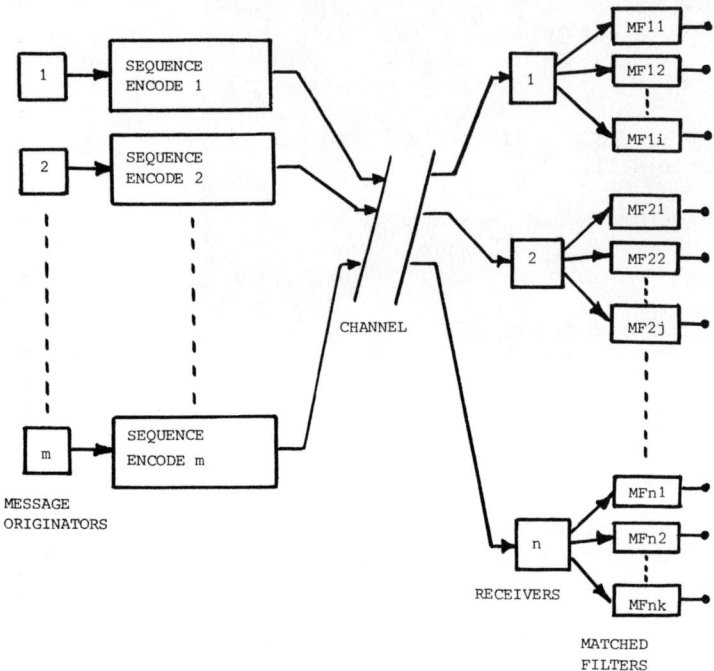

Fig. 18 Code-division multiple-access communication system

10. CONCLUDING REMARKS

This paper has attempted to present both new and established methods of generating sets of completely uncorrelated PR signals. Applications of such sets in the fields of LTI system identification and multiple-access communications have been discussed briefly. Both periodic and non-periodic PR signals have been considered.

Further work is currently in progress in the following areas:

(i)   extension of the number of PR sequences, all having an identical clock rate, in an uncorrelated set;

(ii) investigation of the synthesis of sets of PR sequences which are uncorrelated over a specified bandwidth of interest but may have a degree of correlation outside that bandwidth;

(iii) the possibility of synthesising sets of uncorrelated analogue, as opposed to discrete - level, PR sequences for greater bandwidth efficiency;

(iv) the synthesis of multi-level (non-binary) sets of uncorrelated complementary sequences.

11. REFERENCES

[1] Stiffler, J.J., (1971) Theory of synchronous communications, Prentice-Hall.

[2] Hazlerigg, A.D.G. and Noton, A.R.M., (1965) Application of crosscorrelating equipment to linear - system identification, Proc. IEE, Vol. 112 (12).

[3] Golomb, S.W., (1967) Shift register sequences, Holden - Day.

[4] Darnell, M., (1975) The synthesis and applications of uncorrelated sets of pseudorandom sequences, Symposium on Theory and application of Walsh functions, Hatfield.

[5] Darnell, M., (1968) Multi-level pseudorandom signals for system evaluation, Ph.D. Thesis, University of Cambridge.

[6] Harmuth, H.H., (1972) Transmission of information by orthogonal functions, Berlin: Springer-Verlag.

[7] Lee, Y.W., (1960) Statistical theory of communication, Wiley.

[8] Beale, M., (1986) Private correspondence.

[9] Briggs, P.A.N. and Godfrey, K.R., (1966) Pseudorandom signals for the dynamic analysis of multivariable systems, Proc. IEE, Vol. 113(7).

[10] Darnell, M., (1967) Generation of quadratic residue sequences, Elec. Letts., Vol. 3(2).

[11] Golay, M.J.E., (1961) Complementary series IRE Trans. on Info. Th., Vol. IT-7.

[12] Darnell, M., (1975) Principles and applications of binary complementary sequences, Symposium on Theory and applications of Walsh functions, Hatfield.

[13] Tseng, C.C. & Liu, C.L., (1972) Complementary sets of sequences, IEEE Trans. on Info. Th., Vol. IT-18(5).

[14] Godfrey, K.R., (1969) The theory of the correlation method of dynamic analysis and its application to industrial processes and nuclear power plant, Measurement and Control.

[15] Corran, E.R., Cummins, J.D. and Hopkinson, A., (1964) Identification of some cross flow heat exchanger dynamic responses by measurement with low level binary pseudo - random input signals, UKAEA Report AEEW-R 373.

[16] Johnson, D.A.H., (1969) Cross-correlation techniques and their application to communication channel evaluation, Radio and Electronic Engineer, May.

[17] Utsal, J., (1965) Pseudorandom binary noise for system identification, Ph.D. Thesis, University of Cambridge.

[18] Ream, N., (1967) Testing a 2 - input linear system with periodic binary sequences, Proc. IEE, Vol. 114(2).

APPENDIX A: UNCORRELATED SEQUENCES OF THE SAME LENGTH [8]

Consider two sequences S_A and S_B of length

$$N = 2q^2 \qquad (A1)$$

where q is a prime integer (>2). These sequences will have zero crosscorrelation at all shifts if the following construction is employed:

A.1 Sequence S_A

The general format is

$$\boxed{\overrightarrow{A} \mid \overleftarrow{A}} \qquad (A2)$$

where $\overrightarrow{A}$ represents the first half of the sequence and $\overleftarrow{A}$ the same half-sequence, written in the reverse sense. A may be synthesised by the procedure below

$$A = \underbrace{a\ \bar{a}\ a\ \bar{a}\ - - - - a}_{\text{q repetitions of sub-block a with alternate repetitions inverted}} \qquad (A3)$$

where the sub-block a, of length q, is formed by:

$$\left. \begin{array}{l} a_i = 1 \ ; \ \text{for } 0 \leqslant i \leqslant (q-1)/2 \\[4pt] 0 \ ; \ \text{for } (q+1)/2 \leqslant i \leqslant (q-1) \end{array} \right\} \qquad (A4)$$

A.2 Sequence S_B

The general format is

$$\boxed{\vec{B} \mid -\vec{B}} \qquad (A5)$$

where $\vec{B}$ represents the first half of the sequence and $-\vec{B}$ the same half-sequence with all digits inverted, ie an inverse-repeat sequence. B may be synthesised as follows:

$$B = b\ b\ b\ b\ ----\ b \qquad (A6)$$

q repetitions of sub-block b

where the sub-block b, of length q, is formed by:

$$b_i = \begin{array}{l} 1 : \text{for i even} \\ 0 : \text{for i odd} \end{array} \qquad (A6)$$

A.3 Example for q = 3

$$a = 110 \qquad (A8)$$
$$\vec{A} = 110\ 001\ 110 \qquad (A9)$$
$$S_A = 110\ 001\ 110\ 011\ 100\ 011 \qquad (A10)$$
$$b = 101 \qquad (A11)$$
$$\vec{B} = 101\ 101\ 101 \qquad (A12)$$
$$S_B = 101\ 101\ 101\ 010\ 010\ 010 \qquad (A13)$$

Making the transformation

$$\begin{array}{l} 1 \to -1 \\ 0 \to +1 \end{array} \qquad (A14)$$

gives transformed sequences S_A and S_B which have zero crosscorrelation at all values of shift.

APPENDIX B: GENERATION OF BINARY IR SEQUENCES

B.1 Indirect Generation

Section 4 describes a method of synthesising a set of uncorrelated binary PR sequences by multiplying together a binary m - sequence and various rows of a Hadamard matrix. The indirect generation technique implements this combination by making use of the equivalence between modulo-2 addition and analogue multiplication of binary signals, as demonstrated in the truth tables below

Table B1

Truth Tables

$+_2$	0	1
0	0	1
1	1	0

X	+1	-1
+1	+1	-1
-1	-1	+1

a) Modulo-2 Addition   b) Analogue Multiplication

The IR_2 sequence generated by multiplying an m-sequence by row 2 of a Hadamard matrix may also be derived via modulo-2 addition of the m-sequence and the sequence

$$..... 1\ 0\ 1\ 0\ 1\ 0\ 1\ 0\ 1\ 0 ..... \qquad (B1)$$

Similarly, IR_3 and IR_5 sequences may be generated by modulo-2 addition of the m-sequence and the sequences

$$.....1\ 1\ 0\ 0\ 1\ 1\ 0\ 0\ 1\ 1\ 0\ \ 0\ 1\ 1\ 0\ 0 .... \qquad (B2)$$

and
$$...1\ 1\ 1\ 1\ 0\ 0\ 0\ 0\ 1\ 1\ 1\ 1\ 0\ 0\ 0\ 0\ 1\ 1\ 1\ 1\ 0\ 0\ 0\ 0 ....$$
$$\qquad (B3)$$
respectively.

B.2 Direct Generation

It is also possible to generate binary IR sequences directly using feedback shift-registers with the appropriate feedback logic. Table B2 lists the feedback connections for the various lengths of IR sequences; for completeness, feedback connections for binary m-sequence generators are also included.

Table B2

Feedback Connections for m and IR Binary Sequences

UNCORRELATED DIGITAL SEQUENCES 61

Type of Signal (length)	n	Feedback Coefficients															
		a_1	a_2	a_3	a_4	a_5	a_6	a_7	a_8	a_9	a_{10}	a_{11}	a_{12}	a_{13}	a_{14}	a_{15}	a_{16}
m (2^n-1)	3	0	1	1													
	4	0	0	1	1												
	5	0	0	1	0	1											
	6	0	0	0	0	1	1										
	7	0	0	0	1	0	0	1									
	8	0	0	0	1	1	1	0	1								
	9	0	0	0	0	1	0	0	0	1							
	10	0	0	0	0	0	0	1	0	0	1						
	11	0	0	0	0	0	0	0	1	0	1						
	12	0	0	0	0	0	1	0	1	0	0	1	1				

Type of Signal (length)	n	b_1	b_2	b_3	b_4	b_5	b_6	b_7	b_8	b_9	b_{10}	b_{11}	b_{12}	b_{13}	b_{14}	b_{15}	b_{16}
(IR_2) ($2^{n+1}-2$)	3	1	1	0	1												
	4	1	0	1	0	1											
	5	1	0	1	1	1	1										
	6	1	0	0	0	1	0	1									
	7	1	0	0	1	1	0	1	1								
	8	1	0	0	1	0	0	1	1	1							
	9	1	0	0	0	1	1	0	0	1	1						
	10	1	0	0	0	0	0	1	1	0	1	1					
	11	1	0	0	0	0	0	0	1	1	1	1	1				
	12	1	0	0	0	0	1	1	1	1	0	1	0	1			

Type of Signal (length)	n	c_1	c_2	c_3	c_4	c_5	c_6	c_7	c_8	c_9	c_{10}	c_{11}	c_{12}	c_{13}	c_{14}	c_{15}	c_{16}
$(IR)_3$ ($2^{n+2}-4$)	3	0	0	1	1	1											
	4	0	1	1	1	1	1										
	5	0	1	1	0	0	0	1									
	6	0	1	0	0	1	1	1	1								
	7	0	1	0	1	0	1	1	0	1							
	8	0	1	0	1	1	0	1	0	0	1						
	9	0	1	0	0	1	0	1	0	1	0	1					
	10	0	1	0	0	0	0	1	0	1	1	0	1				
	11	0	1	0	0	0	0	0	1	0	0	0	1				
	12	0	1	0	0	0	1	0	0	0	1	1	1	1	1		

Type of Signal (length)	n	d_1	d_2	d_3	d_4	d_5	d_6	d_7	d_8	d_9	d_{10}	d_{11}	d_{12}	d_{13}	d_{14}	d_{15}	d_{16}
$(IR)_5$ ($2^{n+3}-8$)	3	0	1	1	1	0	1	1									
	4	0	0	1	0	0	0	1	1								
	5	0	0	1	1	1	0	1	0	1							
	6	0	0	0	1	1	1	0	0	1	1						
	7	0	0	0	0	0	0	1	1	0	0	1					
	8	0	0	0	0	1	1	0	0	1	1	0	1				
	9	0	0	0	1	1	0	0	0	0	0	0	1				
	10	0	0	0	1	0	0	1	0	0	1	1	0	1			
	11	0	0	0	1	0	0	0	0	1	0	1	0	1	0	1	
	12	0	0	0	1	0	1	0	1	0	1	1	0	0	0	1	1

$(IR)_x$ indicated IR sequence derived using the xth row of the 8th order Hadamard matrix.

It can be shown that, for IR generators, an additional external input '1' must be introduced into the feedback logic [5].

An equivalent generator can be synthesised by incorporating a binary inverter into the feedback logic, rather than the external '1' input.

APPENDIX C: CALCULATION OF THE ACF OF THE COMPOSITE SEQUENCE FORMED BY INTERLEAVING ALTERNATE DIGITS FROM TWO EQUAL-LENGTH COMPONENT SEQUENCES

If two arbitrary component sequences, each N digits in length, are denoted by

$$\left[1_i \right]_{i=1}^{N} \quad \text{and} \quad \left[2_i \right]_{i=1}^{N} \tag{C1}$$

then the composite sequence

$$\left[3_i \right]_{i=1}^{2N} \tag{C2}$$

formed by interleaving alternate digits from the component sequences is

$$[1_1 \; 2_1 \; 1_2 \; 2_2 \; 1_3 \; 2_3 \; \ldots \ldots \; 1_N \; 2_N] \tag{C3}$$

The periodic ACF of this composite sequence at $r = 0$, $\phi_{33}(0)$, is given by

$$\phi_{33}(0) = \phi_{11}(0) + \phi_{22}(0) \tag{C4}$$

where $\phi_{11}(r)$ and $\phi_{22}(r)$ are the periodic ACF's of the two component sequences computed independently.

For $r = 1, 2, 3, \ldots, (2N-1)$, the values of $\phi_{33}(r)$ are as listed below

$$\left. \begin{array}{l} \phi_{33}(1) = \phi_{12}(1) + \phi_{12}(0) \\ \phi_{33}(2) = \phi_{11}(1) + \phi_{22}(1) \\ \phi_{33}(3) = \phi_{12}(2) + \phi_{12}(N-1) \\ \phi_{33}(4) = \phi_{11}(2) + \phi_{22}(2) \\ \phi_{33}(5) = \phi_{12}(3) + \phi_{12}(N-2) \\ \quad \cdot \quad\quad\quad \cdot \quad\quad\quad \cdot \\ \quad \cdot \quad\quad\quad \cdot \quad\quad\quad \cdot \\ \quad \cdot \quad\quad\quad \cdot \quad\quad\quad \cdot \\ \phi_{33}(2N-1) = \phi_{12}(0) + \phi_{12}(1) \end{array} \right\} \tag{C5}$$

UNCORRELATED DIGITAL SEQUENCES   63

where $\phi_{12}(r)$ is the periodic CCF between the two component sequences.

In general

$$\phi_{33}(r) = \begin{rcases} \phi_{11}(r/2) + \phi_{22}(r/2) \ ; \ r \text{ even or zero} \\ \phi_{12}((r+1)/2) + \phi_{12}(N-(r-1)/2) \ ; \ r \text{ odd} \end{rcases}$$
$$(\text{modulo-}N) \qquad (C6)$$

APPENDIX D: PERIODIC & NON-PERIODIC CORRELATION FUNCTION EVALUATION

The distinction between periodic and non-periodic correlation function evaluation will now be explained by means of simple examples.

Consider first the evaluation of the periodic ACF of a periodic 7-bit signal, derived from the corresponding binary m-sequence: the process is illustrated below.

(i) Example of Periodic ACF Evaluation

```
Delay                          Signal                                ACF

         | + + + - - + - | + + + - - + - | + + + - - + - | + .....
  0      | + + + - - + - |
                                                                      +7
  1Δt    |   + + + - - + | -
                                                                      -1
  2Δt    |     + + + - - | + -
                                                                      -1
  3Δt    |       + + + - | - + -
                                                                      -1
  4Δt    |         + + + | - - + -
                                                                      -1
  5Δt    |           + + | + - - + -
                                                                      -1
  6Δt    |             + | + + - - + -
                                                                      -1
  7Δt    |               | + + + - - + -
                                                                      +7
  8Δt    |               |   + + + - - + | -
                                                                      -1
  .                        .                                           .
  .                        .                                           .
  .                        .                                           .
  .                        .                                           .
```

The following points should be noted:

(a) The 3 operations involved in correlation function evaluation are delay, multiplication and integration (or summation).

(b) Periodic correlation evaluation always requires N digits to be multiplied by N digits at each value of delay.

(c) If the PR signal is periodic, its ACF is also periodic.

(d) The signal is assumed to be clocked at a regular rate with clock interval Δt.

A corresponding example involving the evaluation of the non-periodic ACF for the same 7-bit binary signal is now presented in a similar manner.

(ii) Example of Non-Periodic ACF Evaluation

Delay		Signal		ACF
⋮				
	......Zeros......	+ + + − − + −	......Zeros......	
−7Δt	+ + + − − + −			0
−6Δt	+ + + − − +	−		−1
−5Δt	+ + + − −	+ −		0
−4Δt	+ + + −	− + −		−1
−3Δt	+ + +	− − + −		0
−2Δt	+ +	+ − − + −		−1
−1Δt	+	+ + − − + −		0
0		+ + + − − + −		+7
1Δt		+ + + − − +	−	0
2Δt		+ + + − −	+ −	−1
3Δt		+ + + −	− + −	0
4Δt		+ + +	− − + −	−1
5Δt		+ +	+ − − + −	0
6Δt		+	+ + − − + −	−1
7Δt			+ + + − − + −	0
⋮				
	(NC)	(C)	(NC)	

The following points should be noted in this case:

(a) Non-periodic correlation evaluation requires between 0 and N digits to be multiplied together at different values of delay. The regions labelled (NC) above do not contribute to the value of the ACF; the only contributing region is that labelled (C).

(b) If the PR signal is non-periodic, the corresponding ACF is also non-periodic.

(c) A convenient way to measure a non-periodic correlation function is to set up a digital matched filter (MF) in which the taps correspond to a time-reversed representation of the signal to be correlated. If the input to the MF is an

undistorted version of the tap signal, the MF output will be
proportional to the signal ACF; if the MF input is distorted,
the MF output will be proportional to the CCF between the
input and the tap signal.

INFORMATION THEORY WITHOUT THE FINITENESS ASSUMPTION, III:
DATA COMPRESSION AND CODES WHOSE RATES EXCEED UNITY

G.R. Blakley
(Department of Mathematics, Texas A&M University, U.S.A.)

and

C. Meadows
*(Information Technology Division, Naval Research Laboratory,
Washington, U.S.A)*

ABSTRACT

Codes of all sorts have a group-theoretic structure which can be explicitly stated, and then exploited to define and investigate their properties. The group-theoretic viewpoint helps explain the nature of Gray codes. This paper deals largely with rates of codes, particularly of nonblock codes. The framework within which these calculations can be made appears novel. This paper proves three theorems. One says that every code belonging to the class of what are called Kraft-McMillan equality codes has a rate no smaller than 1. Another describes maximal-rate codes within subclasses of this class. The description is in terms of the rate of a certain natural Huffman code. The third relates the rate of a Kraft-McMillan equality code to the amounts by which it compresses information when viewed, in several ways, as a Huffman code.

1. INTRODUCTION

Hamming codes provide error control. A user pays an overhead in message expansion and accepts a rate smaller than 1. Huffman codes compress text. So a user attains message contraction and expects to enjoy a rate larger than 1. This paper's approach to the rate problem arises from the realization [BL85; BL86] that group-theoretic structures pervade cryptography and information theory, and from the consequent attempt to reformulate these fields in a uniform manner in a group-theoretic context.

2. DEFINITION OF CODES AS GROUP-THEORETIC OBJECTS

We will extend the usual definition [PA66, p. 15] of domain and range of a function [PA66, p. 15] to a definition of domain and range of a relation [PA66, p. 15] as follows. Let R be a relation from A to B, i.e. suppose that R is a subset of the cartesian product [PA66, p. 15] of A and B. Thus $R \subseteq A \times B$. We let

$DOM(R) = \{a \in A : \text{there is some } b \in B \text{ such that } (a,b) \in R\}$,

$RAN(R) = \{b \in B : \text{there is some } a \in A \text{ such that } (a,b) \in R\}$.

Also we will speak of B as being the codomain [PA66, p. 16] of R and write $B = CODOM(R)$.

For any relation $R \subseteq A \times B$, the converse [GR85, p. 88] of R is the set

$CONV(R) = \{(b,a) \in B \times A : (a,b) \in R\}$.

It is obvious that $CONV(CONV(R)) = R$, and hence that $CONV(R) \circ R$ is the diagonal [HE64, p. 5] relation

$DIAG(DOM(R)) = \{(a,a) \in A \times A : a \in DOM(R)\}$

and that $R \circ CONV(R)$ is the diagonal relation

$DIAG(RAN(R)) = \{(b,b) \in B \times B : b \in RAN(R)\}$.

Here, of course, $S \circ R$ is the composite [GR85, p. 131] relation, R followed by S. If $R \subseteq A \times B$ is a function and the converse of R is also a function $CONV(R) \subseteq B \times A$, then this converse is called the inverse [GR85, p. 88] of the function R. But there is a bit more to be said. If we write $R : DOM(R) \to B$ then R might not be surjective (i.e. onto [MO63, p. 495]) and $CONV(R)$ might be merely a left inverse of R. This means that we only know that

$CONV(R) \circ R : DOM(R) \to DOM(R)$

is the identity function with domain $DOM(R)$, but cannot conclude that $R \circ CONV(R)$ is the identity function with domain A. If we write

$CONV(R) : RAN(R) \to A$

then $CONV(R)$ might not be surjective and R might be merely a left inverse of $CONV(R)$. So we would know only that

$$R \circ CONV(R) : RAN(R) \to RAN(R)$$

is the identity function with domain RAN(R), but could not conclude that CONV(R) $\circ$ R is the identity function with domain B. We could, however, be more modest and write either

$$R : DOM(R) \to RAN(R), \text{ or}$$

$$CONV(R) : RAN(R) \to DOM(R).$$

Then we know that CONV(R) is a two-sided inverse of R, so that both R and CONV(R) are bijections [MO63, p. 495] and that R $\circ$ CONV(R) is the identity function on RAN(R) and that CONV(R) $\circ$ R is the identity function on DOM(R).

Definition 2.1: Let P and C be groups [PA66, pp. 78-80], which we will think of as being collections of plaintext symbols, and collections of codetext symbols, respectively. Let E be a relation from P to C, and let D be a relation from C to P. Thus E $\subseteq$ P x C, and D $\subseteq$ C x P. We think of E as an encoding process and of D as a decoding process. Now consider a 4-entry list (P,C,E,D) with P, C, E and D as above. We will call this list (P,C,E,D) a code from (the plaintext group) P to (the codetext group) C if (the decoding process) D is a function [PA66, p. 15] such that the composite [GR85, p. 131] relation D $\circ$ E $\subseteq$ P x R is the identity function [PA66, p. 16] on the set

$$DOM(E \cap CONV(D)).$$

We know that DOM(E) $\subseteq$ P, that RAN(D) $\subseteq$ R, that DOM(D) $\subseteq$ C, and that RAN(E) $\subseteq$ C. But we should be reluctant to infer other relationships among these six sets on the basis of our experience of one or another type of familiar code.

There are codes in which DOM(D) $\neq$ C, whence in these codes there are symbols which cannot be decoded. But the fact that D is a function means that there are no codes with codetext symbols which can be decoded in more than one way. This despite the fact that there are codes in which several different plaintext symbols are encoded by the same codetext symbol, i.e. there are codes in which there is an element c of C, and there are two distinct elements p, π of P, such that both (p,c) and (π,c) belong to E.

We have a (not very important) choice as to whether to write the function D as D : DOM(D) $\to$ RAN(D) or as D : DOM(D) $\to$ P. We will adopt the convention D : DOM(D) $\to$ P.

We will now give exact definitions of what D. Kahn [KA67, pp. xiv., 113] calls homophones, nulls and polyphones.

Definition 2.2: We define H, N, Π and Δ by setting

$H = \{(c,\nu) \; \varepsilon \; \text{RAN}(E) \times \text{RAN}(E) :$ There exists $p \; \varepsilon \; P$ such that

$\{(p,c), (p,\nu)\} \subseteq E\} \}$

$N = C \setminus \text{DOM}(D)$

$\Pi = \{(p,\pi) \; \varepsilon \; \text{DOM}(E) \times \text{DOM}(E) :$ There exists $c \; \varepsilon \; C$ such that

$\{(p,c), (\pi,c)\} \subseteq E\} \}$

$\Delta = P \setminus \text{DOM}(E)$

The members of N are called nulls (codetext symbols which have no plaintext D-descendants). A null may, but does not have to, have an E-ancestor. The members of Δ are called dulls (plaintext symbols which have no codetext E-descendants). A dull may, but does not have to, have a D-ancestor. If $(p,\pi) \; \varepsilon \; \Pi$ then we say that the plaintext symbols p and π are polyphonic (or that p is polyphonic to π). This amounts to saying that they have at least one common codetext E-descendant c. If, additionally, $p \neq \pi$ we say that p and π are nontrivially polyphonic with each other. If $(c,\nu) \; \varepsilon \; H$ then we say that the codetext symbols c and ν are homophonic (or that c is homophonic to ν). This amounts to saying that they have at least one common plaintext E-ancestor p. If, additionally, $c \neq \nu$ we say that c and ν are nontrivially homophonic with one another. Evidently H is a symmetric binary relation on P and Π is a symmetric binary relation on C. Also Π is a reflexive binary relation on DOM(E), but not necessarily on P. In other words a plaintext symbol $p \; \varepsilon \; P$ will not be polyphonic to itself if it does not belong to DOM(E), i.e. if it has no codetext E-descendant, i.e. if it is a dull. Similarly H is a reflexive binary relation on RAN(E) but not necessarily on C. Thus a codetext symbol $c \; \varepsilon \; C$ will not be homophonic to itself if it does not belong to RAN(E), i.e. if it has no plaintext E-ancestor. It is easy, however, to give an example of a code (P,C,E,D) and a codetext symbol c which is not homophonic to itself, but which is not a null. See Section 3 below. Our definition of code allows the existence of nontrivial polyphones p and π even though decoding is unique. Only when we know that two polyphones p and π both belong to RAN(D) can we conclude that $p = \pi$.

Lemma 2.3: If p and π are nontrivially polyphonic then every one of their common E images is a null.

Proof: Suppose that $(p,π) ε Π$ and $p ≠ π$. Now consider any symbol $c ε C$ such that (p,c) and $(π,c)$ belong to E. If $c \notin N$ then there is a pair $(c,q) ε D$. Therefore both (p,q) and $(π,q)$ belong to $D ○ E$. But $(p,q) ≠ (π,q)$. Hence either $(p,q) ≠ (q,q)$ or $(π,q) ≠ (q,q)$. This implies that $D ○ E$ is not a diagonal relation and, consequently, that $D ○ E$ is not an identity function.

The foregoing definition of code is comprehensive enough to embrace the genetic code, many diplomatic and naval secrecy codes [KA67], commercial codebooks [KA67, pp. 836-853] Gray codes, and anti-Gray codes [HA86, p. 12-13, 97-100]. It also includes all error-control codes [BL83; MA78; PE72], all the uniquely decodables codes [HA86, pp. 52-78], all the hashing schemes [HA86, pp. 94-97], and virtually all the cryptosystems [KA67; DE83] the authors are familiar with. It also embraces many objects not hitherto viewed as codes, e.g. Fourier, Laplace and other kinds of transforms (so that deblurring of photographs becomes a decode process), differentiation and integration, Galois connections, etc.

3. EXAMPLE OF A SMALL CODE

We consider a small code (P,C,E,D) in which

P = { 1,2,3,4,5,6,7}

C = {a,b,c,d,e,f,g,h,i,j}

E = {(1,b),(1,c),(1,d),(2,d),(2,e),(2,f),(3,f),(3,g),(4,h)}

D = {(a,1),(b,1),(e,2),(g,3),(i,5)}.

It follows that

$$\text{CONV}(D) = \{(1,a),(1,b),(2,e),(3,g),(5,i)\}$$

$$E \cap \text{CONV}(D) = \{(1,b),(2,e),(3,g)\}$$

$$\text{DOM}(E \cap \text{CONV}(D)) = \{1,2,3\}$$

$$D \circ E = \{(1,1),(2,2),(3,3)\}$$

$$N = \{c,d,f,h,j\}$$

$$\Delta = \{5,6,7\}$$

$$H = \{(b,b),(b,c),(b,d),(c,b),(c,c),(c,d),(d,b),(d,c),$$
$$(d,d),(d,e),(d,f),(e,d),(e,e),(e,f),(f,d),(f,e),$$
$$(f,f),(f,g),(g,f),(g,g),(h,h)\}$$

$$\Pi = \{(1,1),(1,2),(2,1),(2,2),(2,3),(3,2),(3,3),(4,4)\}$$

$$E(\Delta) = \emptyset$$

$$D^{-1}(\Delta) = \{i\}$$

$$D(N) = \emptyset$$

$$E^{-1}(N) = \{1,2,4\}.$$

Note, at this point, that neither (a,a) nor (i,i) nor (j,j) belong to H. Thus the codetext symbol i has no homophone, not even i itself. Note that j is a null but i is not. Neither (5,5) nor (6,6) nor (7,7) belong to Π. Thus of 5 has no polyphone, not even 5 itself. Similarly 6,7. And, of course, all three of these plaintext symbols are dulls. Evidently $D \circ E$ is the identity function with domain and range equal to DOM(E CONV(D)). Also we see that the codetext symbols d and f are nulls, as they must be according to Lemma 2.3, since (1,2) and (2,3) belong to Π.

The group-theoretic structures on P and C are of no import here. There is no harm in taking them to be $Z/7Z$ and $Z/10Z$, respectively, where Z is the ring of integers.

4. THE DEFINITIONS OF THE RATE OF A CODE AS A RATIO OF LOGARITHMIC ASSESSMENTS OF THE SIZES OF DOM(E) and DOM(D)

The informal idea behind the definition of rate is to take the ratio of two logarithms. The numerator is the log of something like the size of the collection of plaintext symbols and the denominator is the log of something like the size of

INFORMATION THEORY   73

the collection of codetext symbols. In block codes such as a Hamming (n,k) code this can become

$$\frac{\log(\text{cardinality}((GF(2))^k))}{\log(\text{cardinality}((GF(2))^n))} = \frac{\dim((GF(2))^k)}{\dim((GF(2))^n)} = \frac{k}{n}$$

where the dimensionality of $(GF(2))^n = GF(2) \times GF(2) \times \ldots \times GF(2)$ is with respect to the underlying field $GF(2)$. It would be tempting, on the basis of this and other block code examples, to expect the general principle to be

$$\text{rate} = \frac{\text{logarithmic assessment of the size of P}}{\text{logarithmic assessment of the size of C}}.$$

But we will argue by example and theorem below that the correct informal definition of rate is

$$\text{rate}((P,C,E,D)) = \frac{\text{logarithmic assessment of the size of DOM}(E)}{\text{logarithmic assessment of the size of DOM}(D)}.$$

In other words, there is no use taking dulls or nulls into account when calculating rates (there are none of either in a sensibly designed block code). The last ratio above sometimes amounts to

$$\frac{\log_b(\text{cardinality}(DOM(E)))}{\log_b(\text{cardinality}(DOM(D)))} = \log_{\text{cardinality}(DOM(D))}(\text{cardinality}(DOM(E))).$$

But this last expression can become useless in infinite structures. However, it can sometimes be replaced by

$$\frac{\dim_F(DOM(E))}{\dim_F(DOM(D))}$$

where both finite dimensionalities are calculated over a common infinite field F. This last expression, in turn can become useless in infinite dimensional cases, and may have to be replaced by

$$\dim_{DOM(D)}(DOM(E))$$

in instances in which DOM(E) is in a natural way a module over DOM(D), considered in some natural way as a ring.

Even further abstraction is possible. We are sometimes able to regain fractional rates for infinite dimensional modules over infinite rings. For example, if in some natural manner,

$$\text{DOM}(E) \times \text{DOM}(E) \times \text{DOM}(E) \simeq \text{DOM}(D) \times \text{DOM}(D)$$

we might be justified in speaking of (P,C,E,D) as a code of rate 2/3. Thus, for example, we know that

$$(\text{GF}(2^4))^7 = \text{GF}(2^4) \times \ldots \times \text{GF}(2^4)$$

can be bijectively mapped onto

$$(\text{GF}(2^7))^4 = \text{GF}(2^7) \times \ldots \times \text{GF}(2^7),$$

and conversely. It is not too hard to use these facts to argue that the Hamming (7,4) code has rate 4/7.

But even this degree of abstraction is not enough if either DOM(E) or DOM(D) is a proper subset, but not a subspace or submodule, of a vector space or a module. And this is the case with the codes we will treat in Example 5.3 below, as well as in Sections 6 and 7. Note that the base b of the logarithm function log has so far been irrelevant to the calculations. But we will presuppose the information theorist's logarithm (to base 2) everywhere below.

5. TWO EXAMPLES OF CODES AND THEIR RATES: GRAY CODES AND KRAFT-McMILLAN EQUALITY CODES

Example 5. A Gray code. Gray codes in general.

In Gray codes we see clearly the value of the group-theoretic approach to codes. A short examination of Table 5.1 will convince the reader that its 81 entries (each entry being a pair of lists of 4 ternary digits) have a special property. You always go from one pair to the next by adding 1 (modulo 81) to the nonnegative integer described in ternary notation by the first entry of the pair, and by adding one of the vectors 1000 or 0100 or 0010 or 0001 to the vector described by the second entry (using positionwise addition modulo 3 without carry).

In other words, we have

$P = Z/81Z$

$C = Z/3Z \otimes Z/3Z \otimes Z/3Z \otimes Z/3Z$

$G = \{1 = 0001\} \subseteq P$

$\Gamma = \{(1,0,0,0) = 1000, (0,1,0,0) = 0100, (0,0,1,0) = 0010,$

$$(0,0,0,1) = 0001\} \subseteq C.$$

G is a singleton set of generators for the (additive) group
P and Γ is a 4-member set of generators for the (additive)
group C. The idea of a Gray code, then, is this. The plaintext
symbol group is a cyclic group $P = Z/\pi^k Z$ of order π^k and the
codetext group is a torus, i.e. is the product $C = (Z/\pi Z)^k$ of
k cyclic groups $Z/\pi Z$ of order π. There is a distinguished
generator g of P and a set of Γ of k distinguished generators
of C. For every p ε P there is a generator γ(p) ε Γ such
that

$$E(p+g) = E(p) + \gamma(p).$$

In other words, as you walk from plaintext symbol to plaintext
symbol by generator-sized steps, the encode process is
producing a corresponding walk through the group of codetext
symbols by generator-sized steps. This description shows the
mathematical essence of Gray codes clearly, and without
reference to extraneous notions. We have, in other words,
merely brought to light a group-theoretic structure which was
there, unrecognized, all along.

What the reader can easily do for Table 5.1 and indeed for
analogous Gray codes specified by any parameters π and k, is
give definitions of E and D which make it evident that
E : P → C and D : C → P are bijections, and in fact are two-
sided inverses of one another, and show that E has the Gray
property (that generator-sized steps in P induce generator-sized
steps in C).

Admittedly, we indulge in an abuse of the + notation. We say
that, in P, 1212 is the integer fifty (modulo eighty one) so
that 1212 + 1212 = 0201, i.e. the integer nineteen. Then we go
on to say that, in C, 1212 is the vector (1,2,1,2) so that
1212 + 1212 = 2121. But it is harmless abuse which cannot
mislead under the circumstances, since it will always be clear
from the context which structure such a string of 4 ternary
digits lies in.

It is obvious, in the example at hand, that the encode
process E : P → C is defined by setting

$E((p(3),p(2),p(1),p(0))) = (p(3), p(2)-p(3), p(1)-p(2), p(0)-p(1))$

and the decode process D : C → P is defined by setting

$D((c(3),c(2),c(1),c(0))) =$

$(c(3), c(3)+c(2), c(3)+c(2)+c(1), c(3)+c(2)+c(1)+c(0)).$

All the addition and subtraction immediately above is, of course,
performed in Z/3Z. The proof that E and D are two-sided

inverses of each other is just the proof of the fundamental theorem of the finite calculus, [RO64, p. 347, BO57, pp. 62-65], viz. that differences undo sums and vice-versa, just as differentiation and integration are inverse operations in the infinitesimal calculus. So it only remains to verify that (P,C,E,D) is really a Gray code. But the reader can easily verify that

$$E(p+1) - E(p) \in \{0001, 0010, 0100, 1000\}$$

(where the subtraction immediately above is performed in C, i.e. modulo 3 in each of the four ternary digit positions independently, but the addition is performed in P, i.e. by considering a list of four ternary digits an integer taken from $\{0,1,2,\ldots,80\}$ and adding 1 to this integer modulo 81) for every $p \in P$.

Thus the code in Table 5.1 is indeed a Gray code.

In the case of our Gray code it would take some effort to provide a natural way to view $Z/81Z$ as a vector space over $Z/3Z$, so we again fall back on the cardinality approach to defining rate and get

$$\text{rate}((P,C,E,D)) = \frac{\log(\text{cardinality}(DOM(E)))}{\log(\text{cardinality}(DOM(D)))} = \frac{\log(81)}{\log(81)} = 1.$$

And this is what we would want for a code which encodes lists of 4 ternary digits into lists of 4 ternary digits.

p	E(p)	p	E(p)	p	E(p)
0000	0000	1000	1200	2000	2100
0001	0001	1001	1201	2001	2101
0002	0002	1002	1202	2002	2102
0010	0012	1010	1212	2010	2112
0011	0010	1011	1210	2011	2110
0012	0011	1012	1211	2012	2111
0020	0021	1020	1221	2020	2121
0021	0022	1021	1222	2021	2122
0022	0020	1022	1220	2022	2120
0100	0120	1100	1020	2100	2220
0101	0121	1101	1021	2101	2221
0102	0122	1102	1022	2102	2222
0110	0102	1110	1002	2110	2202
0111	0100	1111	1000	2111	2200
0112	0101	1112	1001	2112	2201
0120	0111	1120	1011	2120	2211
0121	0112	1121	1012	2121	2212
0122	0110	1122	1010	2122	2210
0200	0210	1200	1110	2200	2010
0201	0211	1201	1111	2201	2011
0202	0212	1202	1112	2202	2012
0210	0222	1210	1122	2210	2022
0211	0220	1211	1120	2211	2020
0212	0221	1212	1121	2212	2021
0220	0201	1220	1101	2220	2001
0221	0202	1221	1102	2221	2002
0222	0200	1222	1100	2222	2000

Table 5.1

A complete listing of the 81 ordered pairs which make up the encode function E in a Gray code (P,C,E,D). Here P = Z/81Z. Its members are written as ternary 4-digit words. Also C = Z/3Z $\tilde{\otimes}$ Z/3Z $\tilde{\otimes}$ Z/3Z $\otimes$ Z/3Z. Its members are written as ternary 4-digit words. The function D is the two sided inverse of the bijection E whose values are tabulated above.

i	1	2	3	4	5	
p(i)	000	001	010	011	100	the 5 plaintext words p(1), p(2), ... , p(5)
E(p(i))	1	01	000	0010	0011	corresponding (P,C,E,D) codetext words
$\overline{E}$(p(i))	00	10	11	010	011	corresponding $(\overline{P},\overline{C},\overline{E},\overline{D})$ codetext words

# of occurrences in the _____ words of corpus _									
# of occurrences in the 1035 words of corpus 1	1000	20	10	3	2	2.848	Y	1.496	N
# of occurrences in the 16 words of corpus 2	8	4	2	1	1	1.600	Y	1.411	N
# of occurrences in the 10 words of corpus 3	4	2	2	1	1	1.363	Y	1.363	Y
# of occurrences in the 12 words of corpus 4	4	2	2	2	2	1.200	N	1.285	Y
# of occurrences in the 8 words of corpus 5	2	2	2	1	1	1.200	N	1.333	Y
# of occurrences in the 5 words of corpus 6	1	1	1	1	1	1.071	N	1.250	Y
# of occurrences in the 11111 words of corpus 7	1	10	100	1000	10000	0.752	N	1.003	N

The ratio of the # of (P,C,E,D) plaintext bits to the # of codetext bits (in corpus j with the frequency distribution shown on the line in question) is

Is there Huffman codetext for this frequency distribution whose word lengths are 1, 2, 3, 4, 4, as they are in (P,C,E,D)?

The ratio of the # of $(\overline{P},\overline{C},\overline{E},\overline{D})$ plaintext bits to the # of codetext bits (in corpus j with the frequency distribution shown on the line in question) is

Is there a Huffman code for this frequency distribution whose codetext word lengths are 2, 2, 3, 3, 3, as they are in $(\overline{P},\overline{C},\overline{E},\overline{D})$?

Table 5.2 Two codes, (P,C,E,D) and $(\overline{P},\overline{C},\overline{E},\overline{D})$, the amounts by which they compress (or, in 1 case out of 14, expand) text when applied to 7 literary corpora whose plaintext word frequencies are shown above, and an answer to the question of whether they amount to Huffman code for these literary corpora.

The rate of (P,C,E,D) is 1.6000, and that of $(\overline{P},\overline{C},\overline{E},\overline{D})$ is 1.3333... .

Example 5.2: Huffman codes described in a Hamming book.

R. Hamming [HA86, pp. 63-68] gives an illuminating example of twin Huffman codes (P,C,E,D) and $(\overline{P},\overline{C},\overline{E},\overline{D})$ which have a common plaintext symbol alphabet $P = \overline{P}$ and a common codetext symbol alphabet $C = \overline{C}$. The common domain $DOM(E) = DOM(\overline{E})$ of the encode relations E and $\overline{E}$ is a 5-member set

$$DOM(E) = DOM(\overline{E}) = \{p(1),p(2),p(3),p(4),p(5)\} \subseteq P.$$

There is some arbitrariness about the group-theoretic structure which one ought to impose on P. There is no harm in letting

$$P = \overline{P} = DOM(E) = DOM(\overline{E}) = Z/5Z.$$

But it seems more natural to set

$$P = \overline{P} = GF(8),$$

i.e. to assume that $DOM(E) = DOM(\overline{E})$ consists of five 3-bit words. The group-theoretic structure on the common codetext symbol alphabet $C = \overline{C}$ is more natural and inevitable. Here $C = \overline{C}$ is the graded algebra [NI59, pp. 222-238] on

$$GF(2) \cup GF(4) \cup GF(8) \cup GF(16) \cup \ldots$$

i.e. the additive group of formal sums s of formal products which look like

$$s = u(1)v(1) + u(2)v(2) + u(3)v(3) + u(4)v(4) + \ldots$$

where, for each i, $u(i) \in GF(2)$ and $v(j)$ belongs to $GF(2^j)$.

In Hamming's twin examples, E and $\overline{E}$ are the mappings:

$E(p(1)) = 1;$	$\overline{E}(p(1)) = 00;$
$E(p(2)) = 01;$	$\overline{E}(p(2)) = 10;$
$E(p(3)) = 000;$	$\overline{E}(p(3)) = 11;$
$E(p(4)) = 0010;$	$\overline{E}(p(4)) = 010;$
$E(p(5)) = 0011;$	$\overline{E}(p(5)) = 011.$

Both E and $\overline{E}$ are injections. We will abuse notation a bit and use the same symbols E, $\overline{E}$ for their restrictions to their common domain

$$E : DOM(E) \to RAN(E)$$
$$\overline{E} : DOM(\overline{E}) \to RAN(\overline{E})$$

These two latter functions are bijections. So let D be the bijection

$$D : RAN(E) \to DOM(E)$$

which is a two-sided inverse of E. Similarly $\overline{D}$ and $\overline{E}$. We have now defined (P,C,E,D) and $(\overline{P},\overline{C},\overline{E},\overline{D})$.

Now Hamming shows that both (P,C,E,D) and $(\overline{P},\overline{C},\overline{E},\overline{D})$ are Huffman code when the plaintext symbol frequencies are as follows:

$$\text{freq}(p(1)) = 0.4;$$
$$\text{freq}(p(2)) = 0.2;$$
$$\text{freq}(p(3)) = 0.2;$$
$$\text{freq}(p(4)) = 0.1;$$
$$\text{freq}(p(5)) = 0.1;$$
$$\text{freq}(p) = 0$$

if p is a member of the set $P \setminus DOM(E) = P \setminus DOM(\overline{E})$.

Huffman code must satisfy the Kraft-McMillan equality (i.e. the equality condition in the Kraft or McMillan inequalities [HA86, pp. 57-63]). To state this equality we let a(i) be the number of members of RAN(E) which belong to $GF(2^i)$ and let $\overline{a}(i)$ be the number of members of RAN($\overline{E}$) which belong to $GF(2^i)$. Then the Kraft-McMillan equality in this case is the requirement that

$$a(1)/2 + a(2)/4 * a(3)/8 + a(4)/16 = 1$$
$$\overline{a}(1)/2 + \overline{a}(2)/4 + \overline{a}(3)/8 + \overline{a}(4)/16 = 1.$$

In our case:

$$a(1) = 1; \quad a(3) = 1; \quad \overline{a}(1) = 0; \quad \overline{a}(3) = 2;$$
$$a(2) = 1; \quad a(4) = 2; \quad \overline{a}(2) = 3; \quad \overline{a}(4) = 0.$$

Hence

$$\Sigma\, a(j)/2^j = 1/2 + 1/4 + 1/8 + 2/16 = 1$$
$$\Sigma\, \overline{a}(j)/2^j = 0/2 + 3/4 + 2/8 + 0/16 = 1.$$

In general a sequence {a(1), a(2), a(3), ... } of nonnegative integers (terminating or otherwise) satisfies the Kraft-McMillan equality if $\Sigma\, a(j)/2^j = 1$.

INFORMATION THEORY   81

If applied to a literary corpus whose 3-bit plaintext symbols have the frequencies given above, the code (P,C,E,D) takes the 30 bits in ten plaintext symbols and yields ten codetext symbols which consist of

$$4*1 + 2*2 + 2*3 + 1*4 + 1*4 = 22$$

bits. Applied to this same literary corpus, the code (P,C,E,D) turns 30 bits into

$$4*2 + 2*2 + 2*2 + 1*3 + 1*3 = 22$$

bits. Each is equally compressive, and obviously each has a rate in excess of 1. But what is rate in a situation such as this?

The major problem in defining rate for Huffman codes is that DOM(D) consists of words of differing lengths. So giving a logarithmic assessment of its size might seem to involve correlating incommensurables. But this is not really the case. The definition of rate we will give for nonblock codes is based on the notion that if you have five 7-bit words you have 5/128 of a 7 dimensional space. So a logarithmic assessment of the size of the set

$$\{\ 0010101,\ 0000000,\ 1110001,\ 1101100,\ 0101010\ \}$$

is $7 * 5/128 = 35/128$.

If we find that DOM(D) = { 00001, 10101, 1011, 1111, 0000, 11 } we can say it has two 5-bit words, three 4-bit words and one 2-bit word. So our logarithmic assessment of the size of DOM(D) is $5*2/32 + 4*3/16 + 2*1/4 = 25/16$. Thus when we use the heuristic definition

$$\text{rate}((P,C,E,D)) = \frac{\text{logarithmic assessment of the size of DOM(E)}}{\text{logarithmic assessment of the size of DOM(D)}}$$

we can say either

$$\text{rate}((P,C,E,D)) = \frac{\log(5)}{1*1/2 + 2*1/4 + 3*1/8 + 4*2/16}$$

or

$$\text{rate}((P,C,E,D)) = \frac{[\log(5)]}{1*1/2 + 2*1/4 + 3*1/8 + 4*2/16}\ .$$

It would appear most natural to assume that Huffman codes are predicated (as Hamming seems [HA86, p. 51-68] to imply) on the problem of doing better than a block code whose words have an integer (rather than an arbitrary real) number of bits. If we did this we would reject the numerator $\log(5) = 2.12\ldots$ in favour of the numerator $\lceil \log(5) \rceil = 3$. But it will turn out that we don't have to reject either alternative. Every theorem, we want to prove is compatible with both possible definitions, as long as we define our denominator appropriately, i.e. in the manner adumbrated above.

So, if we define L by setting

$$L = \text{logarithmic assessment of the size of DOM}(E)$$

then we know, since $\text{DOM}(\overline{E}) = \text{DOM}(E)$,

$$L = \text{logarithmic assessment of the size of DOM}(\overline{E}).$$

Thus (whether $L = \log(5)$, or $L = \lceil \log(5) \rceil = 3$, or L has yet some other value) we can say that

$$\text{rate}((P,C,E,D)) = \frac{L}{1*1/2 + 2*1/4 + 3*1/8 + 4*2/16} = \frac{L}{\Sigma \; ja(j)/2^j} = 8L/15$$

$$\text{rate}((\overline{P},\overline{C},\overline{E},\overline{D})) = \frac{L}{1*0/2 + 2*3/4 + 3*2/8 + 4*0/16} = \frac{L}{\Sigma \; ja(j)/2^j} = 8L/18$$

Consequently

$$\text{rate}((\overline{P},\overline{C},\overline{E},\overline{D})) = (5/6) \; \text{rate}((P,C,E,D)) < \text{rate}((P,C,E,D))$$

no matter how we define L.

The positive real number rate $((P,C,E,D))$ was calculated without reference to any plaintext literary corpus which the code (P,C,E,D) might encode. Similarly rate $((\overline{P},\overline{C},\overline{E},\overline{D}))$. So would it be reasonable to expect to infer from rate $((P,C,E,D))$ very much information regarding how well the code (P,C,E,D) compresses any given plaintext literary corpus? The fact is that rate does tell us quite a bit about compression. To make this clear we need to study Table 5.2 carefully. It describes how much (P,C,E,D) compresses each of seven different plaintext literary corpora, as well as how much $(\overline{P},\overline{C},\overline{E},\overline{D})$ does. It relates the rates of (P,C,E,D) and $(\overline{P},\overline{C},\overline{E},\overline{D})$ to these compressions. In each of these 14 cases it tells whether the code in question can be (isomorphic to) Huffman code for the plaintext literary corpus in question.

INFORMATION THEORY 83

An understanding of the information reported by Table 5.2 is necessary for a full understanding of the theorems and lemmas stated in Section 6 below.

6. THREE CODE-RATE THEOREMS FOR CODES WHICH OBEY THE KRAFT-McMILLAN EQUALITY

Definition 6.1: A Kraft-McMillan equality v-code is a code (P,C,E,D) in which the following six conditions are satisfied:

i) cardinality (DOM(E)) = cardinality (RAN(E)) = v;

ii) $P \subseteq GF(2^{\log(v)})$;

iii) $C = GF(2) \cup GF(4) \cup GF(8) \cup \ldots$;

iv) There are a(j) codetext words of length j (bits) belonging to RAN(E) for every positive integer j;

v) $\Sigma\ a(j) = v$;

vi) $\Sigma\ a(j)/2^j = 1$.

The rate of such a code can be defined either as

$$\text{rate}((P,C,E,D)) = \log(v)\ /\ \Sigma\ ja(j)/2^j$$

or as

$$\text{rate}((P,C,E,D)) = \log(v)\ /\ \Sigma\ ja(j)/2^j.$$

Either definition gives rise to all the results of this section.

Theorem 6.2: The rate of a Kraft-McMillan equality of v-code (P,C,E,D) is equal to the compression (i.e. the ratio of number of plaintext bits to number of codetext bits) this code (P,C,E,D) effects on a plaintext literary corpus whose frequencies are as follows. If a plaintext word p is encoded to a codetext word of length i, then the frequency of p is 2^{v-i}. The code (P,C,E,D) is isomorphic to a Huffman code for this plaintext literary corpus, i.e. one of the possible Huffman encodings of this corpus, based on these frequencies, has the same word lengths as (P,C,E,D).

To get a feel for Theorem 6.2 it is useful to look back at Table 5.2. The rate of the first code, (P,C,E,D), is equal to 48/30 = 1.6. There are Huffman codes isomorphic to (P,C,E,D) for frequency distributions 1, 2, and 3, but not for frequency distributions 4, 5, 6, or 7. The compressions the three Huffman codes afford are 2.8486..., 1.6 and 1.3636... respectively. Thus the rate is one of these compressions (associated with frequency distribution 2). Similarly the rate of the second code, $(\overline{P},\overline{C},\overline{E},\overline{D})$; is equal to $24/18 = 1.3333...$. There are Huffman codes isomorphic to $(\overline{P},\overline{C},\overline{E},\overline{D})$ for frequency distribution 3, 4, 5 and 6, but not for frequency distributions 1, 2 or 7. The compressions the four Huffman codes effect are 1.3636..., 1.2857..., 1.3333... and 1.25. Again we find the rate of (P,C,E,D) among them, being the compression effected upon frequency distribution 5.

Theorem 6.2, then, relates the rate of a Kraft-McMillan equality v-code (P,C,E,D) to a large set K of real numbers. This rate, a single real number rate $((P,C,E,D))$, is a member of the set K of compressions achieved by the code on various literary corpora. The compression of (P,C,E,D) on a literary corpus L is a member of K is the occurrence frequencies of symbols in L are such that (P,C,E,D) could be Huffman code for L.

A straightforward argument based on Jensen's inequality [RU74, pp. 63-64] yields the following.

Lemma 6.3 Suppose that

$$a = \{ a(1), a(2), a(3), ... \}$$

is an eventually zero nonnegative integer sequence which obeys the Kraft-McMillan equality $\Sigma\, a(j)/2^j = 1$. Then

$$\log(v) = \log(\Sigma\, a(j)) \geq \Sigma\, j a(j)/2^j.$$

Equality holds if and only if there is an integer j for which $v = 2^j$ and

$$a = \{0, 0, 0, ..., a(j-1) = 1, a(j) = 2^j, a(j+1) = 0, 0, 0, ...\}$$
$$= \{0, 0, 0, ..., 0, 2^j, 0, 0, 0, ...\}.$$

It is now a trivial matter to verify

Theorem 6.4: Suppose that (P,C,E,D) is a Kraft-McMillan equality v-code. Then rate $((P,C,E,D)) \geq 2$. Moreover rate $((P,C,E,D)) = 1$ if and only if the cardinality of DOM(E) is a positive integer power of 2, say 2^y, and RAN(E) = $GF(2^y)$.

In short, a Kraft-McMillan equality code has a rate no less than 1. Moreover, its rate is equal to 1 if and only if it maps a set of cardinality 2^y onto the set of all y-bit words. The low-rate (i.e. rate 1) Kraft-McMillan equality codes are just bijections from one set of cardinality 2^y to another. This amounts to saying that they are just the most trivial sorts of block codes, being essentially permutations of $GF(2^y)$.

Our third theorem has no bite unless the cardinality v of DOM(E) is at least 3. The reason for this is that it would be wasteful of bandwidth to use anything other than 0 and 1 to encode plaintext if there were fewer than 3 plaintext symbols. So the v ≥ 3 hypothesis is not arbitrary or onerous restriction.

Theorem 6.5: Let v be an integer no smaller than 3. Suppose that (P,C,E,D) is a Kraft-McMillan equality v-code. Then rate ((P,C,E,D)) is no greater than rate ($(\overline{P},\overline{C},\overline{E},\overline{D})$) where $(\overline{P},\overline{C},\overline{E},\overline{D})$ is a code for which

$$P = \overline{P}$$

$$C = \overline{C}$$

$$DOM(\overline{E}) = RAN(\overline{D}) = DOM(E) = RAN(D)$$

$$RAN(\overline{E}) = DOM(\overline{D}) = RAN(E) = DOM(D)$$

$$\overline{a}(1) = \overline{a}(2) = \ldots = \overline{a}(v-3) = \overline{a}(v-2) = 1$$

$$\overline{a}(v-1) = 2$$

$$\overline{a}(v) = \overline{a}(v+1) = \ldots = 0.$$

Such a code $(\overline{P},\overline{C},\overline{E},\overline{D})$ does not exist and does satisfy the Kraft-McMillan equality.

One of the things Theorem 6.5 is based on is that the Huffman code whose codetext word lengths are 1, 2, 3, 4, ..., v-3, v-2, v-1, v-1 is a really efficient compressor of information, more so, under the best of circumstances than any other Huffman code with v plaintext symbols. Theorem 6.5 obviously follows from the proof of the following.

Lemma 6.6: Let v be an integer no smaller than 3. Let

$$a = \{ a(1), a(2), a(3), \ldots \}$$

be a sequence of nonnegative integers such that $\Sigma\ a(j) = v$ and $\Sigma\ a(j)k/2^j = 1$. Then

$$\Sigma\ ja(j)/2^j \geq 1/2 + 2/4 + 3/8 + 4/16 + \ldots + (v-4)/2^{v-4} + (v-3)/2^{v-3}$$

$$+ 2(v-2)/2^{v-2}$$

$$= 2 - 1/2^{v-2}$$

In other words $\Sigma\, ja(j)/2^j \geq \Sigma\, j\bar{a}(j)/2^j$ where $\bar{a}$ is a fixed sequence

$\bar{a} = \{1,1,1, \ldots, 1,1, \bar{a}(v-3) = 1, \bar{a}(v-2) = 1, \bar{a}(v) = 2, \bar{a}(v+1) = 0$

$\bar{a}(v+2) = 0, 0,0,0, \ldots \}$

$= \{1,1,1, \ldots, 1,1,1,2,0,0,0,0,0, \ldots\}.$

Thus $\Sigma\, \bar{a}(j) = v$, and $\Sigma\, \bar{a}(j)/2^j = 1$, and $\Sigma\, j\bar{a}(j)/2^j = 2 - 1/2^{v-2}$.

The proof of the lemma is long, difficult and combinatorial, since the use of analytic methods to prove the inequality seem to be ruled out by the finiteness of the set of sequences a corresponding to any v. All the results of this section are best understood by means of their partial exemplification in Table 5.2.

To recap the theory of the kind of variable length codetext word code we call Kraft-McMillan equality v-codes, we know that:

1. Their rates exceed 1, except in the degenerate case of block codes. In this case they equal 1.

2. The rate of any such code happens to coincide with the compression (ratio of plaintext to codetext bits) it effects on one specific literary corpus for which it amounts to Huffman code. Given the code, it is easy to produce this corresponding literary corpus, and to show that the code is isomorphic to (i.e. has the same distribution of codetext word lengths as) a Huffman code for this literary corpus.

3. For fixed v, the rate of any Kraft-McMillan equality v-code is smaller than $\lceil \log(v) \rceil/2$. For fixed v the Kraft-McMillan equality v-code with largest rate is a code with one 1-bit codetext word, one (v-2)-bit codetext word, ..., one (v-3)-bit codetext word, one (v-2)-bit codetext word, and two (v-1)-bit codetext words. This should come as no surprise to people accustomed to dealing with how much Huffman codes can compress information under various circumstances. Also, it is true that you need very big codes to attain large rates. If you want a Kraft-McMillan equality v-codes of rate 10 you must take v near 1,000,000 so as to get $\lceil \log(v) \rceil/2 \geq 10$. If you want a rate of 100 you need approximately $v = 4 \times 10^{66}$ different plaintext symbols. Moreover literary corpora which actually experience codetext

INFORMATION THEORY   87

compressions to 1% of their plaintext size must have a
wide variation in frequency among all these symbols,
with the upshot that such a literary corpus must be more
than 10^{67} bits long. Here, as elsewhere in information
theory, good codes are big codes.

7. SKETCH OF THE PROOF OF LEMMA 6.6

As we have noted above, every result other than Lemma 6.6 is easy to derive. This section is devoted to a sketch of the proof of Lemma 6.6.

Throughout this section we adhere to several blanket hypotheses:

i) v, k, b, A and T are nonnegative integers;

ii) $3 \leq v$;

iii) $2^b \leq v-1$;

iv) x is a complex number unequal to 1;

v) The symbol Σ stands for summation over all positive integer j;

vi) $a = \{ a(1), a(2), a(3), \ldots \}$ is a sequence of nonnegative integers;

vii) $\Sigma a(j) = v$ and, consequently, the sequence a is eventually zero;

viii) $\Sigma a(j)/2^j = 1/2^k$.

ix) The set of all sequences a described above is called $\Lambda(v,k)$.

x) For every v, k, b as above the sequence

$$c_{[v,k,b]} = c = \{ c(1), c(2), c(3), \ldots \}$$
$$= \{ c_{[v,k,b]}(1), c_{[v,k,b]}(2), c_{[v,k,b]}(3), \ldots \}$$

is defined by setting:

$$c(1) = c(2) = \ldots = c(k+b-1) = 0 \quad \text{if } 2 \leq k + b;$$
$$c(k+b) = -1 + 2^b \quad \text{if } 1 \leq k + b;$$
$$c(k+b+1) = c(k+b+2) = \ldots = c(k+b+v-1-2^b) = 1;$$
$$c(k+b+v-2^b) = 2; \text{ and}$$
$$c(k+b+v-1-2^b) = c(k+b+v+2-2^b) = c(k+b+v+3-2^b) = \ldots = 0.$$

For example

$$c_{[3,0,1]} = c_{[3,0,0]} = \{ 1,2,0,0,0, \ldots \}$$
$$c_{[3,5,1]} = c_{[3,5,0]} = \{ 0,0,0,0,0,1,2,0,0,0, \ldots \}$$
$$c_{[9,0,1]} = c_{[9,0,0]} = \{ 1,1,1,1,1,1,1,2,0,0,0, \ldots \}$$
$$c_{[9,0,2]} = \{ 0,3,1,1,1,1,2,0,0,0, \ldots \}$$
$$c_{[9,6,2]} = \{ 0,0,0,0,0,0,0,3,1,1,1,1,2,0,0,0, \ldots \}$$
$$c_{[9,0,3]} = \{ 0,0,7,2,0,0,0, \ldots \}$$
$$c_{[9,4,3]} = \{ 0,0,0,0,0,0,7,2,0,0,0, \ldots \}.$$

It is a triviality to verify

Lemma 7.1:

$$\Sigma\, c_{[v,k,b]}(j) = v,$$
$$\Sigma\, c_{[v,k,b]}(j)/2^j = 1/2^k, \text{ and}$$
$$\Sigma\, j c_{[v,k,b]}(j)/2^j = (k+b)/2^k + 2/2^{(k+b)} - 2^{(1+2^b-k-b-v)}$$
$$= (k+b)/2^k + [2/2^{(k+b)}][1 - 1/2^{(2^b-v)}].$$
$$= (k+b)/2^k + [1/2^{(k+b-1)}][1 - 1/2^{(v-2^b)}].$$

Hence $c_{[v,k,b]}$ is a member of $\lambda(v,k)$.

Lemma 7.2: The entry after the first positive entry of the sequence $c = c_{[v,k,b]}$ is positive

Proof: There are four cases. If $k = b = 0$ and $v = 3$ then $c(1) = c(k+b+1) = 1$ and $c(2) = c(k+b+v-2^b) = 2$. If $k = b = 0$ and $v \geq 4$ then $c(1) = c(k+b+1) = 1$ and $c(2) = c(k+b+2) = c(k+b+v-1-2^b) = 1$. If $k \geq 1$ and $b = 0$ then $c(k-1) = c(k+b-1) = 0$

and $c(k) = c(k+b) = -1 + 2^b = 1$ and $c(k+1) = c(k+b+1) = 1$. If $b \geq 1$ then $c(k+b-1) = 0$ and $c(k+b) = -1 + 2^b \geq 1$. Moreover either $c(k+b+1) = 1$ or $c(k+b+1) = c(k+b+v-2^b) = 2$.

Well known techniques yield

Lemma 7.3:
$$x^{A+1} + x^{A+2} + \ldots + x^{A+T} = x^{A+1}(1-x^T)/(1-x)$$

and

$$(A+1)x^{A+1} + (A+2)x^{A+2} + \ldots + (A+T)x^{A+T}$$
$$= x^{A+1}[A + 1 - Ax - (A+T+1)x^T + (A+T)x^{T+1}]/(1-x)^2.$$

In particular
$$1/2^{A+1} + 1/2^{A+2} + \ldots + 1/2^{A+T} = 1/2^A - 1/2^{A+T}$$

and

$$(A+1)/2^{A+1} + (A+2)/2^{A+2} + \ldots + (A+T)/2^{A+T} = (A+2)/2^A - (A+T+2)/2^{A+T}$$

Lemma 7.4: Let $a(1) = a(2) = \ldots = a(k+1) = 0$. Then
$\Sigma\ ja(j)/2^j \geq (k+2)/2^k$.

More generally, we have

Lemma 7.5: Let b be a positive integer.
Let $a(1) = a(2) = \ldots = a(k+b-1) = 0$. Let $a(k+b) \leq -1 + 2^{b-1}$.
Then $\Sigma\ ja(j)/2^j \geq (k+b+1/2)/2^k + 1/2^{(k+b)}$.

Lemma 7.6: Suppose that $k \geq 1$. Then $a(1) + a(2) + \ldots + a(k) = 0$. If $2 \leq k + b$ then $c(1) + c(2) + \ldots + c(k+b-1) = 0$.

Lemma 7.7: Suppose that $1 \leq k + b$. Then $a(k+b) < -1 + 2^b$.

Theorem 7.8: Suppose that $2 \leq k + b$, and that $a(1) = a(2) = a(k+b-1) = 0$. Then

$$\Sigma\ jc_{[v,k,b]}(j)/2^j = \Sigma\ jc(j)/2^j \leq \Sigma\ ja(j)/2^j.$$

Outline of the proof of Theorem 7.8: The inequality $a(k+b) \geq 2^b$ cannot hold if $k + b$ is a positive integer. So there are three remaining possibilities. It may fail by an immense margin, meaning that $a(k+b) = 0$. This is an easy case to deal with. It may merely fail by a wide margin, meaning that $1 \leq a(k+b) \leq -1 + 2^{b-1}$. We can, in this case, make use of a crude estimate implicit in Lemma 7.7 to obtain the desired result. Lastly, it may barely fail, meaning that $2^{b-1} \leq a(k+b) \leq -1 + 2^b$. This is a delicate situation. The way to treat it is to format the entire proof of Theorem 7.8 as a finite induction on v, with k and b as free parameters. The statement that

$$\Sigma \, j c_{[3,k,b]}(j)/2^j \leq \Sigma \, j a(j)/2^j$$

for every appropriate k, b and every appropriate a is clearly implicit in Lemma 7.7. The statement

$$\Sigma \, j c_{[4,k,b]}(j)/2^j \leq \Sigma \, j a(j)/2^j$$

takes a trifle more doing. The statement

$$\Sigma \, j c_{[5,k,b]}(j)/2^j \leq \Sigma \, j a(j)/2^j$$

is more interesting, and is sufficiently typical to be quite instructive. It involves consideration of several alternatives. After dispensing with the case $v = 5$ we can consider any $v \geq 6$ and assume the truth of the theorem for all smaller values of v (subject to the stipulation that they be no smaller than 3). The induction step is itself a somewhat complicated argument involving numerous cases.

The nature of the induction step is, roughly speaking, as follows. You want to establish the inequality

$$\Sigma \, j c_{[v,k,b]}(j)/2^j \leq \Sigma \, j a(j)/2^j$$

for sequences

$$c_{[v,k,b]} = \{0,0,0,\ldots,0,0,0,-1+2^b,1,1,1,\ldots,1,1,1,2,0,0,0,\ldots\}$$

and

$$a = \{0,0,0,\ldots,0,0,0,a(k+b),a(k+b+1),\ldots\}$$

which both start with $k+ b - 1$ zero terms, and for which $1 \leq a(k+b)$. You find from Lemma 7.5 that the assumption $a(k+b) = 2^b$ and the assumption

$a(k+b) > 1 + 2^b$ both lead to the impermissible conclusion $\Sigma\, a(j)/2^j > 1/2^k$. Hence you know that

$$1 \leq a(k+b) \leq -1 + 2^b = c(k+b).$$

If $b = 1$ an application of the induction hypothesis yields the desired inequality. If $b \geq 2$ and $2^{b-1} \leq a(k+b) \leq -1 + 2^b$ a rather similar argument yields the desired conclusion. If $b \geq 2$ and $1 \leq a(k+b) \leq -1 + 2^{b-1}$ you must take a different tack. But you have more room to manoeuvre and the inequality follows readily. Finally you can ask what happens if a and $c_{[v,k,b]}$ do not start with the same number of zero terms. It is impossible to have more leading zeros in $c_{[v,k,b]}$ than in a. So we must merely deal with the possibility that $c_{[v,k,b]}$ is as above, with $k + b - 1$ zero terms but

$$a(1) = \ldots = a(k+b-1) = a(k+b) = 0.$$

In this (last) case there are several subcases. But they are analogous to what we have already seen, and will be left to the reader to dispose of.

With Theorem 7.8 at our disposal we can now content ourselves with comparing sequences of the form $c_{[v,k,b]}$ for some fixed v.

Theorem 7.9: For every appropriate k and b,

$$\Sigma\, jc_{[v,k,0]}(j)/2^j = \Sigma\, jc_{[v,k,1]}(j)/2^j \leq \Sigma\, jc_{[v,k,b]}(j)/2^j.$$

This last result is a triviality, and it establishes the sequences of the form

$$\{\, 0, 0, 0, \ldots, 0, 0, 0, 1, 1, 1, \ldots, 1, 1, 1, 2, 0, 0, 0, \ldots\,\}$$

as the ones corresponding to the lowest rates. Now specialise to $k = 0$ (whence no leading zeros in the sequence) and you have the desired result, Lemma 6.6. This then yields Theorem 6.5.

8. REFERENCES

[AH66] Ahlfors, L.V., (1967) Complex Analysis, Second Edition, McGraw-Hill, New York.

[BE68] Berklekamp, E.R., (1968) Algebraic Coding Theory, McGraw-Hill, New York.

[BL83]   Blahut, R.E., (1983) Theory and Practice of Error Control Codes, Addison-Wesley, Reading, Massachusetts.

[BL83b] Blahut, R.E., (1983) Theory and Practice of Error Control Codes, Addison-Wesley, Reading, Massachusetts.

[BL85]   Blakley, G.R., (1985) Information theory without the finiteness assumption. I: Cryptosystems as group-theoretic objects, in G.R. Blakley and D. Chaum (editors), Advances in Cryptology: Proceedings of Crypto '84, Lectures Notes in Computer Science, Volume 196, Springer-Verlag, Berlin pp. 314-338.

[BL86]   Blakley, G.R., (1986) Information theory without the finiteness assumption. II: Unfolding the DES, in H.C. Williams (editor), Advances in Cryptology: Proceedings of Crypto '85, Lectures Notes in Computer Science, Volume 218, Springer-Verlag, Berlin, pp. 282-337.

[BO57]   Boole, G., (1983) The Calculus of Finite Differences, Chelsea, New York.

[CO83]   Considine, D.M., (1983) Van Nostrand's Scientific Encyclopedia, Sixth Edition, Van Nostrand Reinhold, New York.

[DE83]   Denning, D.E.R., (1985) Cryptography and Data Security, Addison-Wesley, Reading, Massachusetts.

[GR85]   Grimaldi, R.P., (1985) Discrete and Combinatorial Mathematics: An Applied Introduction, Addison-Wesley, Reading, Massachusetts.

[HA86]   Hamming, R.W., (1986) Coding and Information Theory, Second Edition, Prentice-Hall, Englewood Cliffs, New Jersey.

[HE64]   Herstein, I.N., (1964) Topics in Algebra, Blaisdell, Waltham, Massachusetts.

[HO71]   Hoffman, K. and Kunze, R., (1971) Linear Algebra, Second Edition, Prentice-Hall, Englewood Cliffs, New Jersey.

[KA67]   Kahn, D., (1967) The Codebreakers, MacMillan, New York.

[KO81]   Konheim, A.G., (1981) Cryptography: A Primer, Wiley-Interscience, New York.

[LA65]   Lang, S., (1965) Algebra, Addison-Wesley, Reading, Massachusetts.

[LE86] Lempel, A. and Ziv, J., (1968) Compression of two-dimensional data, IEEE Transactions on Information Theory, vol. IT-32, pp. 2-8.

[LI83] Lidl, R. and Niederreiter, H., (1983) Finite Fields, Volume 20 of the Encyclopedia of Mathematics and its Applications, Addison-Wesley, Reading, Massachusetts.

[MA67] MacLane, S. and Birkhoff, G., (1967) Algebra, MacMillan, New York.

[MA78] MacWilliams, F.J. and Sloane, N.J.A., (1978) The Theory of Error-Correcting Codes, North-Holland, Amsterdam.

[MC77] McEliece, R.J., (1977) The Theory of Information and Coding, Vol. 3 in the Encyclopedia of Mathematics and its Applications, G.-C. Rota (editor), Addison-Wesley, Reading, Massachusetts.

[MO63] Mostow, G.E., Sampson, J.H. and Meyer, J.-P., (1963) Fundamental Structures of Algebra, McGraw-Hill, New York.

[NI59] Nickerson, H.K., Spencer, D.C. and Steenrod, N.E., (1959) Advanced Calculus, Van Nostrand, Princeton, New Jersey.

[PA66] Paley, H. and Weichsel, P.M., (1966) A First Course in Abstract Algebra, Holt, Rinehart and Winston, New York.

[PE72] Peterson, W.W. and Weldon, E.J., (1972) Error-Correcting Codes, Second Edition, M.I.T. Press.

[RO64] Rota, G.-C., (1964) On the Foundations of Combinatorial theory I. The theory of Mobius functions, Zeitschrift fur Wahrscheinlichkeitstheorie und Verwandte gebiete, Vol. 2, pp. 340-368.

[RU74] Rudin, W., (1974) Real and Complex Analysis, McGraw-Hill, New York, Jensen pp. 63-64.

[SH49] Shannon, C.E., (1949) Communication theory of secrecy systems, Bell System Technical Journal, Vol. 28, pp. 656-715.

[ST85] Stebbins, G.L. and Ayala, F.J., (1985) The Evolution of Darwinism, Scientific American, Vol. 253, No. 1, pp. 72-82.

[VI79] Viterbi, A.J., and Omura, J.K., (1979) Principles of Digital Communication and Coding, McGraw-Hill, New York.

[WA65] Watson, J.D., (1965) Molecular Biology of the Gene, W.A. Benjamin, New York.

ADAPTIVE PRODUCT CODES WITH SOFT/HARD DECISION DECODING

P.G. Farrell
(University of Manchester)

B.K. Honary
(Engineering Department, Warwick University)

and

S.D. Bate
(Coventry Polytechnic)

ABSTRACT

Owing to the time-varying nature of the HF channel, error correcting codes of a fixed rate provide unnecessary correction power for much of the time with consequently low data rates. The purpose of an adaptive coding scheme is to permit only the necessary degree of error correction to be applied to the transmitted information according to the channel conditions. Such a coding scheme, based on product codes, is introduced and the improvement compared to similar fixed rate codes is demonstrated.

INTRODUCTION

A major concern in information theory and coding is that of controlling transmission errors caused by the channel noise, so that it is possible to obtain reliable transmission with the highest rate of information flow and lowest implementation complexity possible. An approach to this problem is the application of coding systems. Adaptive coding algorithms are relatively simple and provide high system reliability, by applying the necessary degree of error correction according to the state of the channel.

Hard decision decoders only operate on the ones or zeroes of the receiver's demodulator output. As no account is taken of the amplitude of each bit received, much information which could be of use to the decoder is lost. Soft decision techniques enable the amplitude information to be used by quantizing the demodulator output further, allowing a confidence value to be associated with each bit.

Earlier research has been carried out to find efficient soft decision decoding algorithms for product codes. A particularly effective algorithm for a class of product RS codes has been derived from a technique originally applied to array codes [1] This algorithm proceeds by decoding the row/column sub-codewords alternately, by minimum soft distance decoding (MSDD), in order of diminishing confidence [2]. In addition, the decoding of the rows/columns by MSDD has been replaced by the use of a hard decision algebraic decoding algorithm only. In this case the use of the confidence information is retained so that the required priority of row/column decoding may be found.

In the following sections we will describe the basic soft decision product coding schemes, the adaptive product coding algorithm and a technique which may enable a further improvement in the information rate to be obtained. Results obtained over a simulated Gaussian noise channel and a HF channel are given for the first two cases.

2. THE PRODUCT CODING METHODS

With regard to the requirements as stated in the previous section, a solution employing product codes was chosen. The structure of such codes gives a reduction in decoder complexity for a given block length and these codes should perform well over the HF channel [3]. The techniques developed are given below.

2.1 Hard decision decoding

Product codes may be considered as a matrix in which each row is encoded according to a linear (n_1, k_1, d_1) code and each column according to a (n_2, k_2, d_2) linear code where n,k and d are the block length number of information symbols and Hamming distance respectively (Fig. 1). The product of these codes gives a $(n_1 n_2, k_1 k_2, d_1 d_2)$ code [4]. These codes are useful for correcting both random and burst errors but it is difficult to characterize the correctable error patterns; this depends on the method of decoding [5]. Although the correctability of the product code is $t = [(d_1 d_2 - 1)/2]$, where [x] indicates the integer part of x, some of the error patterns within this limit (permanent errors) are uncorrectable with cascade decoding [6]. Soft decision decoding would enable many of these previously uncorrectable error patterns to be corrected as well as improving the correctability of the code. Our evaluation of hard decision decoding has been performed by decoding rows and columns of the product code alternately, in increasing order of rows and columns.

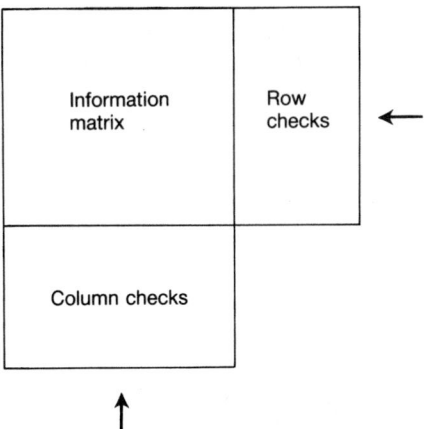

Fig. 1 Cascade decoding

2.2 Soft decision decoding using confidence values

Data receivers using hard decision decoding consist of a demodulator operating on individual data signal elements to determine whether a zero or a one has been received (in the binary case) followed by a decoder operating on these hard decisions. Soft decision decoding techniques make use of the amplitude information which is lost in the case of hard decision decoding. These techniques employ this information by quantizing the demodulator output further, allowing a confidence value to be associated with each bit. The quantization may be linear or non-linear, in fact it has been shown that for the Gaussian channel linear quantization is almost optimum. In the HF case it is unlikely that linear quantization is appropriate for best performance for a number of reasons [7], however this paper considers only linear quantization. The demodulator output is passed to the decoder which can employ full minimum soft distance decoding (MSDD) for short block lengths or, often, a bounded distance decoder capable of decoding errors and erasures, i.e. only errors and/or erasures within the guaranteed correction limit of the code can be corrected (Fig. 2). These techniques therefore yield another degree of freedom in the communication system which can improve the performance of the decoder. An increase in coding gain of approximately 2 dB over the hard decision case can be achieved over a binary symmetric channel and this figure may be exceeded in the case of burst noise channnels.

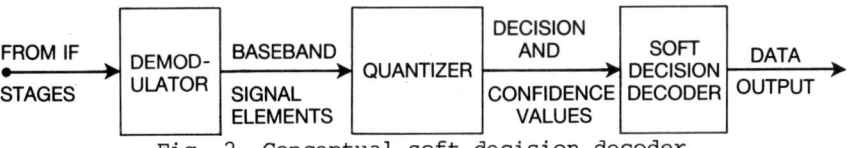

Fig. 2 Conceptual soft decision decoder

The structure of the product code can be employed by assigning a confidence value to each row/column sub-codeword and decoding the rows and columns alternately in order of diminishing confidence (Fig. 3). Two methods of decoding are considered:

(i) Decoding alternate rows/columns as above with successive erasures soft decision decoding of the row/column sub-codewords, S_1.

(ii) As case (i) but using hard decision decoding of row/column sub-codewords, S_2, which should result in a substantial reduction in decoding delay and implementation complexity.

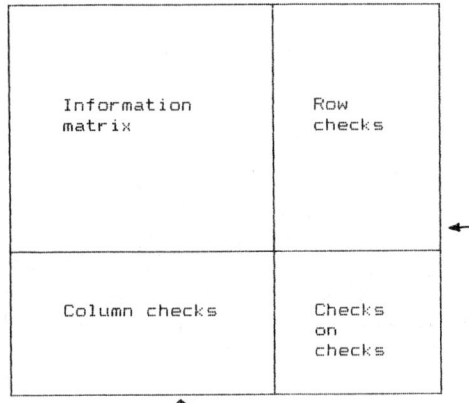

Fig. 3 Soft decision product decoding

Both methods proceed as follows. The received bits are re-arranged in product format by filling the product array row by row with the received symbols. A received symbol consists of p bits since a RS code of length 2^p-1 consists of symbols which are elements of the Galois field $GF(2^p)$. These symbols can be mapped onto binary digits by taking each symbol as a p bit binary number. In the decoder the binary sequences are mapped back onto elements of $GF(2^p)$ using a look up table. The technique then proceeds by:

(i) Computing the row/column confidences. These are the sums of the individual confidence values associated with each symbol of the row/column sub-codewords, given by:

$$\text{row/column confidence} = \sum_{i=1}^{M} |\log(p(r_i|0)/p(r_i|1))| \quad (2.2.1)$$

where for rows $M=n_1$, for columns $M=n_2$ for a full product code and $M=k_2$ otherwise; r_i is the ith demodulated bit.

(ii) the row and column codewords with the greatest confidence values, which have not yet been decoded, are decoded by one or other of the methods, S_1 or S_2 given above.

(iii) After these decodings have been performed the confidence of any symbol found to be in error is set to the minimum and that of the (assumed) correct symbols is set to the maximum. The confidence of each symbol is taken as the sum of the individual bit confidences within the symbol:

$$\text{symbol confidence} = \sum_{i=1}^{p} |\log(p(s_i|0)/p(s_i|1))| \qquad (2.2.2)$$

These steps are then repeated until every sub-codeword has been decoded.

2.3 Soft decision decoding with successive erasures decoding

The optimum method of soft decision decoding is MSDD but this may not be possible for a code with a large number of information symbols, due to the excessive number of comparisons required. For example, the RS(15,9) code has $q^k = 16^9 = 6.9 \times 10^{10}$ codewords, where $q = 2^p$.

Successive erasures decoding [8] is a sub-optimum procedure, which reduces the number of comparisons required by generating a small set of tentative codewords, and is closely related to generalized minimum distance decoding [9]. The number of comparisons is reduced by assuming that the least reliable symbols (those with the lowest confidence values) are in error. The symbols in these positions are passed to the decoder as erasures (errors whose positions are known but whose value can be zero). A code with minimum distance d can correct $2t+e \leq d$ errors and erasures, where t is the number of errors and e is the number of erasures. The technique begins by decoding errors only, next two erasures and the remaining number of errors are corrected, then four erasures and any remaining correctable errors are corrected. This process continues until only erasures can be corrected and the erasure correction limit of the code has been reached.

In the case of the RS(15,9) code, which has been simulated, four possible decodings are produced by considering the following cases:

(i)   t=3, e=0
(ii) t=2, e=2
(iii) t=1, e=4
(iv) t=0, e=6

Odd numbers of erasures are not considered since the same decodings as for the next even number of erasures would result [10].

The word with the smallest soft distance from the received subword is selected as the decoded subword, the soft distance d_s, in the binary sense, being given by:

$$d_s = \sum_{i=1}^{M} C_i \log(p(r_i|0)/p(r_i|1)) \qquad (2.2.3)$$

where C_i is the ith sub-codeword bit.

When this method is employed using Euclid's algorithm for errors and erasures decoding, some of these four decodings may not give codewords. If none of the decodings yield a valid codeword step (ii) of section 2.2 is altered so that the sub-codeword is not changed and the confidence values remain the same.

3. THE ADAPTIVE PRODUCT CODING TECHNIQUE

Product codes generally have a low information rate, which can be a disadvantage, in that when the channel is clear the large redundancy used to correct errors is unnecessary.

Various means exist of counteracting this problem, the simplest being automatic repeat request (ARQ), although under poor channel conditions the number of repetitions becomes excessive. Hybrid ARQ, which provides a degree of error correction, can improve the performance of such systems. These techniques are adaptive in the sense that retransmissions continue until the received block appears to be error free, thus the information rate (throughput efficiency) varies according to the channel conditions. In order to improve the throughput and decoder output error rate, adaptive techniques have been devised such as variable redundancy [11,12] and incremental redundancy [13,14] error control.

The technique applied to the RS product codes is a form of incremental redundancy error control. Such methods operate by transmitting additional parity checks for error correction only when they are needed as opposed to the repetition of information symbols of ARQ methods.

This new algorithm begins by detecting errors in the row and column sub-codewords by sending a reduced number of check symbols for detection only. If errors are detected in particular rows or columns then further check symbols are sent and correction of the erroneous sub-codeword is attempted (Figure 4).

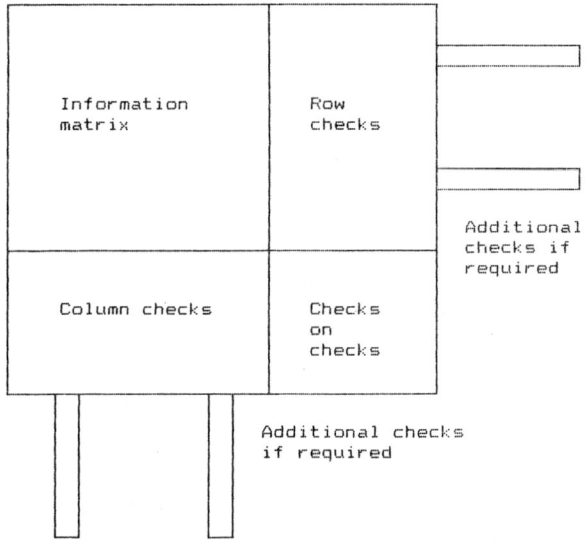

Fig. 4 The adaptive product code format.

In order to reduce the number of check symbols sent in the detection stage the RS codewords are punctured; i.e. certain check symbols are deleted. When a RS code is punctured by p symbols the minimum distance of the code is reduced by p [14]. At the decoder, the symbols in these positions are treated as erasures. Detection of errors in the punctured codewords is performed by considering the modified syndromes [9] formed as follows:

The erasure locator polynomial $\sigma'(x)$ is found from

$$\sigma'(x) = \prod_{i=1}^{m} (x + X_i)$$

$$\sigma'_0 x^m + \sigma'_1 x^{m-1} + \ldots + \sigma'_m \quad (3.1)$$

where X_i is the erasure location (expressed as an element of the field within which the code lies).

The usual syndromes are calculated from

$$S_j = \sum_{i=0}^{n-1} r_i \alpha^{ij} \quad 1 \leq j \leq d-1 \quad (3.2)$$

The r_i in the erased positions can be set to any value but zero is convenient, and α is a primitive element of the field $GF(2^p)$.

A linear transformation yields Forney's modified syndromes

$$T_i = \sum_{j=0}^{m} \sigma'_j S_{i+m+1-j} \quad 0 \leq i \leq d-s-2 \quad (3.3)$$

If any of these syndromes are non-zero then errors have been detected. Only in the case of all the T_i being zero is it assumed that the codewords of the punctured RS code are error-free.

In the case of the simulation results which follow we have used a punctured version of the RS(15,9) code. The last three symbols are punctured so that three errors are detectable, using the first three check symbols. The method of decoding is based on algorithm S_2, where hard decision decoding is performed on the sub-codewords. When errors are detected the remaining three checks are requested, enabling correction of up to three errors.

3.1 The adaptive product code with code cancelling

A method which can give an increased code rate for product codes and concatenated codes has been given in references [15,16]. In the case of product codes this proceeds as below.

A product code is encoded and a RS code over $GF(2^p)$ is superimposed upon the row checks and/or column checks (by modulo 2 addition), where p is the number of row (or column) check bits. The method has been described for binary codes and can be extended to the case of multi-level codes where the check symbols are mapped onto binary digits.

The encoding procedure is shown in Figure 5. Each set of row checks is taken as an element of $GF(2^p)$ and encoded into a RS code of length N. This code can now be superimposed on the checks of the original product code, thus setting the "information" part of the row checks to zero or cancelling them out.

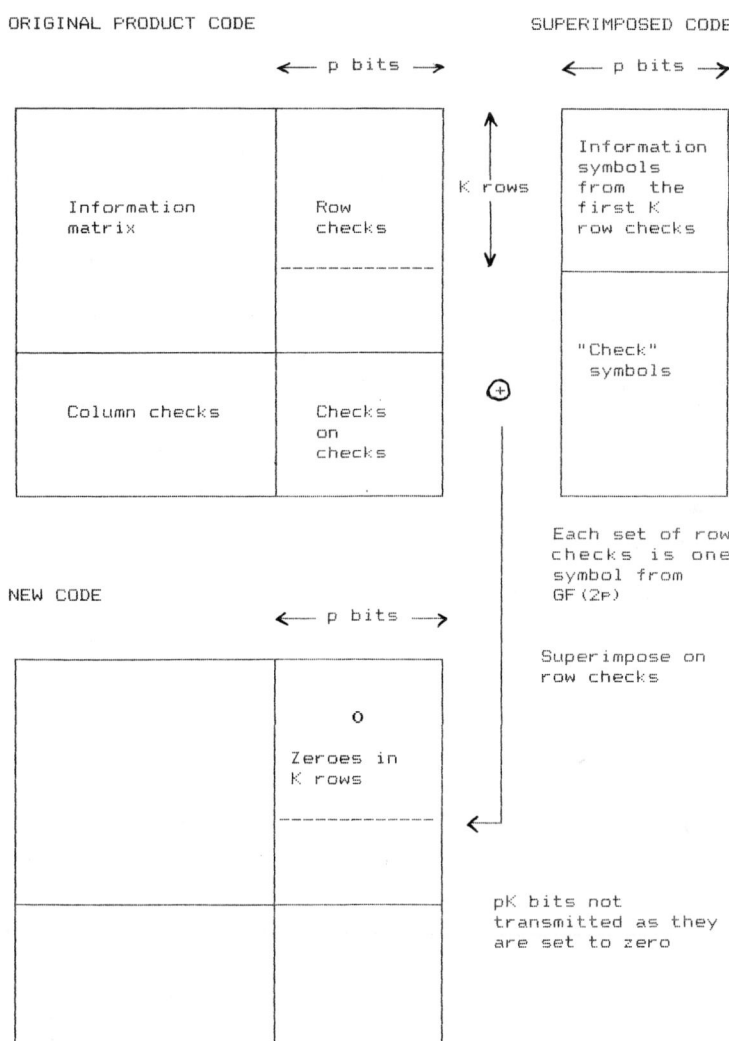

Fig. 5 Encoding a cancelled code

In order to decode such codewords, the original product code can be reconstructed as follows (Fig. 6):

(i) Reconstruct the row checks by re-calculating them from the information part of the product code.
(ii) Add these checks (mod 2) to the received row checks
(iii) Correct errors in the check digits using the RS code. If the correction limit of the RS code is not exceeded the original checks of the product code can be reconstructed.

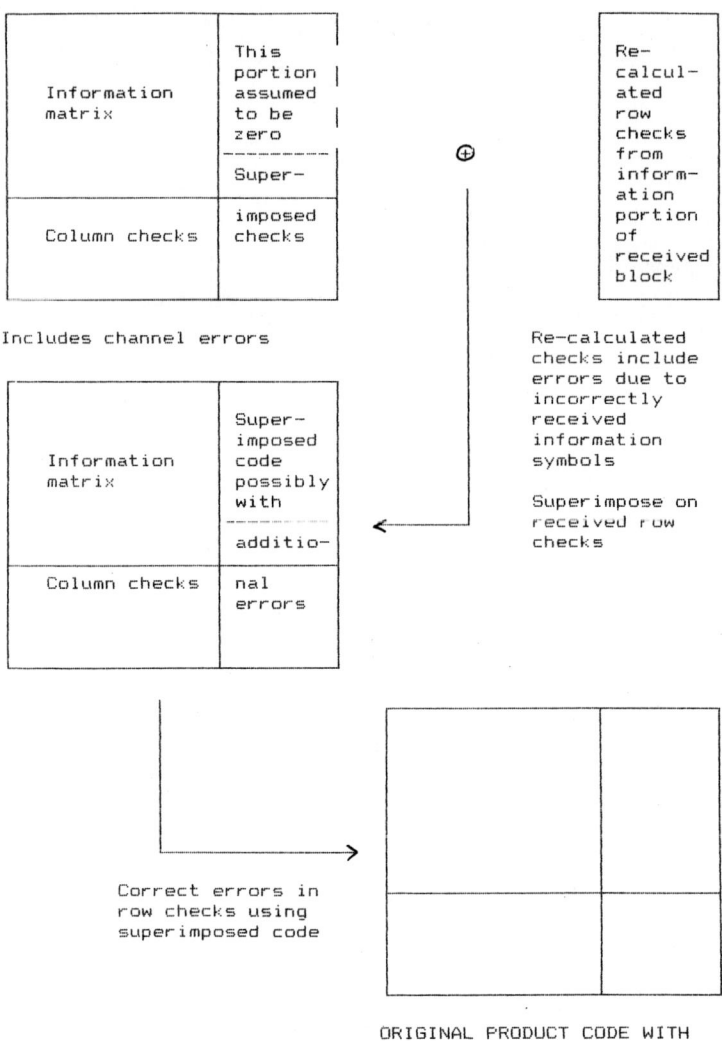

Fig. 6 Decoding a cancelled code

Errors in the product code can now be corrected by a suitable product decoding technique.

An improvement to the throughput available using the adaptive product code may be obtained by applying the code cancelling procedure to its detection stage. We consider here an array code [1], as shown in figure 7 (a product code with a single check symbol), used for error detection (Fig. 7). The maximum throughput is given by

$$R_{max}=k_1k_2/[(k_1+1)(k_2+1)] \qquad (3.1.1)$$

If the cancelling procedure is now applied to both rows and columns (Fig. 8), where K_3 row checks and k_4 column checks are cancelled, then the maximum throughput is now given by

$$R_{max}=k_1k_2/[(k_1+1)(k_2+1)-(k_3+k_4)] \qquad (3.1.2)$$

It can be seen that the maximum throughput can be increased with some reduction in detectability which will be a function of the number of checks cancelled.

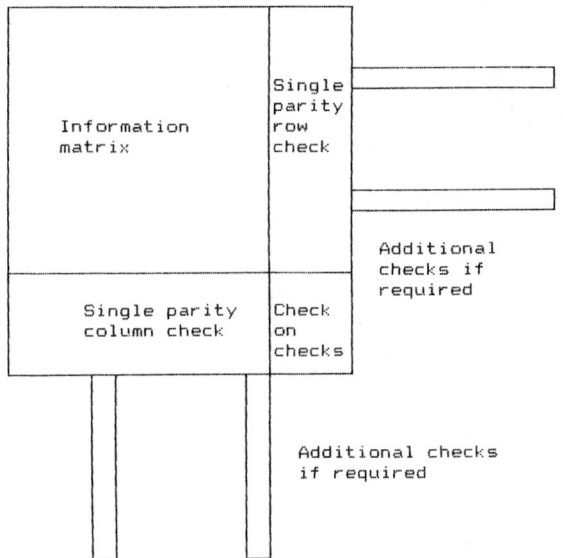

Fig. 7   The adaptive product code in array code format.

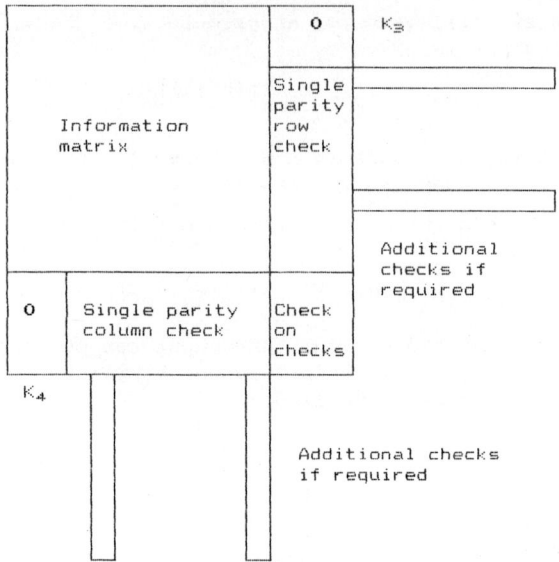

Fig. 8 The adaptive product code with code cancelling

4. RESULTS AND CONCLUSION

The results given apply to product codes whose component codes both comprise a RS(15,9) code. The results obtained for the Gaussian noise channel are given in figures 9 and 10.

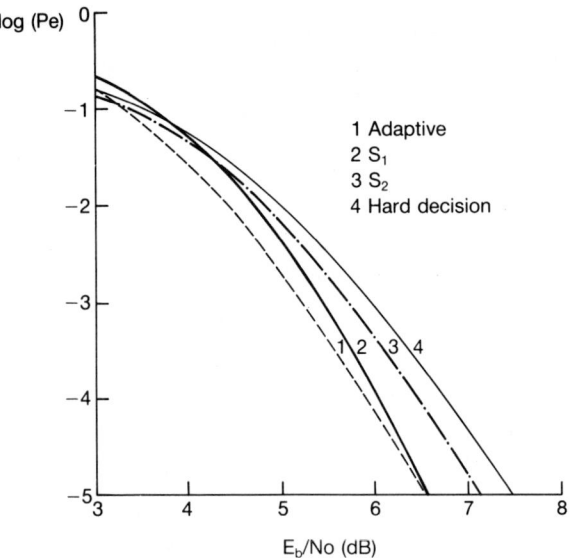

Fig. 9 Probability of error vs. E_b/N_o. AWGN. n=15

The HF channel results were obtained using a generally
accepted multi-purpose HF simulation model. The modem and
channel are considered as a whole, the quantized demodulator
output comprising the received digits. The program used can
simulate a groundwave component and up to four skywave
components. For each of these components the attenuation, pure
time delay, Doppler shift and rms fading frequency can be
specified. In addition an AWGN component can be added, which
has been varied to model differing channels, the error rates and
throughputs being shown in figures 11 and 12. The demodulator
is a coherent matched filter and this is synchronized to the
path of zero time delay, which is usually the groundwave,
although this component is sometimes not present. In order
to compare each method in the HF case a figure of merit is
defined [17] such that

F=decoder input error rate x code rate/decoder output error
rate

which is conveniently plotted as 1/F, thus the code which has
the best performance has the smallest 1/F (Fig. 13).

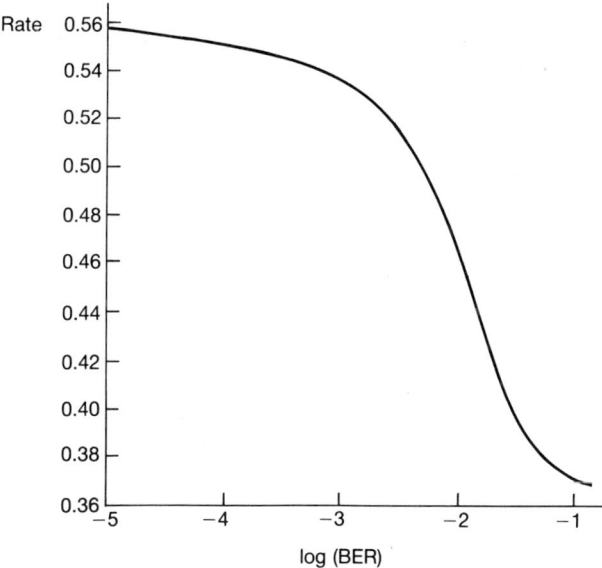

Fig. 10   Throughput efficiency vs. channel error rate.
         AWGN, n=15.

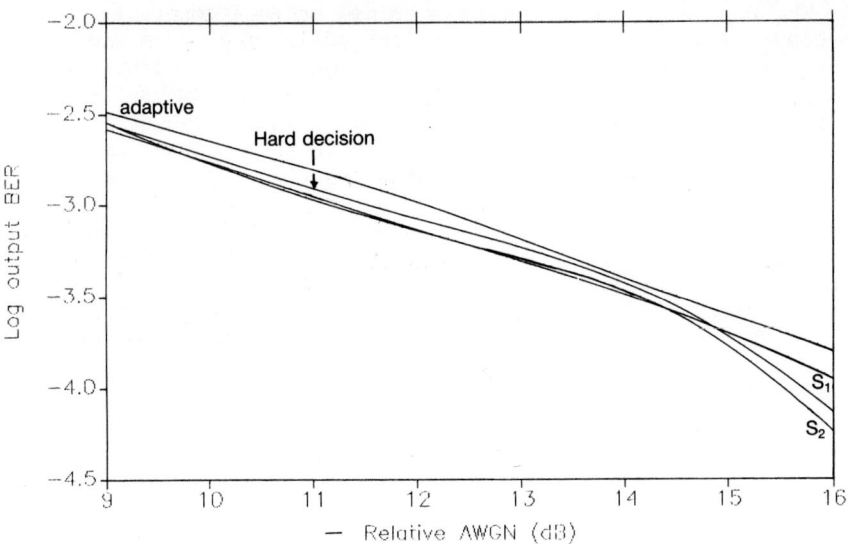

Fig. 11 Output BER vs. relative AWGN block length 15, fade rate = .1Hz.

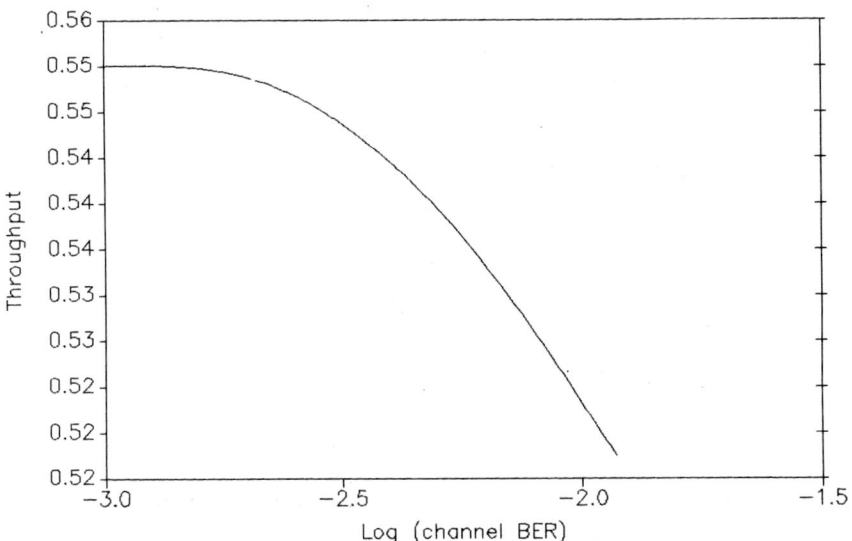

Fig. 12 Throughput vs. channel BER block length 15, fade rate = .1Hz.

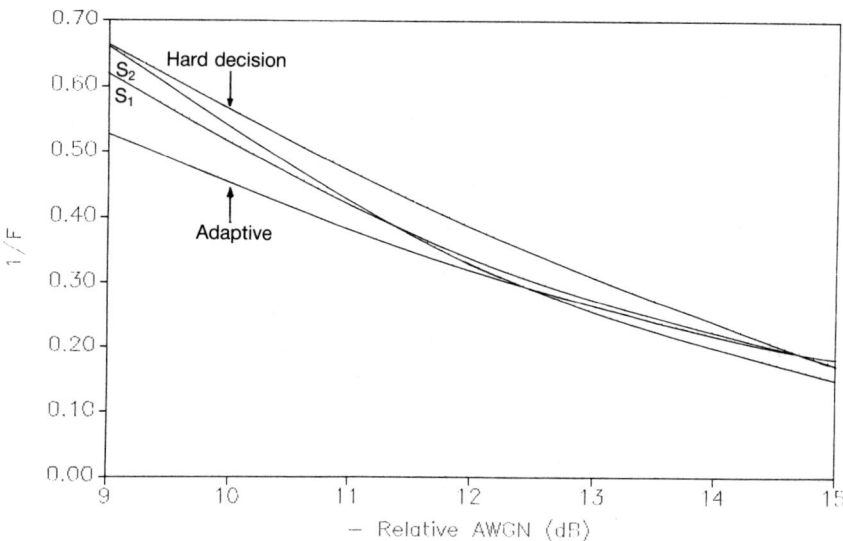

Fig. 13 1/F vs. relative AWGN level block length 15, fade rate = 0.1Hz.

It can be seen that hard decision decoding using confidence values (S_2) is reliable and sometimes gives better performance than S_1, using successive erasured decoding on each sub-codeword. In addition algorithm S_2 gives the advantages of a substantial reduction in implementation complexity and decoding delay compared to algorithm S_1.

The adaptive product code gives an increase in throughput for a given reliability, although a feedback channel is required. We suggest that an increase in the block length of such codes would be preferable to interleaving, since randomizing the burst errors by interleaving would require the transmission of additional checks in many more blocks than would be necessary without interleaving.

Further work is in progress in order to assess the performance of the adaptive product code with code cancelling, which should give further improvements.

REFERENCES

[1] Daniel, J.S. and Farrell, P.G., (1985) "Burst error correcting array codes: further developments" Proc. fourth int. conf. on digital processing of signals in communications, Loughborough.

[2] Honary, B.K. and Farrell, P.G. (1985) "Coding techniques for HF communication systems," Proc. fourth int. conf. on systems science, Coventry.

[3] Farrell, P.G. and Munday, E., (1976) "Economical practical realisation of minimum-distance soft-decision decoding for data transmission," Proc. Zurich Int. Seminar on Digital Communications, pp. B5.1-6.

[4] Elias, P., (1954) "Error free coding," IRE Trans. Inf. Theory, PGIT-4, pp. 29-37.

[5] Honary, B.K., (1981) "Error correction techniques for bursty channels," Ph.D. Thesis, University of Kent at Canterbury.

[6] Abramson, N.M., (1968) "Cascade decoding of cyclic product codes," IEEE Trans. Commun. Technol., Vol. COM-16, pp. 398-402.

[7] Farrell, P.G. and Goodman, R.M.F., (1980) "Soft-decision error control for h.f. data transmission," IEE Proc. F, Vol. 127, No. 5, pp. 389-400.

[8] Einarsson, G. and Sundberg, C.E., (1976) "A note on soft decision decoding with successive erasures," IEEE Trans. Inf. Theory, Vol. IT-22, pp. 88-96.

[9] Forney, G.D., Jr., (1966) "Concatenated Codes," M.I.T. press, Cambridge, Massachusetts.

[10] Clark, G.C. and Cain, J.B., (1981) "Error-correction coding for digital communications," Plenum Press.

[11] Goodman, R.M.F., (1975) "Variable redundancy coding for adaptive error control," Ph.D. Thesis, University of Kent at Canterbury.

[12] Goodman, R.M.F. and Farrell, P.G., (1975) "Data transmission with variable-redundancy error control over a high frequency channel," Proc. IEE, Vol. 122, No. 2.

[13] Mandelbaum, D.M., (1974) "An adaptive-feedback decoding scheme using incremental redundancy," IEEE Trans. Inform. Theory, Vol. IT-20, pp. 388-389.

[14] Dorsch, B., (1983) "Successive check digits rather than information repetition," IEEE International Conference on Communications, Boston, Conference Report pp. 323-327.

[15] Inoue, T. et al., (1985) "New encoding and decoding methods for generalized product codes," Fourth IEEE int. symp. on Information Theory, Brighton.

[16] Kasahara, M. et al., (1976) "New classes of binary codes constructed on the basis of concatenated codes and product codes," IEEE trans. Inform. Theory, Vol. IT-22, pp. 461-468.

[17] Honary, B.K. and Farrell, P.G., (1982) "Error correction methods for HF data channels," Proc. second IEE conf. on HF communication systems and techniques, London.

MINIMUM WEIGHT DECODING FOR CYCLIC CODES

P.G. Farrell, M. Rice and F. Taleb
*(Department of Electrical Engineering,
University of Manchester)*

ABSTRACT

Minimum weight decoding is a reduced-search bounded minimum distance decoding algorithm for cyclic block codes. It is based on a combination of error trapping, trial-and-error (systematic search) and step-by-step syndrome decoding techniques. It can be used to implement an efficient algorithm for hard-decision decoding of the Golay, BCH, RS and other codes. Though it is essentially a syndrome decoding technique, minimum weight decoding can be extended easily to provide erasure and soft-decision decoding of random and burst error control codes. It may also extend to the decoding of convolutional codes.

1. INTRODUCTION

The research on minimum weight decoding described in this paper was motivated by three conjectures. The first arose from the discovery of a very easily determined upper bound on the minimum distance of a binary cyclic code [1]. It appeared that this bounding technique could be used as part of a very simple minimum weight decoding algorithm for cyclic codes. The second conjecture was that by using burst distance [2], and soft distance [3], as metrics, minimum weight decoding could be extended to burst correcting cyclic codes, and soft-decision decoding of binary cyclic codes, respectively. Thirdly, it was conjectured that decoding algorithms for cyclic codes could more effectively exploit the structure exhibited by these codes. It seemed that minimum weight decoding could indeed take advantage of this structure [4, 5].

The overall aim of the research has been to devise simple but effective decoding algorithms for short and medium block length cyclic codes, and to study the trade-offs between decoding complexity and performance. A useful and interesting side effect has been that the relationships between several decoding methods, particularly the syndrome decoding techniques [4, 6], have been elucidated.

2. MINIMUM WEIGHT DECODING

All the code words in a cyclic code, expressed as polynomials in a dummy variable, x, are multiples of $G(x)$, the generator polynomial of the code. Thus, when a word is received from the channel, the easiest way of checking whether it contains a detectable error pattern is to see if it is exactly divisible by $G(x)$, or not. If the remainder of the division process is zero, then the word does not contain a detectable error pattern. If the remainder is non-zero, then a detectable, and possibly correctable, error pattern is present in the word. This remainder is the syndrome [4, 6] corresponding to the error pattern.

If the syndrome is non-zero, then the division process may be continued, as if the received word had been lengthened by adjoining to it a number of zeros. Once a sufficient number of zeros has been so adjoined then either the weight of the remainder falls to t or less, or the pattern of remainders generated by the continued division repeats itself. In the first case, the remainder with weight t or less is, in fact, the error pattern; in the second case, once the remainders repeat, there is no point in continuing. The assumption here is that the code can correct up to t random errors, where $t = \lfloor (d-1)/2 \rfloor$, d is the minimum (Hamming) distance of the code, and $\lfloor \cdot \rfloor$ is the largest integer less than or equal to the argument within the brackets.

It is convenient, and conceptually important, to visualise the continued division process in an alternative way. Instead of adjoining zeros to the received word, $G(x)$ is cyclically folded round to the start of the word, now reduced to zero, of course, by the earlier part of the division process. It is helpful here to pad out the remainders, with zeros in the most significant positions, and the entire received word "brought down"; so that all the "remainders" (partial subtractions) are n-symbol words, where n is the code block length. An example will make this clear.

Consider the Hamming $(n, k, t) = (7, 4, 1)$ binary cyclic code, with generator polynomial $G(x) = x^3 + x + 1 \equiv 1011$, where k is the dimension of the code (number of information digits in each code word). If the transmitted code word is 1001110, and

MINIMUM WEIGHT DECODING

an error occurs in the second digit, then the received word is 1101110. The continued division process (the translation from polynomial to binary word is obvious, and subtraction is modulo-2 addition in GF(2)) then gives:

```
1101110 00 ..
1011
 1101
 1011
  1101
  1011
   1100
   1011
    111 0          syndrome
    101 1
     10 10
     10 11
        01        weight = 1 = t, STOP
```

Or, alternatively

```
                weight
1101110           5
1011
0110110           4
 1011
 0011010          3
  1011
  0001100         2
   1011
   0000111        3  , syndrome
1       101
1000010           2
11      10
0100000           1 = t, STOP
```

Either way, an error in the second digit is indicated.

The folded-round, or cyclic, division makes determination of "remainder" weight easier and more systematic. More importantly, it clarifies what is happening. Each "remainder" is the result of adding (equivalent to subtracting in GF(2)) a shift of G(x) to the previous remainder, and so on back to the first addition of G(x) to the received word. Thus each remainder consists of the sum of a multiple of G(x) (ie, a code word) and the received word. When the multiple of G(x) is the same as the transmitted code word, then the remainder becomes the error pattern. This can only happen, because of the distance properties of the code (all words have a mutual distance of at least d = 2t +1) when the remainder has weight $\leq$ t. If the remainder weight never falls to t or less, then the particular error pattern is not correctable by means of this basic minimum weight decoding algorithm, though it may be within the theoretical error correction power of the code.

It will be recognised that the above simple decoding algorithm is nothing but error trapping [4, 6] in disguise. This follows from the fact that the "remainder", of necessity normally falls within the span of n-k symbols. Hence (with certain rather trivial exceptions) only error patterns spanning n-k symbols or less will be in general correctable. Minimum weight decoding (MWD) deserves its special name, however, because:

i) The above description and example show that the basic form of MWD is a reduced search minimum distance decoding algorithm. The subset of code words compared with the received word are those words generated by the continued division process.

ii) It therefore follows that basic MWD can be extended to burst correction and soft-decision decoding by using the appropriate metric.

iii) Basic MWD can be enhanced in various ways to make it capable of correcting many (in some cases all) non-trappable error patterns.

v) MWD is a very useful concept for evaluating and comparing many decoding algorithms.

The basic MWD algorithms as just set out can be enhanced, as noted in (iii) above, in many ways, including:

a) If the weight of the received word is $\leq$ t, then the all-zero word was transmitted, and the received word is the error pattern.

b) If the cyclic code is binary and contains the all-one word (ie., is transparent, because n is odd and G(x) does not contain the factor (x + 1)), then if the weight of the received word is n-t or more, the zeros in the received word are the error positions, and the all-one word was transmitted. This idea can be extended if the weight structure of the code is known [7], and it applies to multi-level codes (eg. a Reed-Solomon (RS) code [4, 6]) as well.

c) Because of the distance properties of a code, any "remainders" of weight t + 1 can not contain the error pattern (since if it did the distance between a pair of words in code would be < d, a contradiction). This sometimes helps to speed the decoding process when the remainders repeat (ie, when the error is untrappable).

d) If the remainders do repeat (ie, an untrappable error pattern is present), then change the first symbol in the received word to another of the possible symbol values (ie, invert the symbol if the code is binary), and repeat the continued division process. If the errors remain untrappable, then try the other possible values in the first symbol, and/or move on to change successive symbols in the word, each time repeating the division process. In essence, the idea is to test each position in the code word to see if it contains an error. If it does, then suitably changing the symbol value will remove the error, perhaps making the rest of the error pattern trappable. This is trial-and-error decoding [4], called systematic search decoding by Kasami [8]. This form of extended MWD is therefore a combination of error trapping and trial-and-error decoding, which is a form of step-by-step decoding [6], and is also bounded distance decoding. This extended MWD algorithm completely decodes all weight $\leq$ t error patterns for all single and double error correcting codes, the Golay code, RS codes with N $\leq$ 15, and certain other codes (eg. BCH (15, 5, 7), etc). Trapping with trial-and error can also be implemented as a form of trapping with windows [8] or covering polynomials [8, 9]. In this form, its complexity is < 5n.

e) Both the basic and the extended MWD algorithm can be used for burst-correction. The appropriate metric is burst distance (the number of bursts of a given length b in which any pair of words differ) and burst weight (the number of bursts of a given length in a word) [2,10], and the trial-and-error process consists of testing with possible burst error patterns. An example using the binary (7, 3, b = 2) single-burst-correcting code is given below.

		burst (b=2) weight
code word	1010011	3
burst error	0110000	
received word	1100011	2
G(x)	11101	
	0010111	3
	11101	
syndrome	0001010	2
	1 1110	
	1000100	2
	01 111	
	1100011	2
	101 11	
burst error	0110000	1, STOP

3. MINIMUM WEIGHT DECODING FOR REED-SOLOMON CODES

The MWD algorithm was considered for use on non-binary cyclic codes, and in particular for the set of RS(N, K, T) codes with codewords $\underline{C} = (C_N \ldots C_0)$ where $C_i \in GF(2^m)$, $N = 2^m - 1$, $K = N - d + 1$, $T = \lfloor (d-1)/2 \rfloor$, d being the minimum distance of the code. Owing to the extra complexity involved in $GF(2^m)$ arithmetic, the trial-and-error variant was studied for simplicity of implementation. This sets a bound on the number of errors that can be corrected, but all the m = 4 RS codes satisfy $\lfloor N(T-2)/T \rfloor < N-K$ where T is the number of errors that can be corrected by this method and $T = \lfloor (d-1)/2 \rfloor$.

To calculate the new (trial) syndrome $\underline{s}'$ (ie the syndrome that would be formed if a trial error was added to the received code word $\underline{r}$) consider adding the syndrome to the all-zero codeword at the check symbol positions to form an n-tuple $\underline{s} = (0 \ldots s_{N-K-1} \ldots s_0)$. The trial error β can be any of the $2^m - 1$ non-zero elements of $GF(2^m)$. To add β to the (i+1)th symbol to the left of s_{N-K-1}, form a vector

$$\underline{\beta} = (\ldots 0 \underbrace{\beta \ 0 \ldots 0}_{i + N-K}).$$

Then, the new syndrome $\underline{s}' = \underline{\beta} + \beta \cdot G_{N-K-i} + \underline{s}$ where G_{N-K-i} is the (N-K-i)th row of the generator matrix $G = [I : g]$.

The weight of $\underline{s}'$ can then be measured and checked for a value $\leq T-1$. If this is so then the decoded codeword, $\underline{c} = \underline{s}' + \underline{\beta} + \underline{r}$. The same process can be used for all unique syndromes as they are simply formed from cyclic shifts of t.

If all the syndromes are calculated for a given $\underline{r}$ then there is an upper limit on the number of error positions (relative to each syndrome) that must be tried in order to correct T symbols. This can be shown to be $\lfloor K-N/T \rfloor + 1$. (This is the maximum number of trial errors to correct a maximally spread, weight T error pattern). So $0 \geqslant i \geqslant \lfloor K-N/T \rfloor$ must be true to guarantee correction. In fact the number of trial error positions necessary is generally less than $\lfloor K-N/T \rfloor + 1$ because many patterns are equivalent (in a cyclic sense). For the RS(15, K, T) codes only a maximum of three trial errors are required. The decoding complexity of this scheme is governed by five factors:

i) syndrome length, N-K;

ii) number of unique syndromes, N;

iii) maximum number of errors/syndrome, $\leqslant \lfloor K-N/T \rfloor$;

iv) possible error values, 2^m-1;

v) $GF(2^m)$ arithmetic.

A multirate RS(N, K, T) MWD codec has been designed using standard TTL LS logic to run at an encoded data rate of 8 Mb/s. This uses a highly parallel, pipelined architecture, generating all 2^m-1 trial syndromes at once, the syndromes and different error positions being formed in a serial manner. The design involves the use of many fast PROMs (~50) and altogether ~115 chips are required, $GF(q^m)$ arithmetic being implemented by the use of look-up tables. The four different code rates are for T = 1, 2, 3, 4 (ie, N-K = 2, 4, 6, 8).

An alternative design for use at much lower data rates (16-512 kb/s) as part of the payload for an experimental satellite, T-SAT, is made feasible by the use of CMOS semi-custom chip technology. In this case the trade-off between speed and power is biased towards a much more serial system design.

A comparison has been made between the complexities of the above MWD implementation and that of an algebraic RS decoder using transform techniques [11, 12]. The decoder complexities are approximately comparable for T = 1 and 2, but the MWD decoder is significantly less complex for T = 3 and 4.

4. REDUCED SET ZERO-NEIGHBOUR DECODING ALGORITHMS

Minimum weight decoding seeks to find the error pattern by successively adding code words to the received word, under the control of the continued division process, until a "remainder" of weight $\leqslant$ t is found. An alternative method would be to successively add suitable code words to the received word, ensuring that the weight of the sum was always reduced at each step. The set of code words that guarantees successful decoding by this means is called the zero-neighbour code words [13]. If the full set of zero-neighbours is used, then the technique guarantees the performance of full minimum distance decoding (the zero-neighbours decoding (ZND) algorithm).

The set of zero-neighbours N_o are the code words whose domains contain the domain frame of the all-zero code word [13]. If $y = y_o$ is the received word to be decoded, then y_1 is given by $y_1 = y_o + c_1$, where $w(y_o \oplus c_1) < w(y_o)$, $w(x)$ is the Hamming weight of x, and $c_1 \in N_o$. y_i is generated similarly as $y_i = y_{i-1} + c_i$, where $w(y_i \oplus c_i) < w(y_{i-1})$, $c_i \in N_o$, until this condition cannot be fulfilled, at which point the algorithm terminates with $i = M$. The decoded code word is $c = \sum_{i=1}^{M} c_i$.

By applying the algorithm using a subset of N_o, $\hat{N}_o$, sub-optimum decoding can be obtained, but with reduced complexity. The problem is defining the reduced set $\hat{N}_o$ that optimises performance for a given $|\hat{N}_o|$.

4.1 Algorithm to Generate $\hat{N}_o$

i) Generate a small subset of zero-neighbours (ZN); ie, low weight code words (weight d, d+1, d+2 say).

ii) Generate a random code word, x.

iii) Use ZND on x, with $\hat{N}_o$.

iv) If it is not possible to decode x, then a vector c is formed, $c = x + \sum_{i=1}^{m} c_i$ which must belong to N_o in order to decode x. Therefore, add c to $\hat{N}_o$.

v) Repeat (ii) until $\hat{N}_o$ is sufficiently large. If after several iterations, some high weight code words have been accumulated in $\hat{N}_o$, delete these and continue.

These higher weight code words may be some of the original 'seed' subset (if the higher weight code words are in fact zero-neighbours then they will be generated again later).

vi) Having established $\hat{N}_o$ such that ZND can work on code words (ie, when there are no errors) it is now necessary to expand it to decode code words with errors. This is done by generating a random vector e such that $w(e) = w_e$, adding this to x at stage (ii) above to form $y = x + e$ and subtracting e from the low weight vector produced by the decoder when it fails to decode.

$$\text{So, } c = \left(y + \sum_{i=1}^{m} c_i \right) + e = x + \sum_{i=1}^{m} c_i$$

is a new zero-neighbour. In general, w_e is incremented successively from 0 (no error) to t.

Weight d code words are always zero-neighbours. Many code words of weight $d + 1$, $d + 2$, etc, may also be zero-neighbours so there may be no need to throw these away in the above generation process. By constantly refining the subset to contain the lowest weight code words, and regenerating the higher weight zero-neighbours, it is possible to establish their status. NB: this generation method provides lower bounds on the Hamming distance and covering radius of the code; if $\hat{N}_o = N_o$, they are exact.

4.2 Combining ZND with MWD Techniques

ZND has a complexity dependent on $|N_o|$. Using the approximation for $|N_o|$ given in [13], a set of values for some BCH cyclic codes is given in Table 1. By combining with MWD, a reduction in the number of stored code words is possible, because an MWD technique could be used to pre-decode, before starting the ZND algorithm. This pre-decoding might simply be an error trapping algorithm or a permutation decoder [4, 6], for example. The reduction in the number of possible vectors used for ZND means that fewer zero-neighbour code words need to be stored. This new subset is denoted N_o*, and $|N_o*| < |N_o|$, because fewer error patterns are possible as an input for the ZND. This subset N_o* can be generated using the algorithm to generate $\hat{N}_o$. A block diagram for this process is shown in Figure 1.

n	k	t	|No|	|No|/n
7	4	1	7.931144e+00	1.133021e+00
15	11	1	3.355353e+01	2.236902e+00
15	7	2	3.814039e+01	2.542693e+00
31	26	1	1.426491e+02	4.601583e+00
31	21	2	4.941238e+02	1.593948e+01
31	16	3	8.708581e+02	2.809220e+01
31	11	5	5.761981e+02	1.858704e+01
63	57	1	5.903771e+02	9.371065e+00
63	51	2	5.120747e+03	8.128170e+01
63	45	3	3.106922e+04	4.931623e+02
63	39	4	1.248381e+05	1.981557e+03
63	36	5	2.077957e+05	3.298345e+03
63	30	6	3.627553e+05	5.758021e+03
63	24	7	2.876016e+05	4.565105e+03
63	18	10	7.983609e+04	1.267240e+03
63	16	11	4.240982e+04	6.731718e+02
127	120	1	2.401070e+03	1.890606e+01
127	113	2	4.696539e+04	3.698062e+02
127	106	3	7.331777e+05	5.773053e+03
127	99	4	9.161485e+06	7.213768e+04
127	92	5	8.987039e+07	7.076409e+05
127	85	6	6.738371e+08	5.305804e+06
127	78	7	3.731643e+09	2.938302e+07
127	71	9	1.460741e+10	1.150190e+08
127	64	10	3.818196e+10	3.006454e+08
127	57	11	6.184084e+10	4.869357e+08
127	50	13	5.617032e+10	4.422860e+08
127	43	14	2.503482e+10	1.971245e+08
127	36	15	4.638204e+09	3.652129e+07
127	29	21	3.644498e+08	2.869684e+06
255	247	1	9.674941e+03	3.794094e+01
255	239	2	4.059619e+05	1.592007e+03
255	231	3	1.451919e+07	5.693799e+04
255	223	4	4.503042e+08	1.765899e+06
255	215	5	1.209395e+10	4.742725e+07
255	207	6	2.801279e+11	1.098541e+09
255	199	7	5.565448e+12	2.182529e+10
255	191	8	9.420390e+13	3.694271e+11
255	187	9	3.640700e+14	1.427726e+12
255	179	10	4.770605e+15	1.870826e+13
255	171	11	5.203670e+16	2.040655e+14
255	163	12	4.667288e+17	1.830309e+15
255	155	13	3.393167e+18	1.330654e+16
255	147	14	1.966277e+19	7.710891e+16

Table 1 Number of zero-neighbour codewords for BCH codes

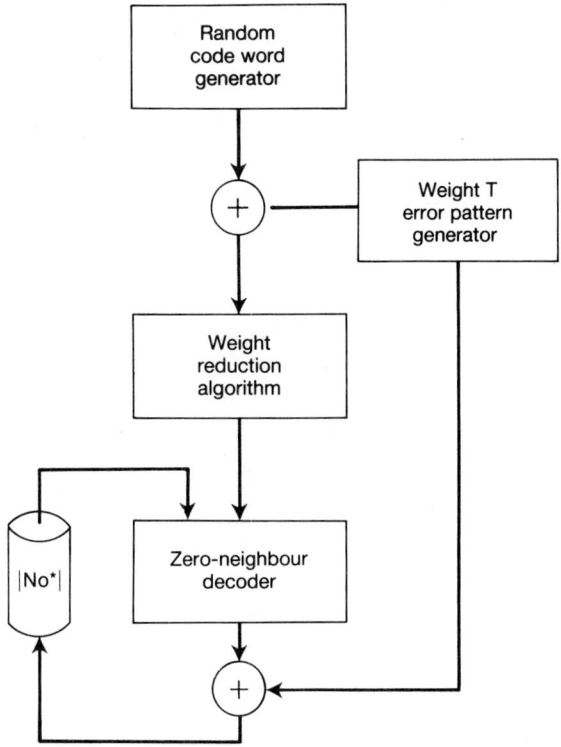

Fig. 1 Zero-neighbour subset generation scheme

By combination of ZND with other (bounded) decoding algorithms, the overall performance can be increased to that of minimum distance decoding without the overhead of large storage. It allows a useful flexibility in choosing between decoder complexity and performance.

4.3 MWD Using Permutations

Code preserving permutations, such as those described in [14], can be used to 'trap' more error patterns than just with the standard error trapping algorithm. This combined algorithm corresponds to a form of minimum weight decoding in the sense that code words (permutations of the generator polynomial) are added to the received vector in a specific sequence (governed by the continued division process) until a weight t or less error pattern is found. Even using all possible unique code preserving permutations, some error patterns are not trappable, but as with simple error trapping the method can be extended by use of trial-and-error. For example, the binary BCH (63, 45, 3) code has many untrappable weight 3 error patterns, when decoded with permutations and trapping alone, or by the use of trial-and-error MWD alone. Combined permutation decoding and trial-and-error leaves only one type of error pattern that cannot be corrected; ie, the maximally spread one. In fact, only 2 permutations are necessary to find all other error patterns. In general, this extension will enhance performance considerably, but at the cost of decoding complexity which would be a factor of n, for trial-and-error, and of v (the smallest integer such that $2^v < n$), for permutation decoding. References [14] and [15] report on improvements due to permutation decoding while both, and in particular [14] show that accurate estimation of performance is not easy. It seems that the best way to assess the performance of these extended MWD algorithms is by means of simulation. Table 2 compares the values of $|N_o^*|$ for the cases mentioned above.

5. SOFT DECISION MINIMUM WEIGHT DECODING

5.1 Soft Decision Decoding of Binary Codes

In an error control-coded binary data transmission system whilst a "hard decision" decoding technique implements a hard 0/1 decision at the receiver on each incoming demodulated signal element, the "soft decision" decoding technique attempts to gain some advantage by assigning a "confidence" value to each output symbol (binary digit) in addition to its hard 0/1 decision. This means that each demodulated binary signal element is quantized into Q>2 levels, rather than Q=2 levels in the hard decision case. Practical values of Q are 8, 16 or 32. The confidence information is then used by the decoding algorithm to improve its performance.

It can be shown [3] that using soft-decision decoding roughly doubles the power of a binary random error correcting code, equivalent to a coding gain of about 2 dB for binary signals in additive white Gaussian noise (AWGN). Similarly, the burst length of a burst-control-code is approximately doubled by the use of soft-decision, and coding gains of much more than 2 dB are achievable for signals perturbed by non-Gaussian noise and fading. This valuable performance improvement makes it of great interest to devise simple and yet effective soft-decision decoding algorithms.

Using soft (Euclidean) distance instead of hard (Hamming) distance as a metric [2, 4, 16] means that soft decision minimum weight decoding of binary cyclic codes is feasible with little additional complexity over the hard decision case. Some classes of linear cyclic block codes, namely the [7, 4, 1]

Hamming code, the [15, 7, 2] BCH code and the [23, 12, 3] Golay code, have been studied to evaluate their performance with the soft decision MWD algorithm, for Q = 4 and 8 [16]. The variant of MWD used is the basic algorithm together with trial-and-error. The metric is soft (Euclidean) distance, which is conveniently calculated by labelling each of the Q soft-decision levels (or regions) with an integer in the range 0 to Q-1. Thus for Q=4, the labelling is as follows:

$$\begin{aligned}\text{high confidence} \quad &1 \to 3 \\ \text{low} \quad " \quad &1 \to 2 \\ \text{low} \quad " \quad &0 \to 1 \\ \text{high} \quad " \quad &0 \to 0.\end{aligned}$$

Then the soft distance between two n-symbol words, V_i and V_j, is given by

$$d_s(V_i, V_j) = \sum_{\ell=1}^{n} |v_{i\ell} - v_{j\ell}|$$

where $v_{i\ell}, v_{j\ell}$ are the symbols in each word. The soft weight of a word V_i is

$$w_s(V_i) = \sum_{\ell=1}^{n} v_{i\ell}.$$

Thus the soft distance between the two words 3003 and 1202 is 5, since the soft weight of 2201 is 5.

The minimum soft distance of a code with hard (Hamming) distance d is $d_s = d(Q-1)$, and the number of soft errors that the code can correct is $t_s = \lfloor (d_s-1)/2 \rfloor$. Thus the "remainder" in the soft decision MWD algorithm must have soft weight $\leq t_s$ if it is to be the soft error pattern.

Figures 1, 2 and 3 show the simulation results for each of the codes studied. By studying these figures one notes that the gain obtained by soft decision over hard decision MWD is about 1 dB, so there is a shortfall of about 1 dB in the expected coding gain. This is partly due to the quantization because depending on where the thresholds are set, the soft weights of the words, and therefore of the remainders formed, change and thus affect the error correcting capability. The optimum threshold values need to be calculated for each code at each number of quantization levels. Another reason for the shortfall is that many of the correctable soft-error patterns are not trappable, even with trial-and-error. It is necessary to use a more enhanced soft MWD algorithm, such as combination with permutation decoding, as discussed in section 4 above, to recover the full soft performance of the code. An attempt was made to improve the performance of the soft MWD algorithm used by changing one of the symbols which had value 1 or $Q-2$, to 0 or $Q-1$, respectively; but this gave only a slightly improved performance.

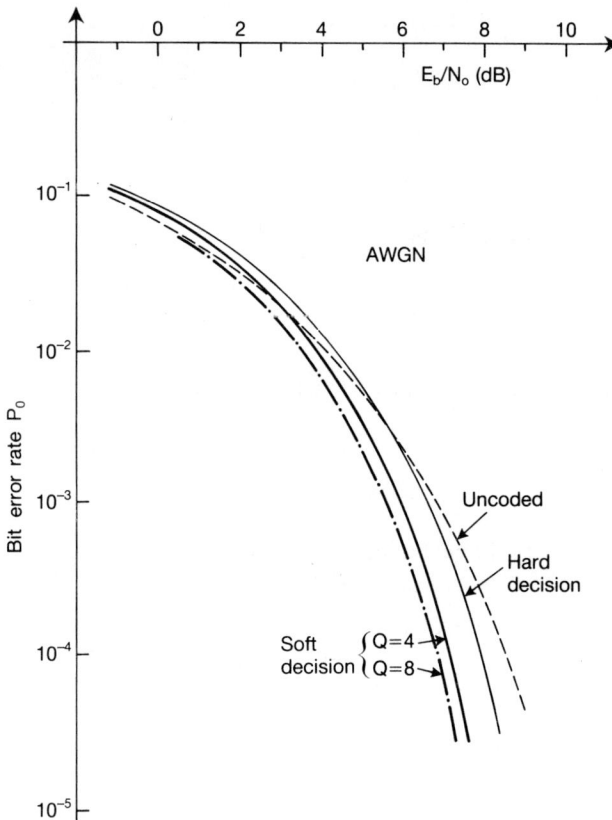

Fig. 2   Hard and Soft Decision MWD Performance of the Hamming (7, 4, 1) Code.

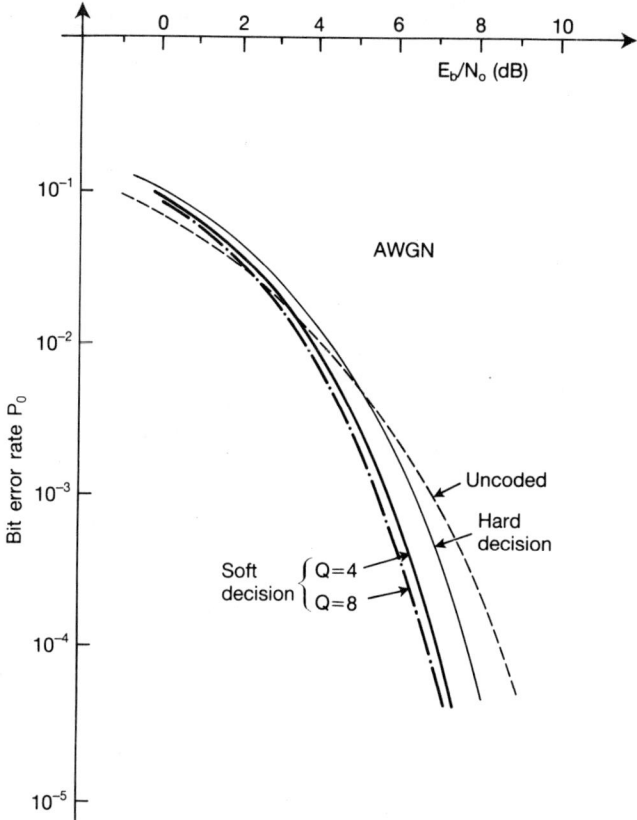

Fig. 3 Hard and Soft Decision MWD Performance of the BCH (15, 7, 2) Code.

5.2 Soft-Decision Decoding of Reed-Solomon Codes

It has been unclear in the past as to how to do soft decision decoding of RS codes (with the exception of erasure or successive erasure [19] decoding). Reference [17] describes a simple technique for maximum-likelihood decoding (MLD) of binary block codes which can be modified for use with non-binary codes. In conjunction with a simple MWD algorithm, a method has been established which implements soft-decision decoding of RS codes.

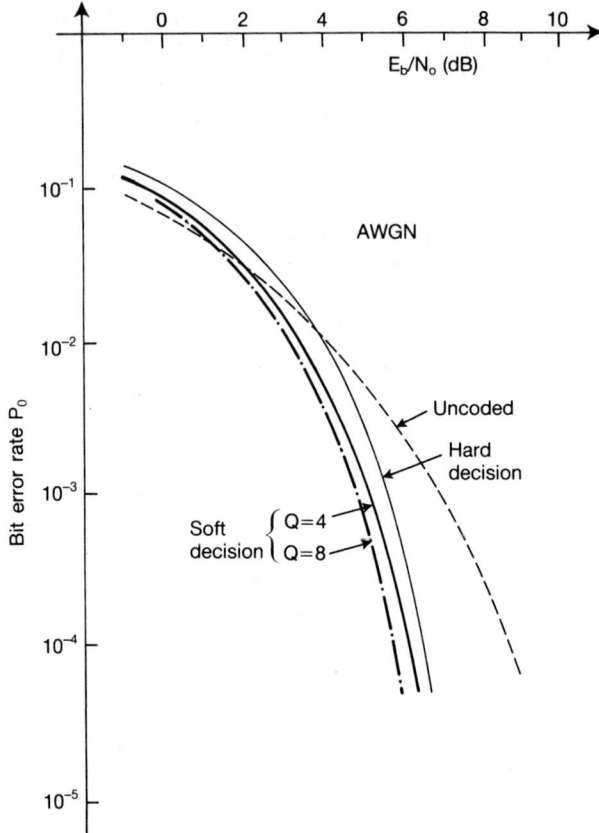

Fig. 4 Hard and Soft Decision MWD Performance of the Golay (23, 12, 3) Code.

The decoding algorithm is as follows:

(i) From the received vector $\underline{r} = (r_{N-1} \ldots r_0)$ generate $\underline{x}_0 = (x_{N-1} \ldots x_0)$, $x_0 \in GF(2^m)$ such that max $\{Pr(r_i/x_i): Pr(r_i/x_i) < Pr(r_i/\beta)\}$ $x_i, \beta \in GF(2^m)$, $x_i \neq \beta$. Set $\alpha = 0$.

(ii) Use MWD on $\underline{x}_\alpha$. If decoding is possible then the algorithm is finished. If not, proceed to (iii).

(iii) Generate $\underline{x}_{\alpha+1}$ such that it is the next most likely vector to have been transmitted after $\underline{x}_\alpha$, ie. max $\{Pr(\underline{r}|\underline{x}_{\alpha+1}): Pr(\underline{r}|\underline{x}_{\alpha+1}) < Pr(\underline{r}|\underline{x}_\alpha)\}$ set $\alpha = \alpha+1$; and go to (ii).

MINIMUM WEIGHT DECODING

The algorithm is near maximum likelihood, and works by gradually moving away from the received vector $\underline{r}$ (in terms of probability) ie, generating quantised estimates of $\underline{r}$, $\underline{x}_i$ until $\underline{x}_i$ comes within the weight threshold t of the MWD decoder.

If the RS code is being used in a multi-level signalling scheme (eg amplitude shift keying), where soft distance can be interpreted as a one-dimensional Euclidean distance (as in the binary case, section 4.1), then a form of soft MWD is feasible. Consider the (3, 2, d=2) RS code in GF(3), with $G(x) = x + 2 \equiv 12$. Its soft distance is $d_s = 2(Q-1) = 6$ if $Q = 4$. Thus $t_s = 2$.
The integer labelling scheme is:

high confidence	"	2 → 6
low	"	2 → 5
low	"	1 → 4
high	"	1 → 3
low	"	1 → 2
low	"	0 → 1
high	"	0 → 0

Assume that the code word 222 ≡ 666 is transmitted, that the error pattern is 020 and that therefore the received word is 646. Soft MWD then proceeds as follows:

```
              soft weight
       646      16
        63
       ---
       016       7
        3 6
       ---
       310       4
        36
       ---
       050       5
        63
       ---
       013       4
        6 3
       ---
       610       7
        63
       ---
       020       2, STOP
```

This soft MWD algorithm could perhaps be extended to two-dimensional signalling schemes, such as quadrature amplitude modulation.

5.3 Soft-Decision Burst Correction

The metric here is soft burst distance or weight [2, 10], by extension from hard burst distance as in section 2(e). Consider again, for example, the binary cyclic [7, 3, b=2] code, which has d_{b2} = 3 as it is single-burst-correcting. If Q = 4, then its minimum soft burst-2 distance is d_{bs2} = d_{b2} (Q-1) = 3(4-1) = 9. Hence t_{bs2} = 4; ie, it is capable of correcting up to four soft bursts of length 2. Soft-burst MWD would then be as follows:

```
                                       soft burst-2 weight
   code word       3030033
   soft errors     0220200
   received word   3210233              8
   G(x)            33303
                   0120133              6
                    33303
                   0113230              7
                   3   3330
                   3110100              5
                   33303
                   0220200              4, STOP
```

6. DISCUSSION

This paper has described minimum weight decoding for random and burst error correcting codes, for binary and non-binary codes, and with both hard and soft-decision decoding. The basic MWD algorithm has low complexity, but is not always maximum likelihood, depending on the code parameters. In this case various extension and enhancements of MWD, in combination with other techniques such as permutation and zero-neighbour decoding, are very interesting and appear to lead to reasonably low complexity algorithms, with performance arbitrarily close to maximum likelihood, as indicated by the results in Table 2.

MWD and ZND have intriguing parallels with a technique called permissible path decoding [18] for convolutional codes. It seems that a variant of MWD may provide a very simple and efficient (but not maximum likelihood) decoding algorithm for convolutional codes, with either hard or soft decisions.

MINIMUM WEIGHT DECODING

Weight reduction Algorithm	$\|No^*\|/n$
None	480
Error trapping alone	150
Error trapping plus trial and error	30
Permutation plus error trapping	78
Permutation plus trial and error	1

Table 2 $\|N_o^*\|$ for the (63, 45, 3) B.C.H. Code

It is clear that an implication of MWD is that to implement full minimum distance decoding, all that is required is to search those code words which have "untrappable" patterns of information symbols of weight $\leq t$. Similarly, full syndrome list (look-up table) decoding is never needed. It is only necessary to list the untrappable error pattern cyclic representatives, thus realising a combined Meggitt [6] and MWD decoder.

The use of MWD with division by words other than $G(x)$ has been explored, but the results have not been very encouraging, except when extended into the various ZND algorithms mentioned in section 4. The idempotent of the code [9], for example, does not help. In general, the use of polynomials of degree higher than that of $G(x)$ (ie, larger than n-k) seems to lengthen the continued division, and does not "trap" significantly more error patterns.

Perhaps the most interesting open question is how to use the simple trapping plus trial-and-error (or windows) version of MWD to efficiently decode error patterns with weights $t > 2$, for codes with relatively long block lengths. The aim here is to avoid multiple test error passes. It is conjectured that the cycle of weights generated by the continued division for each single test error position contains sufficient information to determine whether that position is in error or not.

ACKNOWLEDGEMENTS

Some of the research described in this paper was carried out by P.G. Farrell while a Fairchild Distinguished Visiting

Scholar at the California Institute of Technology, Pasadena, USA. This scholarship is most gratefully acknowledged. M. Rice and F. Taleb gratefully acknowledge support from the Science and Engineering Research Council and the Royal Signals and Radar Establishment (Defford).

REFERENCES

[1] Farrell, P.G. and Campello de Souza, R.M., (1982) An Upper Bound on the Minimum Distance of a Binary Cyclic Code, and a Conjecture; IEEE Int. Symp on Info Theory, Les Arcs, France.

[2] Wainberg, S. and Wolf, J.K., (1972) Burst Decoding of Binary Block Codes on q-ary Output Channels; IEEE Trans, Vol. IT-18, No. 5, pp. 684-686.

[3] Goodman, R.M.F. and Farrell, P.G., (1980) Soft-Decision Error-Control for HF Data Transmission; Proc IEE, Part F, Vol. 127, No. 5, pp. 389-400.

[4] Farrell, P.G., (1985) Code Structure and Decoding Complexity; in "The Impact of Processing Techniques on Communications", ed. J.K. Skwirzynski, Nijhoff, pp. 159-192.

[5] Farrell, P.G. and Rice, M., (1985) Minimum Weight Decoding of Cyclic Codes: IEEE Int. Symp on Info Theory, Brighton, UK.

[6] Peterson, W.W. and Weldon, E.J., (1972) Error Correcting Codes; MIT Press, 2nd Edition.

[7] El-Agami, M.A. and Munday, E., (1986) Reduced Search Soft-Decision Minimum-Distance Decoding for Binary Block Codes; Proc. IEE, Part F, Vol. 133, No. 1, p.34.

[8] Kasami, T., (1964) A Decoding Procedure for Multiple-Error-Correcting Cyclic Codes; IEE Trans, Vol. IT-1-, pp. 134-9.

[9] McWilliams, F.J. and Sloane, N.J.A., (1977) The Theory of Error-Correcting Codes; North-Holland.

[10] Farrell, P.G. and Daniel, J.S., (1984) Metrics for Burst Error Characterisation and Correction; IEE Colloq on "Inference and Crosstalk in Cable Systems", London.

[11] Blahut, R.E., (1983) The Theory and Practice of Error Control Codes; Addison-Wesley.

[12] Sze, H.Y., (1983) A Reed-Solomon Codec Design; MSc Thesis, Univ. of Manchester.

[13] Levitin, L.B. and Hartmann, C.R.P., (1985) A New Approach to the General Minimum Distance Decoding Problem - The Zero Neighbours Algorithm; IEEE Trans, Vol. IT-31, No. 3, pp. 378-384.

[14] Benyamin-Seeyer, A., Shira, S.G.S. and Bhargava, V.K., (1986) Capability of the Error-Trapping Techniques in Decoding Cyclic Codes; IEEE Trans. Vol IT-32, No. 2, pp. 166-180.

[15] Goodman, R.M.F. and Green, A.D., (1978) Microprocessor-Controlled Permutation Decoding of Error-Correcting Codes; Proc. IERE Conf. on "Microprocessors in Automation and Communications", Univ. of Kent, No. 41, pp. 365-376.

[16] Taleb, F., (1986) Minimum Weight Decoding and Soft-Decision Techniques; Postgraduate Res. Rep, University of Manchester.

[17] Tait, D.J., (1983) Soft-Decision Decoding of Block Codes; IEE Colloq on "Practical Applications of Channel Coding Techniques", London, (Digest No. 1983/15).

[18] Ng, W.H. and Goodman, R.M.F., (1978) An Efficient Minimum Distance Decoding Algorithm for Convolutional Error-Correcting Codes: Proc. IEE, Vol. 25, Part 2, pp. 97-103.

[19] Einarsson, G. and Sundberg, C.E., (1976) A Note on Soft Decision Decoding with Successive Erasures; IEEE Trans, Vol. IT-22, No. 1, pp. 88-96.

EMBEDDED ARRAY CODING FOR HF CHANNELS,
THEORETICAL AND PRACTICAL STUDIES

M. Darnell
(University of Hull)

B.K. Honary
(Department of Engineering, University of Warwick)

F. Zolghadr
(Department of Engineering, University of Warwick)

ABSTRACT

In this paper, the principles of embedded array codes, which employ a combination of forward error correction and detection (FEC/FED) for error control in an ARQ environment are described. The reliability and throughput efficiency of the system under additive white Gaussian noise (AWGN) and simulated HF channel conditions are obtained. A new Real Time Channel Evaluation (RTCE) technique is also presented based upon finite-state Markov processes. In this scheme a statistical algorithm is used to analyse the transmitted and the received data prior to decoding; this analysis enables the formulation of the channel model in real time. The model can then be used to predict the channel bit error rate (BER).

1. INTRODUCTION

Propagation effects, noise and man-made interference are extremely variable in the HF (2-30 MHz) band. This results in a continuously varying channel capacity, making optimisation of channel encoding procedures difficult. For this reason, the concept of embedded encoding was proposed [1,2], which is the simultaneous transmission of the same information packets at different rates, in an automatic repeat request (ARQ) environment as shown in Figs. 1&2. The assumption behind the technique is that at least one of the rates will normally be received successfully over a wide range of channel conditions.

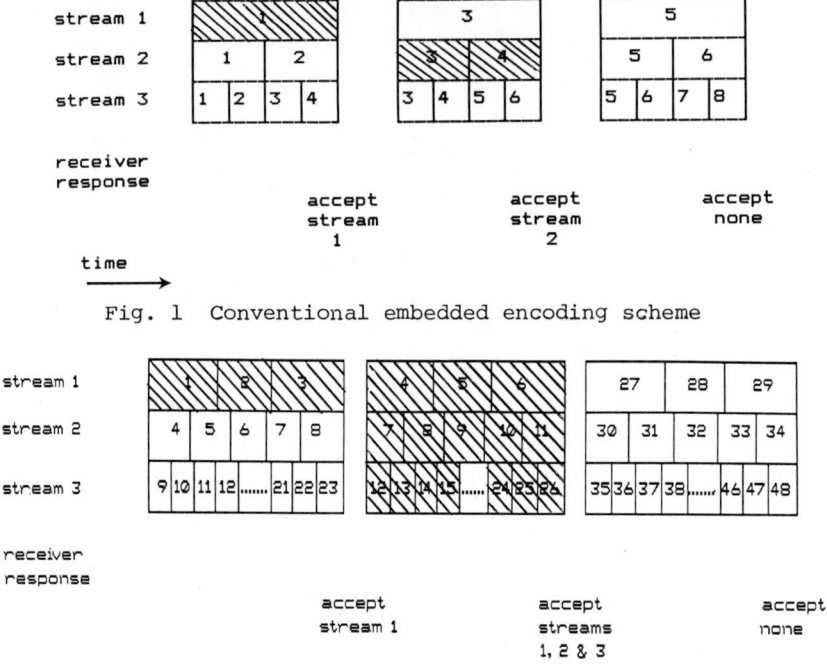

Fig. 1 Conventional embedded encoding scheme

Fig. 2 Modified embedded encoding scheme

The embedded array code [2] is the combination of an inner code for error correction and an outer code for error detection. A retransmission of the erroneous information packets is requested if the outer decoder detects the presence of any errors after the initial correction has been performed by the inner decoder. A modified version of the code which exhibits a superior throughput in the regions of low channel BER is introduced in Section 3.

A RTCE technique [3], employing Markov processes [4-7], which enables the formulation of a channel model is also introduced in Section 4. This model is based upon the statistical analysis of the structure of the encoded data at the receiver and the transmitter.

2. EMBEDDED ARRAY CODES

The embedded encoding approach [1,2] is one in which a message is divided into information packets; these information packets are then encoded at several different rates prior to simultaneous transmission in an automatic repeat request (ARQ) type of communication system. After each block, the receiver indicates to the transmitter the highest rate at which it has been able to decode the information packets in the previous block interval, as shown in Fig. 1. This technique attempts to match the instantaneous reception rate more accurately to the channel capacity available at any time.

The code is comprised of two main codes, D1 and D2. D2 the outer code has a detectability of up to t errors, while D1 is a combination of three inner codes, C1, C2 and C3, capable of correcting F_1, F_2 and F_3 or fewer errors respectively, such that $F_1 > F_2 > F_3$ and

$$F_i = [(d_i-1)/2]$$

where i is an integer ($1 \le i \le 3$), d_i is the Ci code Hamming distance and $[x]$ denotes the integer part of x.

The following is the only constraint on the size of the inner codes C1, C2 and C3:

$$J_1 \cdot N_1 = J_2 \cdot N_2 = J_3 \cdot N_3$$

where J_i is a positive integer with $J_1 < J_2 < J_3$ and, N_i is the code length of Ci.

An example of this code given in [2] is the (52,12) embedded array code, where $J_1=3$, $J_2=6$, $H_3=12$ and $N_1=4$, $N_2=2$, $N_3=1$. The encoding procedure is as follows:

(1) a message of 12 information digits is divided into four information packets, (k1,k2,k3,k4) where;

k1 = $a_1 b_1 c_1$

k2 = $a_2 b_2 c_2$

k3 = $a_3 b_3 c_3$

k4 = $a_4 b_4 c_4$

(2) each information packet is then encoded to form a sub-block, in a manner depending on its position in the main block, using the inner codes C1 and C2 as shown in Fig. 3;

(3) the outer code is then applied to the inner code's information packets to produce an encoded block for transmission.

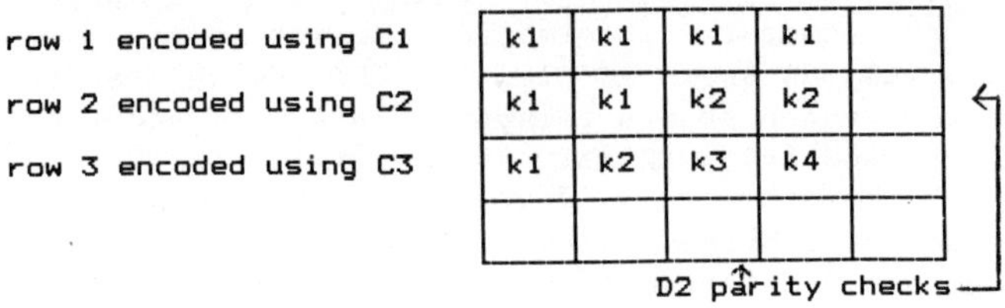

row 1 encoded using C1	k1	k1	k1	k1	
row 2 encoded using C2	k1	k1	k2	k2	
row 3 encoded using C3	k1	k2	k3	k4	

D2 parity checks

Fig. 3 The embedded encoding block structure

The outer code is a shortened array code in which the information digits are arranged as shown in Fig. 4, where P_i are the outer code's parity checks. This arrangement has three advantages:

a) it enables the outer decoder to detect errors within a given sub-block;

b) since each information packet is checked individually, an erroneous sub-block at a higher level will not result in an error in lower-level sub-blocks;

c) the number of detectable errors associated with each information packet is increased, thus resulting in a more powerful code.

a1	b1	c1	0	0	0	0	0	0	0	0	0	P1
0	0	0	a2	b2	c2	0	0	0	0	0	0	P2
0	0	0	0	0	0	a3	b3	c3	a4	b4	c4	P3
P16	P15	P14	P13	P12	P11	P10	P9	P8	P7	P6	P5	P4

Fig. 4 Shortened (52,12) array code

a1	a1	a1	a1	b1	b1	b1	c1	c1	c1	c1	P1
a1	a1	b1	b1	c1	c1	a2	a2	b2	b2	c2	c2	P2
a1	b1	c1	a2	b2	c2	a3	b3	c3	a4	b4	c4	P3
P16	P15	P14	P13	P12	P11	P10	P9	P8	P7	P6	P5	P4

Fig. 5 (52,12) embedded array code block structure

Fig. 5 shows the encoded block prior to transmission.

The decoding starts with error correction within each of the sub-blocks, followed by error detection by the outer decoder. When a block is received, it is decoded by the inner code decoders; if the number of errors in each sub-block, is less than the correctability of the code (F_i), these can be successfully corrected, and the corrected information packet is stored in the outer decoder's buffer. Clearly, the initial correction of these sub-blocks leads to error-free digits in the outer decoder's buffer; however, if the sub-block contains more than the correctable number of errors, the inner decoder will fail to decode successfully, and the output information packet will be in error.

The outer decoder performs error detection on the information packets in the buffer, starting at the 1st packet and proceeding to the 4th. If the number of digits in error at this stage is less than the detectability of the code, the outer decoder will detect the presence of these errors and will accept the error-free information packets, whilst requesting the retransmission of those in error. When the number of digits in error in the outer decoder input buffer is greater than this number, the outer decoder may be unable to detect their presence and the incorrect information packets may be output.

The error control technique described above can be viewed as an adaptive hybrid ARQ scheme [8], in which the information packets are encoded, in the same block, using codes of decreasing error correcting capability. Thus, at times when the channel BER is relatively high, only the information packets encoded with the most powerful code may be accepted, at the expense of low overall code rate and a subsequent reduction in system throughput efficiency. However, when the channel signal-to-noise ratio (SNR) is comparatively high, the information packets encoded using the less powerful code are also accepted, resulting in an increase in the system throughput efficiency.

3. MODIFIED EMBEDDED ARRAY CODE

The embedded array code described in the previous section suffers from low throughput in the regions of low to moderate channel BER. This is the direct result of the additional redundancy of the repeated sub-blocks in the main body of the encoded block. Since in the regions of low channel BER the uncoded information packets are accepted with the greatest probability, under these conditions transmission of the encoded information packets are unnecessary. The modified version of the embedded code described here overcomes the problem by having new sub-blocks in each stream (see Fig. 2), where each information packet consists of one information digit.

The encoding/decoding procedure and the protocols used for this code are the same as the embedded encoding method. As an example, the (64,23) modified embedded array code is shown in Fig. 10, where the a_i are the information digit and P_j are the shortened array code's parity checks.

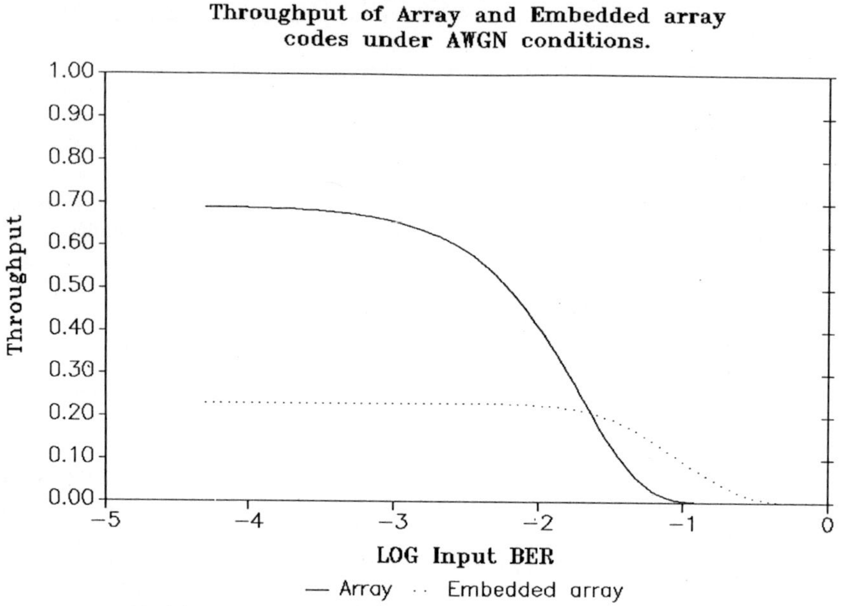

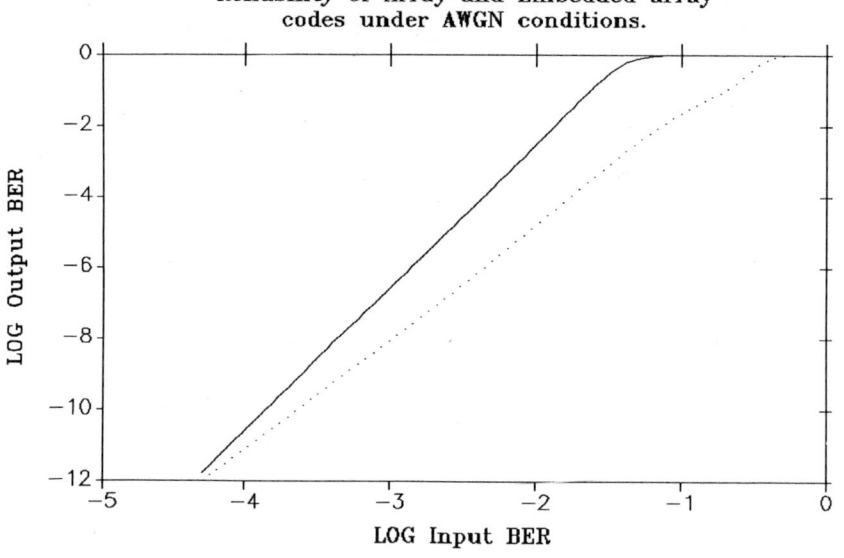

Fig. 6 Theoretical throughputs of array and embedded array codes

Fig. 7 Theoretical reliability of array and embedded array codes

EMBEDDED ARRAY CODING 141

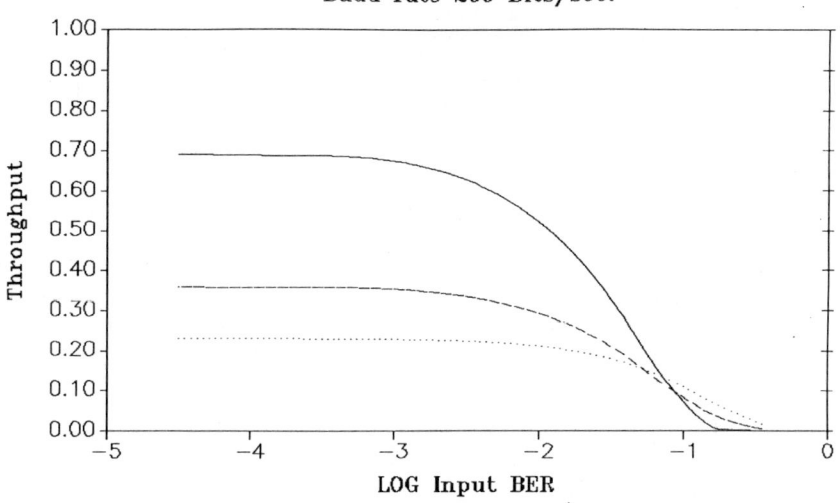

Fig. 8 Simulated throughput comparison of array, embedded array and modified embedded array codes.

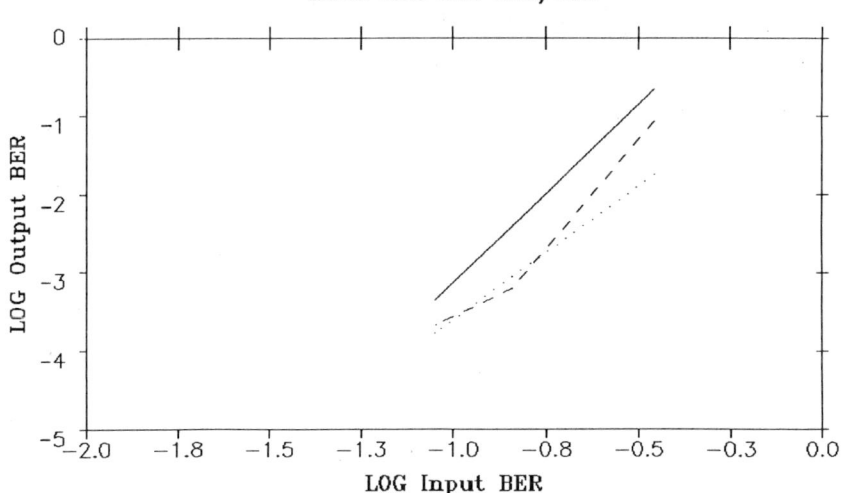

Fig. 9 Simulated reliability comparison of array, embedded array and modified embedded array codes.

k_1	k_1	k_1	k_1	k_1	k_2	k_2	k_2	k_2	k_2	k_3	k_3	k_3	k_3	k_3	P_1
k_4	k_4	k_4	k_5	k_5	k_5	k_6	k_6	k_6	k_7	k_7	k_7	k_8	k_8	k_8	P_2
k_9	k_{10}	k_{11}	k_{12}	k_{13}	k_{14}	k_{15}	k_{16}	k_{17}	k_{18}	k_{19}	k_{20}	k_{21}	k_{22}	k_{23}	P_3
P_{19}	P_{18}	P_{17}	P_{16}	P_{15}	P_{14}	P_{13}	P_{12}	P_{11}	P_{10}	P_9	P_8	P_7	P_6	P_5	P_4

Fig. 10 (64,23) modified embedded array code block structure

4. REAL TIME CHANNEL EVALUATION EMPLOYING MARKOV PROCESSES

The RTCE technique described here, is based upon the statistical analysis of both the transmitted and the received data prior to decoding. This analysis enables the formulation of two basic models, M1 and M2, for the encoded data at the transmitter and the receiver. The technique is then used to derive a channel model, M3, based on finite-state Markov processes [4-7]. In this section a simple two state model, with no memory, is introduced and is extended to a model with one bit memory, as shown in Fig. 11. The analysis that follows, can be easily extended to models with many more states.

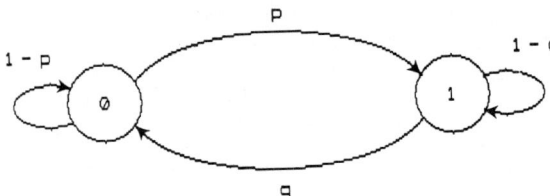

Fig. 11 2-state Markov process state diagram

The basic structure (see Fig. 11), has the following model parameters, where X_i, is the output at step i.

$$Pr(X_n=0/X_{n-1}=1) = q \qquad (1)$$

$$Pr(X_n=1/X_{n-1}=0) = p \qquad (2)$$

$$p+q = 1 \qquad (3)$$

with transition matrix, G, of

$$G = \begin{bmatrix} 1-p & p \\ q & 1-p \end{bmatrix}.$$

It is apparent that the above transition matrix is ergodic [4], (i.e. the state occupancy probabilities reach a steady state as t becomes infinite, regardless of the initial starting conditions). At steady state the ergodic state occupancy probabilities are given by

$$\Gamma(t+1) = \Gamma(t) = \Gamma(t).G \qquad (4)$$

where $\Gamma(t) = [P_0 \quad P_1]$ as time, $t \to \infty$ is the ergodic, state occupancy vector, P_1 is the probability of the process being in state 1, and P_0 is the probability of the process being in state 0.

Solving equation (4) yields

$$P_0/P_1 = q/p \qquad (5)$$

However
$$P_0 + P_1 = 1 \qquad (6)$$

substituting from (6) in (5) for P_0 and P_1 and using equation (3) gives

$$Pr(X_n=1) = p = P_1 \qquad (7)$$

$$Pr(X_n=0) = q = P_0. \qquad (8)$$

The encoded data prior to transmission, is assumed to be statistically stationary, therefore the M1 model is determined off-line. This is achieved by examining an arbitrary sample of the encoded data, of predetermined length, in order to evaluate the state's transition probabilities. The length of the sample is determined, by evaluating the model parameters for increasing sample sizes. A stationary sample is obtained when no further change is observed in the value of the model parameters.

The M2 model, however, is representative of the combined encoded data and the channel; since the channel is continually varying, this model must be evaluated on-line. A finite length buffer is used at the receiver to store the most recent past history of the received encoded blocks. This buffer is updated on the arrival of every block; the size of the buffer is determined by the time variability of the channel (i.e. fade rate etc.). Once a block is received, the RTCE system updates the M2 model, using the stored past history.

The channel model, M3, is then derived using models M1 and M2. Appendix (I), describes the derivation of the channels state transition probabilities, q_c and p_c, where:

$$P_c = \frac{P_r - P_d}{q_d - P_d} \qquad (9)$$

$$q_c = \frac{q_r - P_d}{q_d - P_d} \qquad (10)$$

and P_d, q_d and P_r, q_r are the M1 and M2 model parameters, respectively.

The channel BER can therefore be determined from equations (9, 10 & 7), since the ergodic probability of being in state one is the BER. The memoryless channel BER, BER_r is therefore given by

$$BER_r = P_c. \qquad (11)$$

The memoryless two state model is now extended to a two state case with one bit memory. Consider the state diagram of a two state Markov process as shown in Fig. 11, with the transition matrix, G, given above. In order to find the ergodic, state occupancy probability vector $\Gamma(t)$ as $t \rightarrow \infty$, the solution to equation (4) must be found. Solving equation (4) yields equations (5) and (6) which, after substituting from (6) in (5) for P_0 and P_1, yields

$$Pr(X_n=1) = p/(p+q) = P_1 \qquad (12)$$

$$Pr(X_n=0) = q/(p+q) = P_0. \qquad (13)$$

The channel model, M3, can be derived, in the manner outlined in Appendix (II). The M3 model parameters are given below in terms of the M1 and M2 state transition probabilities.

$$P_c = \frac{P_c(10)}{P_c(11) + P_c(10)} \qquad (14)$$

$$q_c = \frac{P_c(10)}{P_c(00) + P_c(10)} \qquad (15)$$

where $P_c(11)$, $P_c(10)$ and $P_c(00)$ are given in Appendix (II) by equation (A2.3).

The channel BER is again determined by the ergodic probability of state one of model M3 (equation 12); therefore, the channel with memory BER, BER_m, is given by

$$BER_m = \frac{P_c}{P_c + q_c} . \qquad (16)$$

5. PERFORMANCE ANALYSIS

In the case of the embedded array code, the reliability and throughput are calculated by the method described in [2]. The retransmission strategy determines the system throughput; three basic methods exist [9,10] i.e.

(a) stop-and-wait;

(b) go-back-N;

(c) selective-repeat.

In [2], the theoretical expressions of the reliability and throughput efficiency for generalised embedded and array codes incorporated with a selective-repeat ARQ [11] have been derived. The results are shown in Figs. 6&7. A set of simulated throughputs and reliability curves for this code are presented in Figs. 8&9. These results were obtained under simulated HF conditions for a typical fade rate (2.74 Hz), at a transmission rate of 200 bits/sec.

The performance of the modified code and also a (52,36) array code were investigated under simulated HF channel conditions. The channel parameters were identical to those described in Section 2. The throughput and reliability curves are shown in Figs. 8 and 9.

It can be seen from Figs. 8 and 9 that the performance of the modified embedded array code is improved for low channel BERs; however, the throughput in the regions of high channel BER is lower than that of the embedded code. Comparing the throughput curves of these two codes, it is apparent that the desired stable throughput characteristics of the embedded code are preserved in the modified version.

The RTCE system performance was analysed by simulating the encoded data source and the channel separately. A software program was written to determine the M1, M2 and M3 model parameters. Using models M1 and M2, the M3 model parameters were evaluated and compared with the actual values obtained via the simulation programs. The percentage error in the evaluation of the channel model parameters and BERs, for channels with and without memory, against the probability of transmitting a one, are shown in Figs. 13 and 12 respectively.

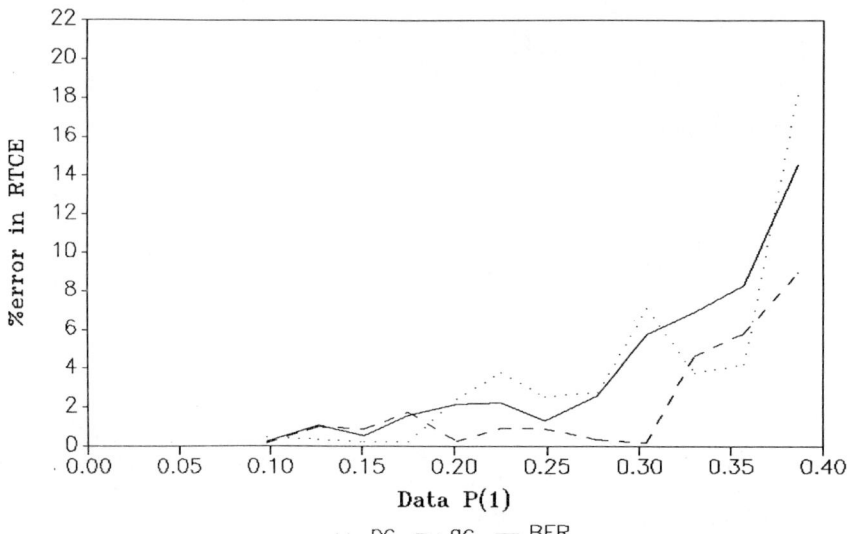

Fig. 12 Simulated % error in the RTCE measurement, memoryless channel

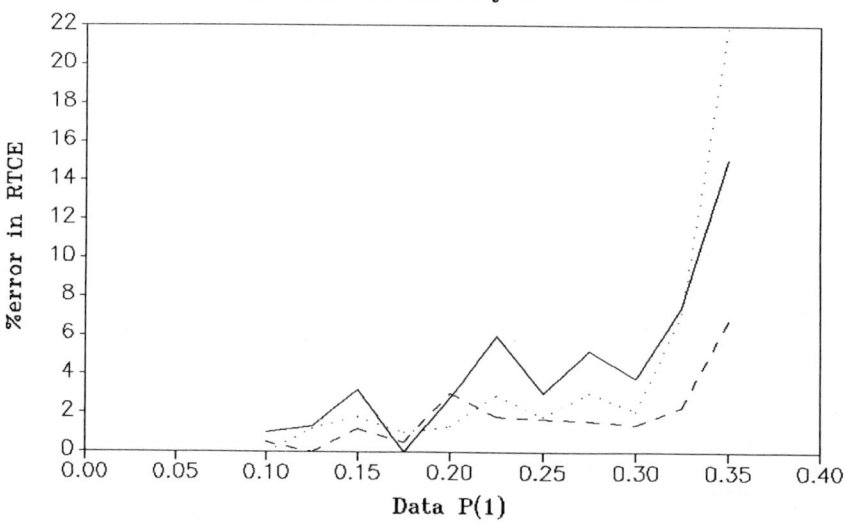

Fig. 13 Simulated % error in the RTCE measurement, channel with memory

It is apparent that once the state transition probabilities of M3 have been evaluated, the channel's BER can be easily determined. The only drawback is the high inaccuracy of the technique as the probability of transmitting a one approaches 0.5. This problem cannot be solved by the conventional encoding methods since the majority of the present codes have an encoded data structure which resembles a random source. A coding scheme which accommodates uneven probabilities of ones and zeros (i.e. in the regions of 0.3/0.7 to allow an accuracy of $\geq$ 5%), would have two advantages:

1) it would incorporate an RTCE system within the code,
2) it would allow error detection using the RTCE system.

Another solution to the above problem can be obtained by considering the source of the data. In some applications (e.g. transmitting digitised speech and English text), the source of the data is not random; therefore, the encoded data would conform to the requirements of the RTCE system. In these circumstances, it could be possible to encode the data even further using the class of codes described above to achieve a better accuracy.

6. CONCLUSIONS

Embedded encoding represents a technique of encoding multiple information packets in the same block in an ARQ system. The information packets are encoded independently, thus allowing a varying number of information packets to be accepted at each block transmission. This arrangement enables the system to operate at very high BER, a situation in which conventional ARQ systems would cease to operate.

A system of this nature has many practical applications. For example, there are certain situations, e.g. associated with transmissions of vocoded digitised speech, in which the significance of the digits comprising the data stream to be transmitted varies. In the case of vocoder, the significance of say the digits describing pitch may be considerably greater than those specifying other parameters of the speech encoding model [12,13]. In these circumstances, it is possible to encode the more significant digits of the data stream with the inner code C1, thus minimising the overall distortion.

The statistical RTCE technique allows the derivation of a channel model in real time. The derived channel model can be used to predict many of the channel's characteristics i.e. BER, average guardspace and burst length etc. The drawbacks of this system were discussed in Section 5. However, the desired encoded data model parameters can be achieved by the use of new coding methods.

A system which has a prior knowledge of the relative bursty nature of the channel can also adaptively adjust the decoding procedure of the decoder in order to reduce the overall error rate. It is possible to implement the evaluation of the channel model parameters on-line; this would require a memory of <10K bits and a bank of logic gates and counters.

6. ACKNOWLEDGEMENT

The authors gratefully acknowledge the financial support of the Science and Engineering Research Council for the work described in this paper.

7. REFERENCES

[1] Darnell, M., (1983) "HF system design principles", AGARD lecture series No. 127 on "Modern HF communications".

[2] Darnell, M., Honary, B.K. and Zolghadr, F., "Embedded coding technique: principles and theoretical studies", submitted to IEE Proc. -F, Comm. Radar and Signal processing.

[3] Darnell, M., (1983) "Real Time Channel Evaluation", AGARD lecture series No. 127, on Modern HF Comm.

[4] Massey, L.D., (1971) "Probability and statistics", McGraw Hill, pp. 88-98.

[5] Kemeny, J.G. and Snell, J.L., (1976) "Finite Markov chains", reprint of the 1960 ed. published by Van Nostrand, Princeton, N.J.

[6] "Clustering in discrete stochastic processes with application to channels having memory", (1970), Tech. Re. Grant AFOSR 68-1390, Dep. Elec. Eng., Lehigh Univ.

[7] Laveen, N. and Sastry, A.R.K., (1978) "Models for channels with memory and their applications to error control", Proc. IEEE, Vol. 66, No. 7, pp. 724-744.

[8] Farrell, P.G., Honary, B.K. and Bate, S.D., (1986) "Adaptive product codes with soft/hard decision decoding", IMA Conference on Cryptography and Coding.

[9] Lin, S. and Costello, D.J., (1983) Error control coding: Fundamentals and applications, New Jersey: Prentice-Hall.

[10] Shu, and Costello., (1984) "A survey of various ARQ and hybrid ARQ schemes, and error detection using linear block codes". IEEE communication magazine, Vol. 22, No. 12.

[11] Yu, P.S. and Lin, S., (1981) "An efficient selective-repeat ARQ scheme for satellite channels and its throughput analysis", IEEE Trans. Commun. COM-29, pp. 353-363.

[12] Jewett, W.M. and Cole, R., (1978) "Modulation and coding stduy for the advanced narrowband digital voice terminal", Naval Research Lab. (Washington DC) Report 3811.

[13] Goodman, D.J. and Sundburg, C.W., (1984) "The effect of channel coding on the efficiency of cellular mobile radio systems", Proc. of Seminar on "Digital Communications", Zurich.

APPENDIX (1)

Memoryless channel model derivation

The channel can be considered as a binary error generating process whose output is added (mod-2) to the transmitted encoded data, to form the received binary sequence as shown in Fig. A1.

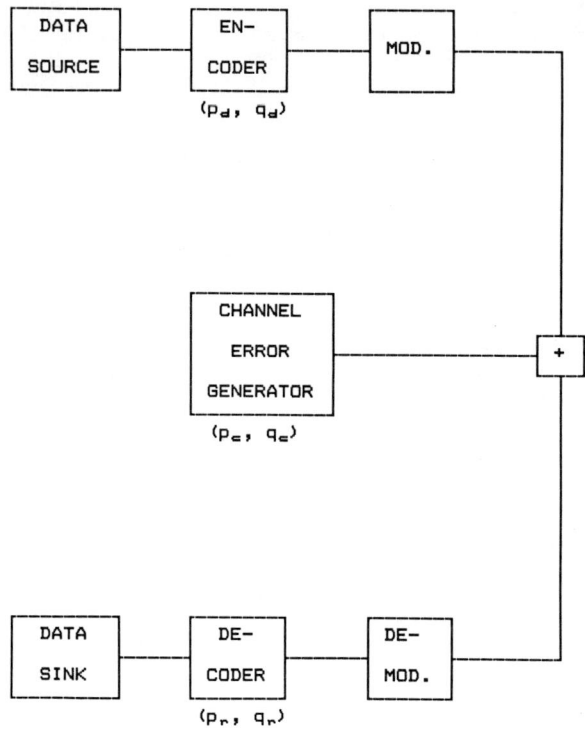

Fig. A1   Block diagram of the communication system with specified model parameters.

In the memoryless channel condition, the encoded data and the channel error bits are assumed to be totally unconditional. Thus the probability of receiving a one or a zero prior to decoding is given by

$$P_r(1) = P_c(0).P_d(1) + P_c(1).P_d(0) \qquad (A1.1)$$

$$P_r(0) = P_c(0).P_d(0) + P_c(1).P_d(1) \qquad (A1.2)$$

where $P_r(X)$, $P_c(X)$ and $P_d(X)$ are the probabilities of X at the receiver, channel and the transmitter, respectively.

Substituting from equations 7 and 8 yields

$$P_r = q_c \cdot P_d + P_c \cdot q_d \quad (A1.3)$$

$$q_r = q_c \cdot q_d + P_c \cdot P_d \quad (A1.4)$$

Solving the above simultaneous equations for qc and pc, bearing in mind that p+q=1, yields

$$P_c = \frac{P_r - P_d}{q_d - P_d} \quad (A1.5)$$

$$q_c = \frac{q_d - P_r}{q_d - P_d} \quad (A1.6)$$

where P_r, q_r and P_d, q_d are the encoded data model parameters at the receiver and the transmitter respectively; and P_c and q_c are the channel's error sequence, model parameters.

APPENDIX (II)

Channel with memory model derivation

In this case the encoded data and the channel are assumed to have one bit dependency (i.e. every bit is dependent on the previous one). The probability of receiving all possible pairs of binary digits at the receiver prior to decoding is given by

$$P_r(11) = P_c(00) \cdot P_d(11) + P_c(01) \cdot P_d(10) + P_c(10) \cdot P_d(01) + P_c(11) \cdot P_d(00)$$

$$P_r(10) = P_c(00) \cdot P_d(10) + P_c(01) \cdot P_d(11) + P_c(10) \cdot P_d(00) + P_c(11) \cdot P_d(01)$$

$$P_r(01) = P_c(00) \cdot P_d(01) + P_c(01) \cdot P_d(00) + P_c(10) \cdot P_d(11) + P_c(11) \cdot P_d(10)$$

$$P_r(00) = P_c(00) \cdot P_d(00) + P_c(01) \cdot P_d(01) + P_c(10) \cdot P_d(10) + P_c(11) \cdot P_d(11)$$

where $P_r(XY)$, $P_d(XY)$ and $P_c(XY)$ are the probabilities of X and Y at the receiver, transmitter and the channel, respectively.

It is clear that the Prob(10) = Prob(01), therefore the above set of equations in matrix form is given by

$$\underline{R} = \underline{D}.\underline{C} \qquad (A2.1)$$

where $\underline{R}^T = [P_r(11) \quad P_r(10) \quad P_r(00)]$,

$\underline{C}^T = [P_c(00) \quad P_c(10) \quad P_c(11)]$

and

$$\underline{D} = \begin{bmatrix} P_d(11) & 2xP_d(10) & P_d(00) \\ P_d(10) & P_d(11)+P_d(00) & P_d(10) \\ P_d(00) & 2xP_d(10) & P_d(11) \end{bmatrix} \qquad (A2.2)$$

Clearly $\underline{C}$ is given by

$$\underline{C} = \underline{D}^{-1}.\underline{R} \qquad (A2.3)$$

Once $P_c(00)$, $P_c(10)$ and $P_c(11)$ have been evaluated from the above equation, the channel model parameters can be obtained. Clearly $P_c(11)$ and $P_c(10)$ are given by:

$$P_c(11) = P_c(1).P_c(1/1) \qquad (A2.4)$$

$$P_c(10) = P_c(1).P_c(0/1) \qquad (A2.5)$$

substituting from equation (1) for the conditional probabilities $P_c(1/1)$ and $P_c(0/1)$ yields

$$P_c(11) = P_c(1).(1-q_c) \qquad (A2.6)$$

$$P_c(10) = P_c(1).q_c \qquad (A2.7)$$

solving equations (A2.6 & A2.7) for q_c and P_c yields

$$q_c = \frac{P_c(10)}{P_c(11) + P_c(10)} \qquad (A2.8)$$

$$P_c = \frac{P_c(10)}{P_c(00) + P_c(10)} \qquad (A2.9)$$

OPTIMUM BINARY WORDS FOR FRAME SYNCHRONISATION

M. Beale and R.T.C. Kwok
*(Department of Electrical Engineering,
University of Manchester)*

1. INTRODUCTION

In many data communication systems, the data are organised in blocks or frames - e.g. when using a block cipher for encryption or a block code for error detection or correction. In such systems, frame synchronisation at a receiver is essential if data blocks are to be correctly decoded. A widely used strategy for attaining frame synchronisation is to precede the transmitted data by a carefully chosen synchronisation pattern, often called a sync. word or unique word; correlation techniques are then used at the receiver to detect the sync. word and hence obtain frame timing. If necessary, the sync. word can be inserted into the stream of data frames at periodic intervals to ensure that synchronisation is maintained. For detecting a known sync. word surrounded on both sides by random data, a conventional correlator is known to be suboptimum, and substantial improvements are possible by subtracting a correction term from the correlator output [1].

However, in many applications (e.g. [2]), the sync. word is itself preceded by another preamble, chosen to facilitate bit-timing at the receiver, such as ...101010... . An optimum frame synchronisation detector in this case would treat the bit-sync preamble as part of the frame sync. word, using the concatenation of these as the reference signal in the correlator, with the correction term subtracted as before. Unfortunately, this reference signal is often too long to make such a detector practical. Instead, the reference signal used in the correlator usually comprises the frame sync. word only. In such systems, synchronisation performance (in particular, the false alarm probability) is strongly influenced by the correlation between the sync. word and a delayed version of itself preceded by the bit-sync. preamble.

Despite its practical importance, this type of correlation function appears to have been ignored in the literature. For example, most of the frame sync. words proposed for use in such systems, such as the well-known (but short) Barker sequences [3] and the Neuman-Hofman sync. words [4], have been chosen on the basis of their aperiodic autocorrelation function (AACF). For a sync. word $\underline{s} = (s_0 \ s_1, \ldots, s_{L-1})$, of length L bits, with $s_i = \pm 1$ ($0 \leq i \leq L-1$), the AACF is defined as:-

$$C_s(k) = \sum_{i=0}^{L-k-1} s_i \cdot s_{i+k}, \text{ for } 0 \leq k \leq L-1,$$

with $C_s(k) = 0$ for $k \geq L$, and $C_s(-k) = C_s(k)$ for all k. This function specifies the correlation between the sync. word and a shifted version of itself surrounded by nothing (zero volts for a bipolar sync. word), a situation which never occurs in practice!

Clearly, optimising the choice of sync. word according to the AACF does not necessarily provide an optimum choice for most practical situations, where the sync. word is surrounded by other signals. Although some of the Neuman-Hofman sync. words have been found to perform well when surrounded on both sides by purely random data [1], out investigation have shown that this is not true when a bit-sync. preamble precedes the sync. word. We have therefore carried out, as described in section 2, a systematic study of the correlation functions which influence the frame synchronisation detection process, and an optimisation of the choice of sync. words with respect to these correlation functions. The analysis presented in section 3 then enables the results obtained for the correlation properties of these optimum sync. words to be used to evaluate the corresponding probabilities of detection (P_d) and false alarm (P_{fa}).

2. SYNC. WORD OPTIMISATION

We consider the transmitted signal format in which the sync. word is preceded by a bit-sync. preamble and followed by random data. The false alarm probability during the search for the sync. word is influenced by four types of correlation function, corresponding to the four relative positions of the received signal to the stored copy of the sync. word, identified as A, B, C and D in Figure 1. In addition, region E should be considered, but here, the false alarm probability is independent of the correlation properties of the sync. word. Thus, region E is not considered when choosing sync. words.

FRAME SYNCHRONISATION

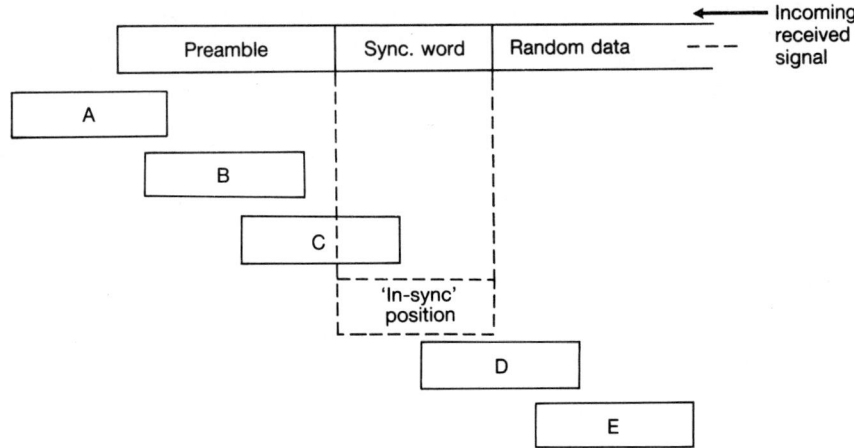

Fig. 1 A, B, C, D and E represent various positions of the reference copy of the sync. word relative to the received signal

From these considerations, one approach to the optimisation of the choice of sync. word is to treat the correlation values obtained in all four of the regions A, B, C and D as a single cross-correlation function (CCF), and to select sync. words for which the peak magnitudes of this CCF are minimised. We are usually interested in the <u>magnitudes</u> of the correlation values because of the possibility of the entire signal being received inverted. This is particularly true in systems employing phase-shift-keying (PSK) modems, where the frame synchronisation detector is often also used to resolve the 180° carrier phase ambiguity associated with such modems [2].

For region D in Figure 1, the best that can be done is to minimise the AACF sidelobe magnitudes, $|C_s(k)|$ for all $k \neq 0$, since the presence of the random data (assumed to be a sequence if independent, identically-distributed bits, with equiprobable values of ± 1) is equally likely to increase or decrease the values of $C_s(k)$. The CCF to be considered is therefore the concatenation of the AACF and the cross-correlation values for regions A, B and C in Figure 1.

We have carried out an exhaustive search of all binary sequences with lengths in the range 8-24 bits, to determine those for which the peak magnitudes of the above CCF are minimised. The bit-sync. preamble was assumed to be of the form 1010...10, in all of the results presented here. Other types of bit-sync preamble were also considered but, for these, sync. word optimisation was carried out only for a few selected word lengths (these results are reported in [2]). Table I summarises the results of the search for optimum sync. words. For ease of comparison with the results of Neuman and Hofman [4] (who considered the AACF alone), the sidelobe peak of the AACF of each sync. word is indicated separately from the CCF peak over regions, A, B and C. Although the actual sync. words obtained by our optimisation procedure are different from those reported in [4] (except for the 11-bit Barker sequence, which popped out of both searches), it can be seen that their AACF behaviour is almost as good and, in several cases, is the best possible. Thus, taking all the extra cross-correlation values into consideration does not incur a significant penalty in terms of the AACF. However, it has the advantage of ensuring that the false alarm probabilities, for all time-shifts of the received signal prior to (as well as after) the 'in-sync' position, are minimised.

Table I

Length	Sync. Word	Max. magnitude of CCF over regions A, B & C	Max. magnitude of AACF sidelobes (Best results from [4] in brackets)
8	00011011	2	2 (2)
9	010110111	3	2 (2)
10	1001000011	2	3 (2)
11	00011101101	3	1 (1)
12	001000010110	2	3 (2)
14	10000111011011	2	3 (2)
16	0011000000101101	3	3 (2)
18	000011110101100110	4	2 (2)
20	10110100111110001000	5	4 (2)
24	111111000110101001001101	4	4 (4)

3. ANALYSIS OF DETECTION AND FALSE ALARM PROBABILITIES

We consider a binary, symmetric channel (BSC) model with crossover probability P_e. It is assumed that it is possible for the entire signal to be received inverted, so that the detection of frame synchronisation is based on taking the magnitude of the output of a correlator. Although, as noted earlier, an optimum detector would subtract a correction term from the (magnitude of the) correlator output [1], this is not considered here, since the main purpose of this analysis is to establish the performance improvements which can be obtained by choosing the sync. word according to the CCF values discussed in section 2. In any case, the correction term requires soft decision (ideally analogue) information on each received digit, and is therefore inapplicable to the BSC model considered here.

Now, for the BSC model, the probability that an L-bit sync. word is received with E errors ($0 \leq E \leq L$) is given by:-

$$P_{L,E} = \binom{L}{E} P_e^E (1-P_e)^{L-E} . \qquad (1)$$

Synchronisation is detected by comparing the magnitude of the correlator output, $|C|$, with a certain set threshold, T. For convenience, we consider the correlator output, C, to be unnormalised, such that its 'in-sync' value, in the absence of errors, is +L. Suppose that the threshold T is set such that the sync. word will be detected as long as it is received with r errors or less (for any r in the range $0 \leq r \leq L$). Then $T = L - 2r$ and the probability of detection, P_d, is a function of r given by:-

$$P_d(r) = \text{Prob } \{|C| \geq T\} = \text{Prob } \{C \geq L-2r\} + \text{Prob } \{C \leq -L+2r\}$$

or

$$P_d(r) = \sum_{E=0}^{r} P_{L,E} + \sum_{E=L-r}^{L} P_{L,E} . \qquad (2)$$

When considering the false-alarm probability, P_{fa}, we distinguish between two cases: (a) P_{fa} prior to the 'in-sync' position, which is influenced by the CCF corresponding to regions A, B and C in Figure 1, and (b) P_{fa} after the 'in-sync' position, corresponding to regions D and E. Note that case (a) influences performance on every attempt to achieve frame synchronisation, whereas case (b) relates only to those situations where a failure to detect the 'in-sync' position occurs. Since, in most applications, a reasonably high detection probability, say $P_d \simeq 0.99$, is specified, case (a) is usually far more important than case (b) in determining synchronisation performance. For this reason, we concentrate here on case (a). For comparison, region E in Figure 1 is also considered. A complete analysis of case (b) (regions D and E) is included in [2].

Firstly, consider region E, where we are interested in the correlation between the L-bit sync. word and a string of L random data bits. A false alarm will occur whenever the correlation magnitude becomes $|C| \geq T = L-2r$ (where, as before, r is the maximum permissible number of errors in the received sync. word to ensure its detection). If n is the number of data bits which agree with corresponding sync. word bits, a correlation value of C implies that $C = n - (L-n) = 2n-L$. Thus, a false alarm will occur if and only if (iff) $|2n-L| \geq L-2r$, i.e., iff $n \geq L-r$ OR $n \leq r$. Now, the probability of exactly n agreements (and therefore L-n disagreements) occurring is simply:-

$$\binom{L}{n} (0.5)^n (0.5)^{L-n} = 2^{-L} \binom{L}{n}.$$

Hence, the false alarm probability becomes:-

$$P_{fa}(r) = 2^{-L} \left[\sum_{n=0}^{r} \binom{L}{n} + \sum_{n=L-r}^{L} \binom{L}{n} \right]$$

and, by symmetry of the binomal coefficients, this reduces to:-

$$P_{fa}(r) = 2^{-L+1} \cdot \sum_{n=0}^{r} \binom{L}{n}, \text{ for region E.} \qquad (3)$$

Now consider regions A-C in Figure 1 and suppose that, in the absence of errors, the CCF between the received string of L bits and the stored copy of the L-bit sync. word takes the value C (as evaluated in section 2). This implies that there are $a = (L+C)/2$ agreements and $d = (L-C)/2$ disagreements between corresponding bits, in the absence of errors. With a received bit error probability of P_e, the probability of exactly n agreements occurring can be derived as follows. First, consider the case where $n \geq a$. If the original a agreements still occur, which happens with probability $(1-P_e)^a$, an extra n-a agreements must occur in the remaining L-a bit positions (all of which were disagreements in the error-free case), and this occurs with probability:

$$\binom{L-a}{n-a} P_e^{n-a} (1-P_e)^{L-n},$$

so the joint probability of these independent events is:

$$\binom{L-a}{n-a} P_e^{n-a} (1-P_e)^{L-n+a}.$$

Next, suppose that one of the original agreements becomes a disagreement, which occurs with probability:

$$\binom{a}{1} P_e (1-P_e)^{a-1}.$$

We then require exactly n-a+1 agreements in the remaining L-a bit positions, which occurs with probability:

$$\binom{L-a}{n-a+1} P_e^{n-a+1} (1-P_e)^{L-n-1},$$

yielding the joint probability:

$$\binom{a}{1}\binom{L-a}{n-a+1} P_e^{n-a+2} (1-P_e)^{L-n+a-2}.$$

Continuing in this fashion, it can be seen that, in general, the joint probability that k of the original agreements (0 ≤ k ≤ a) become disagreements, and n-a+k agreements occur in the remaining L-a bit positions, is given by

$$\binom{a}{k}\binom{L-a}{n-a+k} P_e^{n-a+2k} (1-P_e)^{L-n+a-2k}.$$

Since the events corresponding to each value of k are mutually exclusive, the total probability that exactly n agreements occur is given by:

$$P_a(n) = \sum_{k=0}^{a} \binom{a}{k}\binom{L-a}{n-a+k} P_e^{n-a+2k} (1-P_e)^{L-n+a-2k}, \quad (a \leq n \leq L-a) \quad (4)$$

The restriction that n ≥ a was imposed at the outset of the above derivation. The further restriction, n ≤ L-a, follows by considering the upper limit, k = a, in the above summation, for which all n of the resulting agreements must occur in the L-a bit positions where disagreements occurred in the error-free case. These restrictions on n can be removed as follows.

Note that if n < a, the first term (smallest k) in (4) is that for which n-a+k=0, so that meaningless binomial coefficients are avoided; i.e. for n < a, the sum starts at k = a-n instead of k = 0. The restriction n ≥ a can therefore be removed by replacing the lower limit of the sum in (4) by k = max (0, a-n). Similarly, when n > L-a, the last term in the sum is that for which n-a+k = L-a, i.e. for k = L-n (<a). Again, the restriction n ≤ L-a can be removed, by replacing the upper limit of the sum in (4) by k = min (a, L-n). Thus, for all possible values of n (0 ≤ n ≤ L), the probability of exactly n agreements occurring, given that a = (L+C)/2 agreements occur in the absence of errors, can be expressed as:

$$P_a(n) = \sum_{k=\max(0,a-n)}^{\min(a,L-n)} \binom{a}{k} \binom{L-a}{n-a+k} P_e^{n-a+2k} (1-P_e)^{L-n+a-2k}. \quad (5)$$

Finally, as noted earlier, a false alarm will occur iff n ≥ L-r OR n ≤ r, so the false alarm probability becomes:-

$$P_{fa}(r) = \sum_{n=0}^{r} P_a(n) + \sum_{n=L-r}^{L} P_a(n), \text{ for regions A-C.} \quad (6)$$

Thus, P_{fa} for all time-shifts of the received signal prior to the 'in-sync' position can be evaluated from equations (5) and (6), using a knowledge of the number of agreements in the error-free case, a = (L+C)/2, where C is a CCF value for regions A-C, as determined in section 2 for the optimum sync. words.

To illustrate the excellent performance that can be achieved using sync. words chosen by the optimisation procedure in section 2, consider the 24-bit sync. word in Table I to be transmitted over a rather poor channel, with a bit error probability of P_e = 0.03. Firstly, for any 24-bit sync. word, the detection probability is found from equations (1) and (2) to be P_d = 0.97 and 0.995, for detection thresholds of T = L-4 (i.e. r = 2 permissible errors in the received sync. word) and T = L-6 (i.e. r = 3 permissible errors), respectively. Using the computed CCF for the 24-bit sync. word in Table I, together with equations (5) and (6), the false alarm probability in regions A-C is found to be P_{fa} = 1.8 x 10^{-11} and 1.6 x 10^{-9} for r = 2 and 3, respectively. For comparison, under the same conditions, the false alarm probability due to the correlation of purely random data with any 24-bit sync. word (region E) is, from equation (3), $P_{fa} = 3.6 \times 10^{-5}$ and 2.8×10^{-4} for $r = 2$ and 3, respectively.

4. CONCLUSIONS

Most of the frame sync. words that have been proposed in the literature have been chosen solely on the basis of their aperiodic autocorrelation function. Although this function does have some bearing on synchronisation performance, there are many applications where other types of correlation function, as identified here, play a much more major role. Taking these correlation functions into account leads to a new optimisation procedure for the choice of sync. words. Although this procedure imposes extra constraints on the sync. words, it has been shown that no significant penalty is incurred in terms of the aperiodic autocorrelation values. However, as shown by the analysis presented here, this procedure ensures that the false alarm probability for all time-shifts of the received signal prior to the 'in-sync' position is reduced by several orders of magnitude, compared with those that occur after the 'in-sync' position has been missed. Since the latter is a rare event in any system designed to have a reasonably high detection probability, the approach described here appears to offer significant practical advantages.

REFERENCES

[1] Massey, J.L., (1972) 'Optimum frame synchronisation'. *IEEE Trans. Commun.*, Vol. COM-20, pp. 115-119.

[2] Beale, M., (1985) 'Study and development of error control techniques for mobile communications - Task 1200: synchronisation'. Report to the European Space Agency and Racal-Decca Advanced Development Limited, under ESA Contrast 6176/85/NL/GM(SC).

[3] Barker, R.H., (1953) 'Group synchronisation of binary digital systems', in 'Communication Theory', W. Jackson (Ed.), Butterworth, p. 273.

[4] Neuman, F. and Hofman, L., (1971) 'New pulse sequences with desirable correlation properties'. Conf. Record, Nat. Telemetering Conf., Washington D.C., U.S.A., pp. 277-282.

AN OVERVIEW OF COMPUTER SECURITY

R.A. Kemmerer
(Department of Computer Science, University of California)

ABSTRACT

As more business activities are being automated and an increasing number of computers are being used to store vital and sensitive information the need for secure computer systems becomes more apparent. These systems can be achieved only through systematic design; they can not be achieved through haphazard seat-of-the-pants methods.

This paper introduces some known threats to computer security, categorizes the threats, and analyzes protection mechanisms and techniques for countering the threats.

1. INTRODUCTION

Computer security consists largely of defensive methods used to detect and thwart would-be intruders. The principles of computer security thus arise from the kinds of threats intruders can impose. This paper begins by giving examples of known security threats in existing systems. The second section presents a classification of security threats, and the last section presents some protection mechanisms and techniques for ensuring the security of a computer system. This paper does not address the topics of physical security, communication security, and breaches of trust by personnel with access to sensitive information.

2. THREATS

Probably the most publicised threat is the result of an intruder guessing a user's password. With the advent of personal computers and dial-up modems this has become much more of a problem. Penetrators have lists of commonly used passwords and they can try them all with the aid of their personal computer. In addition, if passwords are short they are easily found by an exhaustive search [20]. There are also standard accounts with default passwords that are distributed with systems, and that may not have been changed.

Another common threat is called "spoofing". This is accomplished by fooling a user into believing that he/she is talking to the system, resulting in information being revealed. For instance, the spoofer may display what looks like the system login prompt on a terminal to make the terminal appear to be idle. Then when an unsuspecting user begins to use the terminal, the spoofer retrieves the login name and asks for the user's password. After obtaining this information, the spoofer displays a message to try again and returns ownership of the terminal to the system.

Another threat is user browsing for sensitive information. This occurs when a legitimate user peruses any files that are available and gleans useful information. For instance, a browser may locate a password inadvertently left in a publicly readable file.

A more sophisticated threat, commonly known as the "Trojan horse", is the result of a program doing more than it is supposed to. For instance, a backgammon program may be made public. However, when the unsuspecting user plays against the backgammon program, the Trojan horse, executing with the user's own access rights to his own files surreptitiously reads the user's files (in addition to beating the user at the game).

Another threat is the result of a devious user exhausting a shared resource so that legitimate users can not complete their work. For instance, the devious user of a network front-end might use all of the available message buffers making it impossible for the legitimate users to accomplish any useful work. The intentional crashing of the system causing all work to halt is a further example of this type of threat.

Another class of threats is the result of a user of a statistical database being able to infer sensitive data from non-sensitive information returned by the database. For instance, if Morgan is the only Economics major in a particular class one could deduce Morgan's grade from the average grade for the course and the average grade of all non-economics majors in the class.

The reader may be asking, "If there is so much computer crime why haven't I heard about it?" Statistics show that approximately 1% of all computer crime is detected, 7% of the detected crimes are reported, 1 out of 33 criminals reported is convicted, and 1 out of 22,000 ends up in jail [17]. One reason most of these

crimes are not reported is that a successful attack often reveals
vulnerabilities that can be exploited by other potential
attackers. In addition, the adverse publicity discourages new
clients and makes shareholders unhappy. Furthermore, many of
the crimes are viewed as pranks, and the people who detect them
do not think they are serious enough to report to the police [23].

3. THREAT CLASSIFICATION

This section attempts to categorize the various threats.
The classifications used were first introduced by Denning [5].

Browsing describes the method of searching through main and
secondary memory for residue information. The browser is
usually not looking for anything in particular, but is alert
to possibly useful information. The browser may find files
containing sensitive information or containing information that
helps to access other sensitive information. The most useful
deterrent to browsing is the use of controls that restrict
users to only accessing information in their own data space.
Enciphering data also deters browsing.

Leakage is the transmission of information to an unauthorized
user from a process that is allowed to access the data. The
public backgammon game is an example of this type of threat.

An *inference threat* exists if a user can deduce sensitive
information from non-sensitive data. This is usually the result
of correlating information about groups of individuals to obtain
information about an individual. The inference controls
presented in the next section are used to counter this type of threat.

Tampering refers to the process of making unauthorized
changes to the value of information stored in the computer.
An example of tampering is a student changing his/her grade in
the grade file. Tampering is avoided by allowing users to
modify only their own files. *Cryptography check summing* can be
used for detecting tampering. This method uses cryptographic
techniques, such as cipher block chaining, to generate a check
sum for each file. This technique only detects changes; it
does not prevent them.

Accidental data destruction although often innocent, can be
costly. Accidental destruction may be caused by both hardware
and software failures. For instance, faulty software could
allow a program to write beyond its data space and overwrite
another user's data. Access control techniques can be used to
limit overwriting to the user's own data space, but there is
no protection against hardware failures such as a head crash.
Cryptographic check summing can also be used for detecting
accidental data destruction. For dealing with both tampering
and accidental destruction it is necessary to have a backup
recovery plan.

Browsing, leakage and inference are threats to the secrecy of data, and tampering and accidental destructions are threats to the integrity of data. Two threat classifications that fit in neither the secrecy nor integrity category are masquerading and denial of service. Masquerading refers to the process where an intruder gains access to the system under another user's account. Spoofing and password guessing are masquerading threats. In the first the intruder is posing as the system, and in the second the intruder is posing as a legitimate user.

Denial of service threats prevent legitimate users from getting useful work done. The devious user exhausting all available resources is an example of this threat.

4. PROTECTION MECHANISMS

This section introduces protection mechanisms used to enhance computer security. The mechanisms presented are grouped into authentication mechanisms, access control, and inference control. In addition, the methods of penetration analysis, formal verification techniques, and covert channel analysis are introduced.

Authentication Mechanisms - Authentication mechanisms primarily address the masquerading threat. The first mechanism discussed is the *secure attention key*. This key, when hit by a user at a terminal, kills any process running at the terminal except the true system listener and thus guarantees a trusted path to the system. This will foil attempts at spoofing the unsuspecting user. However, it is important that users make a habit of always hitting the secure attention key to begin a dialogue with the system. One way of ensuring this is for the system to only display the login prompt after the key is depressed.

Simple guidelines can be used to deter password guessing. One should choose a long password (at least eight characters) that is not obvious, and should not use easily guessable passwords like a spouse's first name, a middle name, or a login name. In addition, a password should not be written down, or if it is it should not be written in an obvious place. Furthermore, users should be trained to change their passwords at appropriate intervals. Most of these guidelines can be enforced by the system. For instance, the password program can require long passwords and can check the password chosen against a list of obvious passwords. The login program can also inform the user that it is time to change passwords.

Password files stored in the system may be compromised like any other file. Therefore, it is not good practice to store passwords in the clear! Instead, a *one way function* (i.e., a function whose inverse is computationally infeasible to

determine) is used to encipher passwords and the result is
stored in the password file. When a user's password is
presented at login time it is enciphered and compared to the
stored value. By using one-way functions to encipher passwords
the login file can be made public.

Access Control - Assuming that by using authentication mechanisms
and good password practice the system can guarantee that users
are who they claim to be, the next step is to provide a means
of limiting a user's access to only those files that policy
determines should be accessed. These controls are referred to
as *access control*.

When describing access control policies and mechanisms it is
necessary to consider the *subjects* and *objects* of the system.
Subjects are the users of the system along with any active
entities that act on behalf of the user or the system (eg. user
processes). Objects are the resources or entities of the system
(eg. files, programs, memory, devices). Subjects may also be
objects (eg. procedures). The *access control mechanism*
determines for each subject what *access modes* (sometimes called
access rights), such as read, write, or execute, it has for
each object.

A convenient way of describing a protection system is with
an access *matrix*. In the access matrix rows correspond to
subjects and columns correspond to objects. Each entry in the
matrix is a set of access rights that indicate the access that
the subject associated with the row has for the object
associated with the column. The following is an example access
matrix. From this matrix one can determine that subject S3 has
read and write access to object O2 and execute access to object
O3.

	OBJECTS				
SUBJECTS	O1	O2	O3	O4	O5
S1	R		W	RW	W
S2		E		R	
S3		RW	E		
S4	RE		RW		RE

Example Access Matrix

There are two common ways of representing an access matrix in a computer system: access control lists (sometimes called authorization lists) and capability lists (often called c-lists). With the access list approach each object has an access list associated with it. This list contains the name of each subject that has access to the object along with the modes of access allowed. In contrast the capability list approach associates a list with each subject. The elements of the list are *capabilities* which can be thought of as tickets that contain an object name and the modes of access allowed to the object. A subject's capability list defines the environment or *domain* that the subject may directly access.

The reader should note that an access list corresponds to a column in the access matrix and a capability list corresponds to a row.

An important aspect of either approach is that both the capabilities and the elements of access lists must be unforgeable or else the entire protection mechanism breaks down. One way of guaranteeing the unforgeability of these elements is by restricting access to them through an intermediary trusted piece of code. The reference monitor introduced below is one such mechanism.

Access control policies enforced by the access control mechanisms often incorporate *access hierarchies*. That is, subjects may have different ranks ranging from the most to the least privileged, where the more privileged user automatically gets the rights of the less privileged user. For instance, in a UNIX* system a subject with superuser privilege can access any object in the system.

The Multics system introduced a ring structure, with each ring representing a higher privilege class. It provides eight hierarchical rings that separate the operating system from system utilities and users, and the users from each other.

As an example of an access control policy that incorporates access hierarchies, consider the *mandatory control policy*. In this model every subject and every object has an access class made up of a level (eg. unclassified, confidential, and secret) and a (possibly empty) set of categories (eg. crypto, nuclear, and intelligence). Levels are ordered and categories are not. When comparing access classes the result can be equal, less than, greater than, or not comparable. For instance, the access class with level secret and category set containing only crypto is greater than the access class with level unclassified

---

* UNIX is a trademark of Bell Laboratories.

and an empty category set. Furthermore, secret/{crypto} is less
than secret/{crypto,nuclear}, and secret/{crypto} is not
comparable to confidential/{nuclear}. The access rules for
this policy are as follows. A subject may obtain read
permission to an object if its access class is greater than or
equal to the access class of the object. This is known as
the *simple security property*. In addition, a subject may write
an object if the subject's access class is less than or equal to
the access class of the object. This is known as the *-property
(pronounced star property).

To assure that all access control policies are enforced a
means of mediating each access of an object by a subject is
needed. The reference monitor[2] provides this mediation. A
reference monitor has three basic properties.

1. It must be tamperproof. That is, it should be isolated
   from modification by system entities.
2. It must always be invoked. That is, it must mediate
   every access.
3. It must be small enough to be subjected to analysis and
   tests, the completeness of which can be assured.

Reference monitors are often called *security kernels* in the
literature.

Inference Controls - The last class of security mechanisms
in this paper is inference controls. These controls attempt
to restrict access to sensitive information about individuals
while providing access to statistics about groups of individuals.
The ideal is a statistical database that discloses no sensitive
data.

Two approaches to solving this problem are to restrict
queries that reveal certain types of statistics and to add
"noise" to the results returned. To foil small and large query
set attacks, such as the Morgan example in the first section,
a technique called *query-set-size control* is introduced. This
forbids the release of any statistics pertaining to a group
less than some predetermined size n or greater than N-n, where
N is the total number of records in the database. Other
techniques, restrict queries with more than some predetermined
number of records in common or with too many attributes
specified.

Among the techniques that add noise to the statistical results
returned are *systematic rounding, random rounding,* and *controlled
rounding*. The third alternative requires the sum of rounded
statistics to equal their rounded sum. The idea is that it is
all right if the querier knows the exact answer about a large

sample, but nothing should be released about a small sample. *Random sample query control* is another promising approach to solving the inference problem [4]. With this approach each statistic is computed using 80-90% of the total number of records and a different sample is used to compute each statistic. For an excellent presentation of these techniques see [5].

Systematic Methods to Enhance Security - Systematic techniques are used to enhance the security of computer systems. Among these methods are penetration analysis, formal specification and verification, and covert channel analysis. None of these methods guarantees a secure system. They only increase one's confidence in the security of the system.

Penetration Analysis - One approach to locating security flaws in computer systems is *penetration analysis*. This approach uses a collection of known flaws, generalizes these flaws, and tries to apply them to the system being analyzed. Usually a team of penetrators, called a *tiger team* is given the task of trying to enter the system. Flaws in several major systems have been located by using this approach [9,15].

The problem with the tiger team approach is that like testing, "penetration teams prove the presence, not absence of protection failures" [21]. This observation has led to the use of *formal specification* and *verification techniques* to increase ones confidence in the reliability and security of a computer system.

Formal verification - Formal verification demonstrates that an implementation is consistent with its requirements. This task is approached by decomposing it into a number of easier problems. The requirements, which are initially and usually a natural language statement of what is desired, are first stated in precise mathematical terms. This is known as the *formal model* or *criteria* for the system. This formal model expresses the critical requirements for the system. For example, for a security system the criteria could be that information at one security level does not flow to another security level. Next, a high level formal specification of the system is stated. This specification gives a precise mathematical description of the behaviour of the system omitting all implementation details such as resource limitations. This is followed by a series of less abstract specifications each of which implements the next higher level specification, but with more detail. Finally, the system is coded in a high order language (HOL). This HOL implementation must be shown to be consistent with the original requirements.

It should be emphasized that demonstrating that HOL code is consistent with security requirements is a difficult process.

The process is made tractable by verifying the design at every step. The first step of the verification process is to informally verify that the formal model properly reflects the security requirements. This is the only informal step in the process. Since the formal model is at a high level of abstraction and should contain no unnecessary details, it is usually a simple task to review the formal model with the persons who generated the requirements and determine whether the model properly reflects the critical requirements. Next, it is necessary to prove that the highest level specifications are consistent with the formal model. Both a state machine approach [10] and an algebraic approach [7] are possible.

After the highest level formal specification has been shown to be consistent with the formal model it is necessary to show that the next lower level specification, if one exists, is consistent with the level above it. This process continues from level to level until the lowest level specification is shown to be consistent with the level above it. Finally, it is necessary to show that the HOL implementation is consistent with the lowest level specification. By transitivity, the implementation is thus shown to be consistent with the formal model. For a detailed description of the current state-of-the-art in formal verification systems see [12].

The advent of the security kernel as a means of encapsulating all security relevant aspects of the system makes formal verification feasible. That is, by developing kernel architectures that minimize the amount and complexity of software involved in security decisions and enforcement, the chances of successfully verifying that the system meets its security requirements are greatly increased. Because the remainder of the system is written using the facilities offered by the kernel, only the kernel code must be verified. Examples of work in this area are [18,24,25].

Covert Channel Analysis - When performing a security analysis of a system both overt and covert channels of the system must be considered. *Overt channels* use the system's protected data objects to transfer information from one subject to another. That is, one subject writes into a data object and another subject reads from the object; thus, information is transferred from one subject to another. The channels are overt because the entity used to hold the information is a data object; i.e., it is an object that is normally viewed as a data container. Examples of objects used for overt channels are buffers, files, and devices. *Covert channels* in contrast, use entities not normally viewed as data objects to transfer information from one subject to another. These nondata objects such as file locks, device busy flags, and the passing of time, are needed to register the state of the system.

Overt channels are controlled by enforcing the access control policy of the system being designed and implemented. Covert channels are more elusive. As stated above, objects used to hold the information being transferred are normally not viewed as data objects, but can often be manipulated maliciously to transfer information. Two types of covert channels are considered in a covert channel analysis: *storage channels and timing channels* With a storage channel the sending process alters a particular attribute and the receiving process detects and interprets the value of the altered attribute to receive information covertly. With a timing channel the sending process modulates the amount of time required for the receiving process to perform a task or detect a change in an attribute, and the receiving process interprets this delay or lack of delay as a bit of information.

There are many examples of covert channels and methods for blocking these channels [1,8,11,13,14,16,19,22]. For example, depleting and restoring resources from a common resource pool is a typical storage channel. A technique commonly used for blocking this type of channel is to have a separate resource pool for each security class and allowing resources to be moved from one pool to another only under the supervision of a flow control method that introduces random delays.

5. CONCLUSIONS

This paper has attempted to give a brief overview of the topic of computer security. There are many good references on the topic. In particular, [3,5,6,21] provide good surveys of the area.

REFERENCES

[1] Ames, S.R. and Millen, J.K., (1978) "Interface Verification for a Security Kernel," System Reliability and Integrity, Vol. 2, Infotech State of the Art Report, INFOTECH Int., Ltd., Maidenhead, Berkshire, UK.

[2] Anderson, J.P., et al., (1972) "Computer Security Technology Planning Study", Deputy for Command and Management Systems, HQ Electronic Systems Division (AFSC), ESF-TR-73-51 Vol. 1.

[3] Special issue on security technology, Computer, Vol. 16, No. 7, July 1983.

[4] Denning, D.E., (1980) "Secure Statistical Databases Under Random Sample Queries," ACM Transactions on Database Systems, Vol. 5, No. 3.

[5] Denning, D.E., (1982) Cryptography and Data Security, Addison Wesley, Reading, Massachusetts.

[6] Gasser, M., (1987) Building a Secure Computer System, Van Nostrand Reinhold, Inc.

[7] Guttag, J., Horowitz, E. and Musser, D., (1978) "Abstract Data Types and Software Validation," Communications of the ACM, Vol. 21, No. 12, pp. 1048-1064.

[8] Haigh, J.T., Kemmerer, R.A., McHugh, J. and Young, W.D., (1987) "An Experience Using Two Covert Channel Analysis Techniques on a Real System Design," IEEE Transactions on Software Engineering, Vol. SE-13, No. 2.

[9] Hebbard, B., et al., (1980) "A Penetration Analysis of the Michigan Terminal System," ACM Operating Systems Review, Vol. 14, No. 1.

[10] Hoare, C.A.R., (1972) "Proof of Correctness of Data Representations", Acta Informatica, Vol. 1, pp. 271-281.

[11] Kemmerer, R.A., (1983) "Shared Resource Matrix Methodology: An Approach to Identifying Storage and Timing Channels," ACM Transactions on Computer Systems, Vol. 1, No. 3.

[12] Kemmerer, R.A., (1986) "Verification Assessment Study Final Report", C3-CR01-86, National Computer Security Center, Fort George Meade, Maryland.

[13] Kline, C.S., (1980) "Data Security: Security, Protection, Confinement, Covert Channels, Validation," Ph.D. Dissertation, Computer Science Department, UCLA, Los Angeles, California.

[14] Lampson, B.W., (1973) "A Note on the Confinement Problem," Communications of the ACM, Vol. 16, pp. 613-615.

[15] Linde, R.R., (1975) "Operating System Penetration, "Proceedings of National Computer Conference, Vol. 44, AFIPS Press, Montvale, N.J.

[16] Lipner, S.B., (1975) "A Comment on the Confinement Problem," Proceedings of the Fifth Symposium on Operating Systems Principles, The University of Texas at Austin.

[17] Lipner, S.B. and Mason, D., (1983) private communications, Digital Equipment Corporation.

[18] McCauley, E. and Drognowski, P., (1979) "KSOS: The Design of a Secure Operating System," Proceedings of the National Computer Conference, AFIPS Press.

[19] Millen, J.K., (1976) "Security Kernel Validation in Practice," Communications of the ACM, Vol. 19, pp. 243-250.

[20] Morris, R. and Thompson, K., (1979) "Password Security: A Case History," Communications of the ACM, Vol. 22, No. 11.

[21] Popek, G.J., (1974) "Protection Structures," Computer.

[22] Schaefer, M., Gold, B., Linde, R. and Scheid, J., (1977) "Program Confinement in KVM/370," Proceedings of the 1977 Annual Conference ACM, Seattle, Washington, pp. 404-410.

[23] Schrage, M., (1983) "Teen Computer Break-Ins: High-Tech Rite of Passage," Washington Post.

[24] Silverman, J.M., (1983) "Reflections on the Verification of the Security of an Operating System Kernel," Communications of the ACM.

[25] Walker, B.W., Kemmerer, R.A. and Popek, G.J., (1980) "Specification and Verification of the UCLA Unix Security Kernel," Communications of the ACM, Vol. 23, pp. 118-131.

AN ALGEBRAIC CONSTRUCTION OF SONAR SEQUENCES USING M-SEQUENCES*

R.A. Games
(The MITRE Corporation, Bedford, Massachusetts)

ABSTRACT

An algebraic construction of sonar sequences that is based on the properties of q-ary M-sequences for q a prime power is presented. Sonar sequences give two-dimensional synchronization patterns that have two-dimensional spatial aperiodic autocorrelation functions with minimum out-of-phase values. The best sonar sequences with length $q^m \leq 128$ that are obtained from the construction are tabulated. Based on a comparison with the limited number of known optimal values, the construction performs quite well, producing optimal sonar sequences in the majority of applicable cases.

1. INTRODUCTION

This paper describes an algebraic construction of sonar sequences that is based on the properties of q-ary M-sequences--maximum period linear recursive sequences over GF(q) for a prime power q. An M by N <u>sonar sequence</u> $a_1, a_2, \ldots, a_N$ has integer values in the range 0 to M - 1 and satisfies the <u>synchronization</u> property: for each k from 1 to N - 1, the list of differences $(a_{i+k} - a_i : i = 1, 2, \ldots, N - k)$ contains distinct entries.

A sonar sequence can be pictured as an M by N <u>sonar array</u> (with rows and columns numbered 0 to M - 1 and 1 to N, respectively) in which column i has a single dot in row a_i. The synchronization property is equivalent to the fact that any horizontal and/or vertical shifted copy of the M by N array will agree with the original in at most one dot [5]. In other

---

* This work was supported by the MITRE-Sponsored Research Program.

words, the two-dimensional spatial <u>aperiodic autocorrelation</u> function of the array has out-of-phase values of at most 1. Figure 1 shows a 4 by 8 sonar sequence and array.

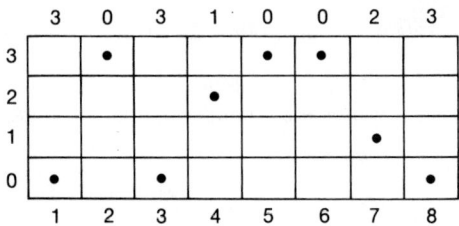

Fig. 1   A 4 by 8 Sonar Array

In applications, the sonar sequence corresponds to a sequence of transmitted tones; a horizontal shift of the array corresponds to elapsed time; a vertical shift corresponds to a Doppler shift in frequency. The synchronization property guarantees that out-of-phase shifts result in "correlations" of at most one, which is small compared to the matched value of N. See [2,5,6] for more on these and other related two-dimensional synchronization patterns.

The fundamental problem for sonar sequences is to determine for fixed M the largest value of N for which there exists an M by N sonar sequence. It is not hard to see that with M rows, the maximum number of columns is at most 2M. However the following known optimal values, given in [8], indicate that as M increases the maximum value of N is probably closer to M than 2M: 1 x 2, 2 x 4, 3 x 6, 4 x 8, 5 x 9, 6 x 11, 7 x 12, 8 x 13, 9 x 14, 10 x 16, 11 x 17, and 12 x 18.

This paper contains an algebraic construction that produces for q a prime power and m a positive integer, a sonar sequence with q^m columns. Initially, the sonar sequence produced has $q^m - 1$ rows, however, the sequence satisfies a stronger synchronization property that allows the rows of the sonar array to be rotated cyclically while still preserving the synchronization property. Thus, a better sonar sequence for this case can be obtained by rotating empty rows to the top (or bottom) and deleting them. The decrease in the number of rows from $q^m - 1$ that can be obtained depends on the primitive polynomial used in the construction. A further decrease, which depends on an integral multiplier, is sometimes possible. The parameters of the best sonar sequences obtained from the construction are listed in a table along with a corresponding primitive polynomial and multiplier for all cases q and m with

$q^m \leq 128$. Based on a comparison with the limited number of known optimal values, the construction performs quite well, producing optimal sonar sequences in the majority of applicable cases.

2. M-SEQUENCES AND SHIFT SEQUENCES

The construction for sonar sequences is based on the properties of q-ary M-sequences. A q-ary M-sequence s of span n and period $q^n - 1$ is determined by choosing a primitive polynomial $f(x)$ over $GF(q)$ of degree n. The sequence is formed by choosing initial conditions $s_0, s_1, \ldots, s_{n-1}$ and generating the sequence using the linear recursion that has characteristic polynomial $f(x)$. The sequence is denoted by $s = (s_0, s_1, \ldots, s_{q^n-2})$, and s is identified with its $q^n - 1$ cyclic shifts $E^k s$, $k = 0, 1, \ldots, q^n - 2$, where E is the sequence shift operator; i.e., Es is the sequence with i^{th} term $(Es)_i = s_{i+1}$. Each cyclic shift of s corresponds to a distinct choice of initial conditions.

It is well known [1,7] that if m divides n (so that $q^m - 1$ divides $q^n - 1$) and if the sequence $s = (s_0, s_1, \ldots, s_{q^n-2})$ is arranged in a $(q^m - 1)$ by $v = (q^n - 1)/(q^m - 1)$ array:

$$A(s) = \begin{bmatrix} s_0, & s_1, & \ldots, & s_{v-1} \\ s_v, & s_{v+1}, & \ldots, & s_{2v-1} \\ & & \vdots & \\ s_{(q^m-2),v}, & s_{(q^m-2)v+1} & \ldots, & s_{(q^m-1)v-1} \end{bmatrix}$$

then each column of this array is either identically zero or a shift of the same M-sequence of span m. If the column sequence is denoted by t, then the ith column of $A(s)$ is either identically 0 or has the form $E^{e_i} t$ for some integer e_i with $0 \leq e_i \leq q^m - 2$.

Using the convention that $E^\infty t = 0$, i.e., $e_i = \infty$ if column i is identically zero, we obtain the corresponding sequence $(e_0, e_1, \ldots, e_{v-1})$ for the M-sequence s.

A sequence e of period $q^n - 1$ is defined by the array

$$A(e) = \begin{bmatrix} e_0 & e_1 & \cdots & e_{v-1} \\ e_0 + 1 & e_1 + 1 & \cdots & e_{v-1} + 1 \\ & & \vdots & \\ e_0 + (q^m - 2) & e_1 + (q^m - 2) & \cdots & e_{v-1} + (q^m - 2) \end{bmatrix}$$

Here we use the convention $\infty + i = \infty$. For example, the entries in row 2 of $A(e)$ correspond to the shifts of the column sequence involved in the array $A(E^v s)$. The finite elements of $A(e)$ are regarded as elements of $Z/(q^m - 1)$, the integers modulo $q^m - 1$, to obtain entries in the range $0 \le e_i \le q^m - 2$. For a fixed integer m dividing n, the sequence e of period $q^n - 1$ is determined, up to cyclic shifts, by the primitive polynomial $f(x)$ and is called the <u>shift sequence associated with $f(x)$ and m</u>. The difference properties of this shift sequence are used in the sonar sequence construction.

3. THE SONAR SEQUENCE CONSTRUCTION

Let q be a prime power and let $m \ge 1$ be an integer. The construction uses a q-ary M-sequence of span 2m. In this case $v = (q^{2m} - 1)/(q^m - 1) = q^m + 1$. Let $f(x)$ be a primitive polynomial of degree 2m over $GF(q)$, and let $e = (e_0, e_1, \ldots, e_{q^{2m}-2})$ be the associated shift sequence. For $a \in Z/(q^m - 1)$, we use the convention that $a - \infty = \infty - a = \infty$.

The following facts are special cases of results proved in [4]. (The results in [4] are stated for the case $q = 2$, however, the proofs remain valid for q any prime power.)

<u>Fact 1.</u> In any v consecutive terms of e, there is exactly one ∞ [4, theorem 1].

<u>Fact 2.</u> For fixed $k \in Z/(q^{2m} - 1)$, $k \not\equiv 0 \pmod{v}$, the list of differences $(e_{i+k} - e_i : i = 0, 1, \ldots, v - 1)$ contains each element of $Z/(q^m - 1)$ exactly once [4, theorem 2].

If $e = (e_0, e_1, \ldots, e_{q^{2m}-2})$ is the shift sequence associated with a primitive polynomial over $GF(q)$ of degree 2m, then e can be shifted so that $e_0 = \infty$. Then fact 1 implies that $e_1, e_2, \ldots, e_{q^m}$ are all elements of $Z/(q^m - 1)$. Furthermore, fact 2 implies that the sequence $e_1, e_2, \ldots, e_{q^m}$ has the synchronization property, since certainly, for $1 \leq k \leq q^m - 1$, the differences ($e_{i+k} - e_i : i = 1, 2, \ldots, q^m - k$) being distinct modulo $q^m - 1$ means they are distinct as integers. Thus $e_1, e_2, \ldots, e_{q^m}$ forms a $(q^m - 1)$ by q^m sonar sequence.

However, more is true. Consider the sequence $f_1 = e_1 + 1$, $f_2 = e_2 + 1, \ldots, f_{q^m} = e_{q^m} + 1$, where each entry is considered modulo $q^m - 1$. The differences ($f_{i+k} - f_i : i = 1, 2, \ldots, q^m - k$) do not change modulo $q^m - 1$, and so $f_1, f_2, \ldots, f_{q^m}$ is also a $(q^m - 1)$ by q^m sonar sequence, which corresponds to the sequence E^vs. The new sonar array is formed by cyclically rotating the rows of the former sonar array up by one. This, of course, can be repeated.

In general, the sequence $a_1, a_2, \ldots, a_N$ of integers in the range 0 to $M - 1$ satisfies the <u>strong synchronization</u> property if for each k from 1 to $N - 1$, the list of differences ($a_{i+k} - a_i \pmod{M} : i = 1, 2, \ldots, N - k$) contains distinct entries. As has already been seen, a sonar sequence with the strong synchronization property can be "rotated" to yield another sonar sequence. In general, this is not the case. If an M by N sonar array with the strong synchronization property has d consecutive empty rows, then an improved $M - d$ by N sonar array can be obtained by rotating these empty rows to the bottom and deleting them. The resulting array can no longer have the strong synchronization property.

Example 1. $q = 2$, $m = 3$.

The polynomial $f(x) = x^6 + x^5 + x^2 + x + 1$ is primitive over $GF(2)$. Starting with the state $(0,0,0,0,0,1)$ the following binary M-sequence s is obtained (arranged as a 7 by $v = (2^6 - 1)/(2^3 - 1) = 9$ array)

$$A(s) = \begin{bmatrix} 0 & 0 & 0 & 0 & 0 & 1 & 1 & 1 & 1 \\ 0 & 0 & 1 & 0 & 0 & 1 & 0 & 1 & 0 \\ 1 & 0 & 0 & 1 & 1 & 0 & 1 & 0 & 0 \\ 0 & 0 & 1 & 0 & 0 & 0 & 1 & 0 & 1 \\ 1 & 0 & 1 & 1 & 1 & 1 & 1 & 1 & 0 \\ 1 & 0 & 1 & 1 & 1 & 0 & 0 & 0 & 1 \\ 1 & 0 & 0 & 1 & 1 & 1 & 0 & 1 & 1 \end{bmatrix}$$

The column M-sequence is 0010111 (taken from the first column). The shifts of this sequence occurring in the other columns determine the first 9 terms of the shift sequence:

$$0, \infty, 1, 0, 0, 5, 2, 5, 6$$

The remaining terms of the shift sequence continue as

$$|1, \infty, 2, 1, 1, 6, 3, 6, 0|2, \infty, 3, 2, 2, 0, 4, 0, 1|3, \infty, 4, \ldots$$

Shift the ∞ term to the beginning and the next 8 terms form the 7 x 8 sonar sequence.

$$1, 0, 0, 5, 2, 5, 6, 1$$

The differences for this sequence are

```
-1    0    5   -3    3    1   -5
   -1    5    2    0    4   -4
        4    2    5    1   -1
             1    5    6   -4
                  4    6    1
                       5    1
                            0
```

The array corresponding to this sonar sequence is shown in figure 2. Figure 3 shows the sonar array obtained by rotating the empty rows to the top and deleting. The corresponding sonar sequence is 3,2,2,0,4,0,1,3. To obtain the best sonar sequence for this case, all primitive polynomials of degree 6 over GF(2) must be considered. The next section describes how this can be done by just considering decimations.

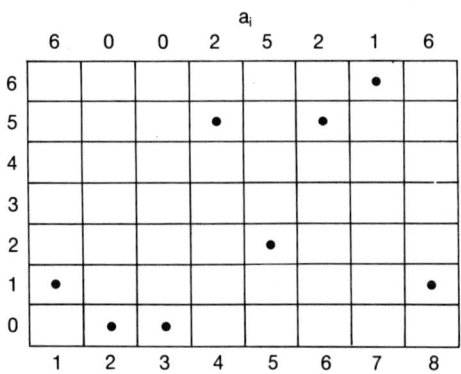

Fig. 2 A 7 by 8 Sonar Array

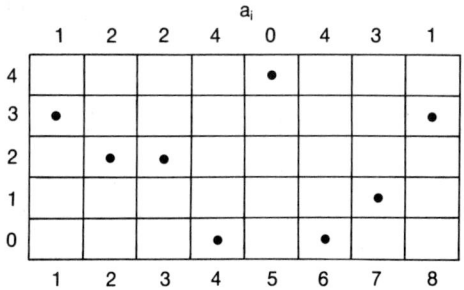

Fig. 3 A 5 by 8 Sonar Array

4. SONAR SEQUENCES OBTAINED FROM DECIMATIONS

All q-ary M-sequences of span n can be obtained from a single q-ary M-sequence of span n by decimating by integers r with $(r, q^n - 1) = 1$. For a fixed integer m dividing n, the associated shift sequences can be obtained by decimations along with one additional multiplication. For a sequence $s = (s_0, s_1, \ldots, s_{q^n-2})$ and an integer r, the <u>r-decimation</u> of s is denoted by $s[r]$ and has i^{th} term $(s[r])_i = s_{ri}$.

THEOREM 1. Let m be an integer dividing n and let $e = (e_0, e_1, \ldots, e_{q^n-2})$ be the shift sequence associated with m and a primitive polynomial $f(x)$ over $GF(q)$ of degree n, equivalently, with the M-sequence $s = (s_0, s_1, \ldots, s_{q^n-2})$ generated by $f(x)$. If r is an integer with $(r, q^n - 1) = 1$, then the shift sequence $f = (f_0, f_1, \ldots, f_{q^n-2})$ associated with m and the M-sequence $s[r]$ satisfies

$$f_i = r^{-1} e_{ri} \pmod{q^m - 1}.$$

<u>Proof</u>. Since $q^m - 1$ divides $q^n - 1$, $(r, q^n - 1) = 1$ implies $(r, q^m - 1) = 1$, and so $r^{-1} \pmod{q^m - 1}$ exists. If s is shifted so that $s_0 \neq 0$, then the first column of $A(s)$ can be taken as the column sequence for $A(s)$. This sequence is $t = (t_0, t_1, \ldots, t_{q^m-2})$ with j^{th} term $t_j = s_{jv}$. The first column of $A(s[r])$ is $(s_{0r}, s_{vr}, s_{2vr}, \ldots, s_{(q^m-2)vr})$, which is $t[r]$.

By definition of the shift sequence $E^{e_i}(s_i, s_{i+v}, s_{i+2v}, \ldots, s_{i+(q^m-2)v}) = t$, i.e., for $i = 0, 1, \ldots, q^n - 2$, $j = 0, 1, \ldots, q^m-2$,

$$s_{jv} = s_{i+(j+e_i)v} = s_{i+jv+e_i v}. \qquad (1)$$

The proof involves writing the indices in equation (1) in terms of the decimation value r. For fixed i, j, and e_i, since $(r, q^n - 1) = (r, q^m - 1) = 1$, i', j' and f_i' can be determined so that $i = ri' \pmod{q^n - 1}$, $j = rj' \pmod{q^m - 1}$ and $e_i = rf_i' \pmod{q^m - 1}$. Note that $\{i' : i = 0, 1, \ldots, q^n - 2\} = \{0, 1, \ldots, q^n - 2\}$ and $\{j' : j = 0, 1, \ldots, q^m - 2\} = \{0, 1, \ldots, q^m - 2\}$. So for $i' = 0, 1, \ldots, q^n - 2$, $j' = 0, 1, \ldots, q^m - 2$, substituting into equation (1),

$$s_{vrj'} = s_{ri'+vrj'+vrg_i} = s_{r(i'+v(j'+f_i'))}$$

or equivalently $t[r] = E^{f_i'}(s_{ri'}, s_{r(i'+v)}, s_{r(i'+2v)}, \ldots,$
$s_{r(i'+(q^m-2)v)}) = E^{f_i'}(s[r]_{i'}, s[r]_{i'+v}, \ldots, s[r]_{i'+(q^m-2)v})$.

Thus $f = (f_0, f_1, \ldots, f_{q^n-2})$ is the shift sequence for $s[r]$ where for $i = 0, 1, \ldots, q^n - 2$, $f_i = r^{-1} e_{ri} \pmod{q^m - 1}$.

Theorem 1 can be used to obtain sonar sequences for each $r \in Z^*_{q^{2m}-1} = \{i : 0 \leq i \leq q^{2m} - 2, (i, q^m - 1) = 1\}$.

Actually, it suffices to decimate by a set of representatives of the cosets of $Z^*_{q^{2m}-1} / \{1, q, q^2, \ldots, q^{2m-1}\}$, since elements of the same coset correspond to the same primitive polynomial. Example 2 illustrates the process for the sequence considered in example 1.

Example 2. $q = 2$, $m = 3$.

From example 1, the shift sequence of the primitive polynomial $f(x) = x^6 + x^5 + x^2 + x + 1$ is

$$A(e) = \begin{bmatrix} \infty & 1 & 0 & 0 & 5 & 2 & 5 & 6 & 1 \\ \infty & 2 & 1 & 1 & 6 & 3 & 6 & 0 & 2 \\ \infty & 3 & 2 & 2 & 0 & 4 & 0 & 1 & 3 \\ \infty & 4 & 3 & 3 & 1 & 5 & 1 & 2 & 4 \\ \infty & 5 & 4 & 4 & 2 & 6 & 2 & 3 & 5 \\ \infty & 6 & 5 & 5 & 3 & 0 & 3 & 4 & 6 \\ \infty & 0 & 6 & 6 & 4 & 1 & 4 & 5 & 0 \end{bmatrix}$$

To obtain other examples, decimate by $r \in Z^*_{63}$. The cosets of $Z^*_{63}\{1, 2, 4, 8, 16, 32\}$ are:

cosets	representative r	r^{-1} (mod 7)
{ 1, 2, 4, 8, 16, 32}	1	1
{ 5, 10, 20, 40, 17, 34}	5	3
{11, 22, 44, 25, 50, 37}	11	2
{13, 26, 52, 41, 19, 38}	13	6
{23, 46, 29, 58, 53, 43}	23	4
{31, 62, 61, 59, 55, 47}	31	5

The sequence $e[11]$ begins

$$\infty, 1, 0, 1, 5, 0, 0, 3, 1, \infty, \ldots$$

So that the shift sequence $(11^{-1})e[11] = 2e[11]$ begins

$$\infty, 2, 0, 2, 3, 0, 0, 6, 2, \infty, \ldots$$

The sonar sequence is 2,0,2,3,0,0,6,2, which also results in a 5 x 8 sonar array when the two consecutive empty rows are rotated to the bottom and deleted. Decimating by 5, 13, 23, and 31 similarly produce 5 x 8 arrays, although in general some decimation values will result in a different number of rows.

There is an additional transformation which can improve the sonar sequence obtained from the construction. If $a_1, a_2, \ldots, a_N$ is an M by N sonar sequence with the strong synchronization property and r is an integer with $(r,M) = 1$, then $ra_1, ra_2, \ldots, ra_N$ (mod M) also has the strong synchronization property. However, the latter sequence can correspond to a sonar array with more consecutive empty rows, and a better sonar array can be obtained for this case.

Example 3. $q = 2$, $m = 3$.

The sonar sequence 2,0,2,3,0,0,6,2, of example 2 when multiplied by $r = 2$ becomes 4,0,4,6,0,0,5,4. This latter sequence corresponds to a sonar array with empty rows at 1, 2, and 3. Thus a 4 by 8 sonar sequence, which is optimal, can be obtained in this case.

This sonar array is pictured in figure 1 and can be computed directly using the shift sequence of the primitive polynomial $f(x) = x^6 + x^5 + 1$ with multiplier $r = 2$.

5. THE BEST SONAR SEQUENCES OBTAINED FROM THE CONSTRUCTION

When tabulating the best sonar sequences obtained from the construction, the next theorem implies that only polynomials over $GF(p)$, p a prime, need to be considered.

THEOREM 2. Let m and r be positive integers and $q = p^r$, p a prime. Let $e = (e_0, e_1, \ldots, e_{q^{2m}-2})$ be the shift sequence associated with m and a primitive polynomial $f(x)$ over $GF(q)$ of degree $2m$. Then there exists a primitive polynomial $g(x)$ over $GF(p)$ of degree $2mr$ such that e is the shift sequence associated with mr and $g(x)$.

Proof. In this case $v = q^m + 1 = p^{mr} + 1$. The polynomial $f(x)$ can be used to construct $GF(q^{2m}) \cong GF(p^{2mr})$ where a root α of $f(x)$ can be taken as a primitive element. Let $g(x)$ be the minimal polynomial of α over $GF(p)$; i.e., $g(x) = (x - \alpha)(x - \alpha^p) \ldots (x - \alpha^{p^{2mr-1}})$. Then $g(x)$ is a primitive polynomial over $GF(p)$ of degree $2mr$. To see that the shift sequence associated with $f(x)$ and m is identical to the shift sequence associated with $g(x)$ and mr, the trace function definition of M-sequences is used. The trace function $Tr_q^n : GF(q^n) \to GF(q)$ is defined for $x \in GF(q^n)$ by $Tr_q^n(x) = x + x^q + \ldots + x^{q^{n-1}}$. The M-sequence $s = (s_0, s_1, \ldots, s_{q^{2m}-2})$ generated by $f(x)$ is determined, up to cyclic shift, by $s_i = Tr_q^{2m}(\alpha^i)$, $i = 0, 1, \ldots, q^m - 2$. Similarly, the M-sequence $u = (u_0, u_1, \ldots, u_{p^{2mr}-2})$ generated by $g(x)$ is determined, up to cyclic shift, by $u_i = Tr_p^{2mr}(\alpha^i)$, $i = 0, 1, \ldots, p^{2mr} - 2$. However

$$\text{Tr}_p^{2mr}(x) = \text{Tr}_p^r(\text{Tr}_{p^r}^{2m}(x))$$

and so $u_i = \text{Tr}_p^r(s_i)$, $i = 0, 1, \ldots, p^{2mr} - 2$. In other words, the $p^{mr} - 1$ by v array $A(u)$ is obtained by applying the function $\text{Tr}_p^r : GF(q) \to GF(p)$ to each term of the $q^m - 1$ by v array $A(s)$. Thus, the column shifts involved in each array are identical; i.e., the shift sequence associated with $f(x)$ and m is identical to the shift sequence associated with $g(x)$ and rm.

Table 1 contains the parameters of the best sonar sequences with 128 or fewer columns that can be obtained from the construction. For each prime p and integer m with $p^m \leq 128$, a primitive polynomial over $GF(p)$ of degree $2m$ and a multiplier r used to obtain a sonar sequence with these parameters is listed. Table 1 lists these parameters with the number of columns in increasing order. The difference between the number of columns and the number of rows is also indicated.

The optimal sonar sequence parameters are known for 18 or fewer columns. For a fixed number of columns N, the minimum number of rows M possible can be determined from the results of [8] given in section 1. There are 11 prime powers less than 18 for which the present construction applies. Of these 11 cases, eight have optimal parameters (1 x 2, 2 x 3, 2 x 4, 3 x 5, 4 x 7, 4 x 8, 10 x 16 and 11 x 17), while the remaining three cases have only one extra row (6 x 9, 7 x 11 and 9 x 13).

6. CONCLUSION

An algebraic construction of sonar sequences with q^m columns, q a prime power and m an integer, was presented. The construction was based on the properties of the shift sequence obtained from a q-ary M-sequence of span $2m$. The best sonar sequences obtained from the construction were tabulated for the number of columns $q^m \leq 128$. Based on a comparison with the limited number of known optimal values, the construction performed quite well, producing optimal sonar sequences in eight out of 11 applicable cases and being off by 1 in the remaining three cases.

A subject for future research is the asymptotic performance of the construction, including a comparison with the parabolic construction of [3]. Also, the results suggest that it should be possible to improve the upper bound of 2M on the number N of columns of an M x N sonar sequence.

q	m	M	N = q^m	N - M	primitive polynomial													multiplier
2	1	1	2	1	1	1	1											1
3	1	2	3	1	1	1	2											1
2	2	2	4	2	1	1	0	1										1
5	1	3	5	2	1	1	2											1
7	1	4	7	3	1	1	3											1
2	3	4	8	4	1	1	0	0	0	0	1							2
3	2	6	9	3	1	1	0	0	2									1
11	1	7	11	4	1	1	7											1
13	1	9	13	4	1	11	6											1
2	4	10	16	6	1	0	1	1	0	0	1	0	1					4
17	1	11	17	6	1	8	6											3
19	1	13	19	6	1	11	3											1
23	1	16	23	7	1	22	19											9
5	2	19	25	6	1	1	0	2	3									5
3	3	21	27	6	1	0	2	0	1	1	2							9
29	1	22	29	7	1	7	2											9
31	1	23	31	8	1	24	17											11
2	5	24	32	8	1	0	0	0	0	1	0	0	1	1	1			2
37	1	29	37	8	1	31	15											5
41	1	32	41	9	1	32	7											19
43	1	34	43	9	1	10	5											19
47	1	38	47	9	1	19	22											21
7	2	40	49	9	1	3	3	2	3									23
53	1	44	53	9	1	30	33											3
59	1	49	59	10	1	49	11											15
61	1	52	61	9	1	1	44											19
2	6	54	64	10	1	1	1	0	0	0	0	0	0	1	0	1		17
67	1	57	67	10	1	4	2											5
71	1	61	71	10	1	33	21											29
73	1	62	73	11	1	48	31											19
79	1	67	79	12	1	54	63											31
3	4	71	81	10	1	1	2	0	2	2	1	0	2					9
83	1	72	83	11	1	3	24											27
89	1	77	89	12	1	15	58											17
97	1	85	97	12	1	52	39											17
101	1	88	101	13	1	28	63											27
103	1	91	103	12	1	39	86											29
107	1	94	107	13	1	33	97											25
109	1	97	109	12	1	82	65											13
113	1	100	113	13	1	30	54											33
11	2	109	121	12	1	3	2	10	2									43
5	3	112	125	13	1	3	4	3	0	3	2							59
127	1	114	127	13	1	2	23											41
2	7	117	128	13	1	1	1	1	0	1	0	1	0	1	1	0	1 1 1	45

Table 1 Parameters of the Best M x N Sonar Sequences Obtained from the Construction; N ≤ 128.

ACKNOWLEDGEMENT

The author is indebted to Michael S. Chao and Robert A. Meyer for providing the programming support required to generate table 1.

REFERENCES

[1] Baumert, L.D., (1971) Cyclic Difference Sets, Lecture Notes in Math., 182, Springer, Berlin.

[2] Costas, J.P., (1984) A study of a class of detection waveforms having nearly ideal range-Doppler ambiguity properties, *IEEE Proceedings*, vol. 72, pp. 996-1009.

[3] Gagliardi, R., Robbins, J. and Taylor, H., "Acquisition sequences in PPM communications," preprint, Dept. of Elec. Engineering, Univ. of Southern California.

[4] Games, R.A., (1984) Crosscorrelation of M-sequences and GMW-sequences with the same primitive polynomial, *Discrete Applied Math.*, vol. 12, pp. 139-146.

[5] Golomb, S.W. and Taylor, H., (1982) Two-dimensional synchronization patterns for minimum ambiguity, *IEEE Trans. Inform. Theory*, vol. IT-28, pp. 600-604.

[6] Constructions and properties of Costas arrays, (1984) *IEEE Proceedings*, vol. 72, pp. 1143-1163.

[7] Gordon, B., Mills, W.H. and Welch, L.R., (1962) Some new difference sets, *Canad, J. Math.*, vol. 14, pp. 614-625.

[8] Robbins, J. and Taylor, H., (1984) Sonar sequences and PPM sequences, part 1, No. CSI-84-12-01, Communication Sciences Institute, Univ. Southern Calif., Los Angeles, CA.

PUBLIC-KEY CRYPTOGRAPHY AND RE-USABLE SHARED SECRETS

R.A. Croft and S.P. Harris
(Plessey Electronic Systems Research Limited, Hampshire)

ABSTRACT

The paper describes how Shamir's secret sharing method can be combined with the trap-door properties of exponentiation/logarithmisation modulo a large prime number as used in the Diffie-Hellman secret number exchange method.

The object of this combination is to preserve the secrecy of the numbers held by the participants of the shared secret, whilst at the same time permitting them to transmit information in the clear which, when issued by sufficient of the participants, enables either

(i) authorisation of a transaction (e.g. h out of n signatories for a cheque), or

(ii) mutually authenticated base key exchange, pairwise between the participants.

Since the secrecy of the numbers held by the participants is preserved, this means that the participants can, on future occasions, either authorise further transactions or exchange further base keys using the same, uncompromised secret numbers.

1. INTRODUCTION

Shamir's secret sharing scheme [1] offers a way of 'spreading' a secret number among many individuals. Only when a certain minimum number of individuals co-operate can the secret number be reconstructed.

The Diffie-Hellman public key distribution scheme (PKDS) [2] offers a way for two individuals to agree a secret number between them, although all their exchanges are carried out over a public medium.

This paper describes how Shamir's secret sharing method can be combined with the trap-door properties of exponentiation/ logarithmisation modulo a large prime as used in the Diffie-Hellman secret number exchange method.

The object of this combination is to preserve the secrecy of the numbers held by the participants of the shared secret, whilst at the same time permitting them to transmit information in the clear which, when issued by sufficient of the participants, enables either

(i) authorisation of a transaction (e.g. h out of n signatories for a cheque), or

(ii) mutually authenticated base key exchange, pairwise between the participants.

Since the secrecy of the numbers held by the participants is preserved, this means that the participants can, on future occasions, either authorise further transactions or exchange further base keys using their same, uncompromised secret numbers.

The theory of the proposed scheme is discussed in Section 2, and the specific theory and an example of each of applications (i) and (ii) is discussed in Section 3. Section 4 offers some notes about the method.

2. THEORETICAL DISCUSSION

Any polynomial of degree n in one variable is completely defined when n+1 points through which it passes are specified. This statement is true when the coefficients belong to any field, and in particular to the field $GF(P1)$ of integers modulo a prime number $P1$. If these points are (X_i, Y_i), for $i=1,\ldots,n+1$, the value of Y corresponding to any value of X is given by the Lagrange interpolation formula:

$$Y = \sum_{r=1}^{n+1} A_r . Y_r \pmod{P1} \qquad (2.1)$$

where $A_r = \displaystyle\prod_{\substack{s=1 \\ s<>r}}^{n+1} (X-X_s)/(X_r-X_s) \pmod{P1}$, for $r=1,\ldots,n+1$ (2.2)

In the proposed scheme the abscissae, X, are publicly known quantities and, since the Ar depend solely on them, these are also publicly known.

(It should be noted that as well as the X and Y, the Ar, being derived by arithmetical operations modulo P1 from the X, are also members of the field GF(P1), i.e. are integers modulo P1. The divisions required in their derivation can be carried out, for example, by using the Euclidean algorithm.)

The ordinates, Y, however are kept secret by the participants and never directly transmitted by them. Instead they are used as exponents to raise some common and publicly known base number, b, to different powers to give another set of numbers, M. This exponentiation process is carried out modulo a second prime number, P2. The base number b and the resulting M's are therefore members of the field GF(P2). Thus

$$M_r = b^{Y_r} \pmod{P2} \quad (2.3)$$

These exponentiations may be performed efficiently using the 'exponentiation by repeated squaring and multiplication' algorithm, which is widely used in public key cryptography, and described, for example, by Rivest Shamir and Adleman [3].

As in the Diffie-Hellman PKDS, provided P2 is a well chosen prime, knowledge of b, P2 and the M's does not reveal the corresponding Y's, since logarithmisation modulo a well-chosen prime is a computationally hard process.

The prime numbers P1 and P2 are chosen so that they are related to each other by the equation:

$$P2 = 1 + k*P1 \quad (2.4)$$

where, P1 having been chosen to be prime, k is conveniently chosen from the ascending sequence of even numbers 2,4,6,... to be the least positive integer which makes P2 prime.

This relationship has two purposes. First, it guarantees that P2-1 has a large prime factor, which is a necessary condition for ensuring that logarithmisation module P2 is computationally hard. (The best known algorithm, Shanks' algorithm [4] requires $O(\sqrt{P2})$ operations to perform the logarithmisation.) Secondly, it provides a method of effectively performing the manipulations between the exponents, Y, required by Equation (2.1), by acting on the corresponding M values. Additions between Y numbers are replaced by multiplications between M numbers. Multiplications of Y numbers by publicly known multipliers (Ar) are replaced by raising the M numbers to the power of these known multipliers. To accomplish this correctly, it is necessary to restrict the choice of base number b as follows:

$$b = c \hat{\ } k \pmod{P2}, \quad \text{for} \quad 2 <= c <= P2-1 \text{ and } b <> 1 \tag{2.5}$$

By Fermat's Simple Theorem:

$$c \hat{\ } (P2-1) = 1 \pmod{P2} \quad \text{for any} \quad c <> 0 \pmod{P2} \tag{2.6}$$

Hence

$$b \hat{\ } P1 = (c \hat{\ } k) \hat{\ } P1 = c \hat{\ } (P2-1) = 1 = b \hat{\ } 0 \pmod{P2} \tag{2.7}$$

i.e.

$$b \hat{\ } P1 = b \hat{\ } 0 \pmod{P2} \tag{2.8}$$

so that provided that Equation (2.5) holds, the exponents of b behave, as we require them to, as integers modulo P1. It may be noted that this restriction still leaves a choice of P1-1 different potentially usable values for b.

If b is raised respectively to the power of each side of Equation (2.1), the following relationship is obtained:

$$M = b \hat{\ } Y = b \hat{\ } (\sum_{r=1}^{n+1} Ar.Yr) = \prod_{r=1}^{n+1} b \hat{\ } (Ar.Yr) = \prod_{r=1}^{n+1} (b \hat{\ } Yr) \hat{\ } Ar \tag{2.9}$$

i.e.

$$M = \prod_{r=1}^{n+1} (Mr \hat{\ } Ar) \pmod{P2} \tag{2.10}$$

Equation (2.10) is a relationship between n+2 different M's, each of which is derived from one of the n+2 corresponding Y's which satisfy the relationship given in Equation (2.1). Any participant in possession of, or supplied with, a total of n+2 values of M can check whether Equation (2.10) is satisfied. If it is satisfied, then the n+2 values of M, and hence their suppliers, are genuine.

3. APPLICATIONS

3.1 Authorisation of a transaction

3.1.1 Theory

Suppose that a minimum number of h signatories out of a total of N signatories are required to authorise a cheque. Then a polynomial of degree (2*h - 1) is secretly generated. Each signatory is issued with two points on this polynomial, and the Bank with one point.

Then, using the same base number, h authorisers can each supply the bank with two M values. The Bank can generate one M value itself, giving a total of (2*h + 1). These are sufficient for the Bank to check compliance with Equation (2.10).

Once 2*h M values are known, any other M value can be calculated from them, so that the same base number must not be used for another transaction. To prevent this, it is suggested that the base number should incorporate, in some way, a date and time stamp.

3.1.2 Example

A numerical example illustrating the theory described in Section 3.1.1 is given here, making use of small prime numbers to demonstrate the principle of operation. In practice a number of 100 or more decimal digits would be used; Odlyzko [5] discussed the cryptographic strength.

Suppose that a minimum of 2 signatories out of a total of 4 are required to authorise a cheque.

Select P1 = 101 (prime), and then calculate P2 = j*P1 + 1 = 607 (prime), with j = 6.

A computer program is used to select a secret polynomial of degree 3 with coefficients in GF(101). Suppose it selects:

$$Y = 51*X^3 + 80*X^2 + 29*X + 7 \pmod{101} \qquad (3.1.2.1)$$

It then selects 9 abscissae, X, (two for each of the four authorising participants, and one for the Bank). It calculates secretly from Equation (3.1.2.1) the corresponding ordinates, Y:

Participant	X	Y
1a	19	93
1b	32	57
2a	43	7
2b	65	30
3a	90	67
3b	26	100
4a	13	4
4b	72	65
Bank	51	10

The computer supplies all participants with details of everybody's X numbers, and each participant individually with his secret Y number(s). It then erases its memory to destroy the records of the polynomial coefficients it had chosen.

Suppose that Participants 1 and 4 decide to authorise a transaction. They agree with the Bank a number c (= 23, say), linked with the transaction, and from it calculate the base number

$$b = c^k = 23^6 \pmod{607} = 122 \qquad (3.1.2.2)$$

They each send to the Bank two (X,M) pairs, where $M = 122 \wedge Y \pmod{607}$, and Y is the secret ordinate corresponding to the abscissa X. The Bank also calculates its own M:

Participant	Suffix	X	M
1a	1	19	60
1b	2	32	454
4a	3	13	308
4b	4	72	392
Bank		51	329

Using the received abscissa inputs, the Bank calculates, by means of Equation (2.2), the Ar values corresponding to its own abscissa:

$$A1 = \frac{(51-32)*(51-13)*(51-72)}{(19-32)*(19-13)*(19-72)} = \frac{89}{94} = 89*72 = 45 \qquad (3.1.2.3)$$

$$A2 = \frac{(51-19)*(51-13)*(51-72)}{(32-19)*(32-13)*(32-72)} = \frac{17}{18} = 17*73 = 29 \quad (3.1.2.4)$$

$$A3 = \frac{(51-19)*(51-32)*(51-72)}{(13-19)*(13-32)*(13-72)} = \frac{59}{41} = 59*69 = 31 \quad (3.1.2.5)$$

$$A4 = \frac{(51-19)*(51-32)*(51-13)}{(72-19)*(72-32)*(72-13)} = \frac{76}{42} = 76*89 = 98 \quad (3.1.2.6)$$

The Bank now calculates from Equation (2.10) the value of its own M as given by the four received M's to get:

$$M = (60^{\wedge}45)*(454^{\wedge}29)*(308^{\wedge}31)*(392^{\wedge}98) \pmod{607}$$

$$= 242*214*552*489 \pmod{607} \quad (3.1.2.7)$$

$$= 329$$

Since this agrees with its own internally generated M value, the Bank regards the transaction as authorised.

Once this particular base number is used, its future use is no longer secret. The Y numbers do however retain their secrecy and may be re-used with a different base number.

3.2 Mutual Authentication and Base Key Exchange

3.2.1 Theory

The application described above is restricted to the authorisation of a transaction. Also, authentication is one-way only - the Bank authenticates the signatories, but the signatories authenticate neither the other signatories nor the Bank. The application described below is more general, realising a public-key distribution system with mutual authentication of all participants. In this application, all participants have equal status - there is no 'Bank'.

Suppose the total number of participants is N.

For $i=1,\ldots,N$, Participant i is issued with two (X,Y) pairs - a transmission pair (X_{i1}, Y_{i1}) and an authentication pair (X_{i2}, Y_{i2}). From these, he can calculate two (X,M) pairs - a transmission pair (X_{i1}, M_{i1}) and an authentication pair (X_{i2}, M_{i2}).

With a polynomial of degree n (i.e. n+1 secret coefficients), the minimum number of active participants is n+1. If each of n+1 active participants sends his transmission (X,M) pair, then each active participant will know n+2 (X,M) pairs, viz the n+1 transmission pairs together with his own authentication pair. Thus each participant separately can check for compliance with Equation (2.10) to authenticate the other participants.

Having established the authenticity of all the other participants, i and j can communicate, as in the Diffie-Hellman scheme, using the base key

$$Kij = b \char`\^ (Yil*Yjl) \qquad (3.2.1.1)$$

in which i calculates

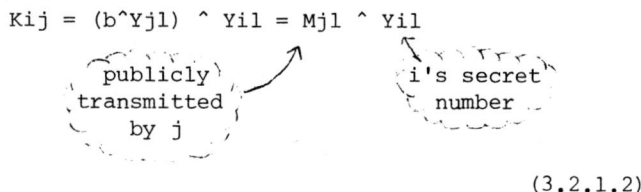

$$(3.2.1.2)$$

and j calculates

$$Kij = (b\char`\^Yil) \char`\^ Yjl = Mil \char`\^ Yjl$$

with publicly transmitted by i, and j's secret number.

$$(3.2.1.3)$$

By the security of the Diffie-Hellman scheme, it is computationally infeasible for anyone other than i and j to find Kij.

Once base keys have been established pairwise between participants, these links can be used, if desired, to establish a net-wide base key.

Once n+1 M values are publicly known, any other M value can be calculated from them, so that the same base number must not be later re-used. To prevent this, it is suggested that the base number should incorporate, in some way, a date and time stamp.

3.2.2 Example

A numerical example of the technique described in Section 3.2.1 is given here. It uses small prime numbers to demonstrate the principle of operation.

Suppose that the number of active participants is 3 out of a total of 5.

Select P1 = 101 (prime).

Then calculate P2 = k*P1 + 1 = 607 (prime), with k=6

A computer program is used to select a secret polynomial of degree 2, with coefficients in GF(101). Suppose it selects

$$Y = 58*X^2 + 4*X + 67 \pmod{101} \qquad (3.2.2.1)$$

It then selects 10 abscissae, X, two for each of the 5 participants. It calculates secretly from Equation (3.2.2.1) the corresponding ordinates, Y:

Participant	Transmission pair		Authentication pair	
	Xi1	Yi1	Xi2	Yi2
1	97	70	43	17
2	69	44	21	75
3	65	48	94	53
4	10	49	27	37
5	82	22	71	31

The computer then supplies all participants with details of everyone's transmission pair X numbers (i.e. the Xi1's), and each participant individually with his authentication pair X number (i.e. Xi2) and his secret Y numbers (Yi1 and Yi2). The computer then erases its memory to destroy the records of the polynomial coefficients it had chosen.

Suppose that Participants 1, 3 and 5 decide to establish base keys for communication between them. They agree a number c = 81, say, and from it calculate the base number

$$b = c^k = 81^6 \pmod{607} = 308 \qquad (3.2.2.2)$$

Each then calculates his own transmission pair (Xi1,Mi1), where

$$Mi1 = 308^{Yi1} \pmod{607} \qquad (3.2.2.3)$$

and an authentication pair (Xi2,Mi2), where

$$Mi2 = 308^{Yi2} \pmod{607} \qquad (3.2.2.4)$$

Participant	Suffix	Transmission pair	Authentication pair
1	1	(97,309)	(43,512)
3	2	(65,369)	(94,329)
5	3	(82,292)	(71,552)

Participant 1 performs the authentication check as follows:

He calculates Ar values corresponding to his own authentication abscissa, i.e. $X_{12} = 43$. Thus

$$A_1 = \frac{(43-65)*(43-82)}{(97-65)*(97-82)} = \frac{50}{76} = 50*4 = 99 \pmod{101}$$

(3.2.2.5)

$$A_2 = \frac{(43-97)*(43-82)}{(65-97)*(65-82)} = \frac{86}{39} = 86*57 = 54 \pmod{101}$$

(3.2.2.6)

$$A_3 = \frac{(43-97)*(43-65)}{(82-97)*(82-65)} = \frac{77}{48} = 77*40 = 50 \pmod{101}$$

(3.2.2.7)

He then calculates, using Equation (2.10), the value his own authentication M should take to comply with the 3 transmitted M's:

$$M = (309\hat{\ }99) * (369\hat{\ }54) * (292\hat{\ }50) \pmod{607}$$

$$= 597 * 478 * 454 \qquad \pmod{607} \quad (3.2.2.8)$$

$$= 512$$

Since this agrees with his own authentication M, Participant 1 can be sure that 3 and 5 are indeed the other participants.

Participants 3 and 5 each perform similar calculations to verify the identities of the other two.

Then, for example, 1 and 3 can communicate using the base key

$$K_{13} = 308\hat{\ }(70*48) \pmod{607} \qquad (3.2.2.9)$$

which 1 calculates as

$$K13 = M31 \wedge 7o = 369 \wedge 7o = 489 \pmod{607}$$

where $M31$ is *publicly transmitted by 3* and $7o$ is *1's secret number*.   (3.2.2.10)

and 3 calculates as

$$K13 = M11 \wedge 48 = 309 \wedge 48 = 489 \pmod{607}$$

where $M11$ is *publicly transmitted by 1* and 48 is *3's secret number*.   (3.2.2.11)

Similarly, base keys can be established between 1 and 5 and between 3 and 5.

Once this particular base number is used, its future use is no longer secret. The Y numbers do, however, retain their secrecy, and may be re-used with a different base number.

4. SOME NOTES

4.1 Vulnerability to captured stations

In both variations of the method, it is assumed that the secret Y numbers are physically stored at the participating stations. This renders the system vulnerable to captured stations - thus it may be useful to have some mnemonic scheme to enable participants to remember their secret numbers. For the 'base key exchange scheme', it is desirable that participants remember two secret numbers, although a lesser degree of security is offered if only one is remembered.

4.2 Participants trust each other

In the 'authorisation of a cheque scheme', it is possible for one participant to impersonate another. Thus it is necessary that all authorising stations trust one another - otherwise one authorising station may gain an advantage by making it appear that another authorised a transaction, rather than himself.

In the 'base key exchange scheme', it is possible for one participant to impersonate another in the authentication process. However, there is no advantage to him in doing so, because the impersonator cannot deduce the base key for communication.

4.3 Amendment to the 'base key exchange scheme' when the minimum number of active participants is 2

According to the proposed scheme, when the minimum number of active participants is 2, f(x) is a polynomial with 2 secret coefficients, i.e. we can write

$$Y = A*X + B \pmod{P1} \qquad (4.3.1)$$

Each participant has two (X,Y) pairs, and can therefore deduce A and B, and hence the secret numbers of all other participants. To avoid this, a polynomial of the following form may be used

$$Y = A*X^3 + B*X^2 + C*X + D \pmod{P1} \qquad (4.3.2)$$

i.e. one having 4 secret coefficients. Each participant is issued with three (X,Y) pairs - two for transmission and one for authentication. Before transmission, each participant has three (X,Y) points on a polynomial with four secret coefficients, and hence can't deduce the coefficients or other participants' secret numbers. After transmission, each participant has five (X,M) pairs, and can hence perform the authentication check by use of Equation (2.10).

4.4 Extensions

Variants on the Shamir secret sharing scheme are discussed by Denning [6], which have their parallels in the method discussed here. These give greater authority to some participants than to others.

4.5 Polynomials in more than one variable

It is possible to adapt the method to use polynomials in more than one variable. This may offer advantages of simplification in practical implementations, and of widening the possible applications of the technique.

5. SUMMARY

This paper has described how the Shamir's secret sharing method can be combined with the trap-door features of exponentiation/logarithmisation modulo a suitable large prime, as used in the Diffie-Hellman secret number exchange method.

This combination allows individuals' components of a shared secret number to be transmitted over a public medium in a disguised form, so that the secrecy of the components and whole of the shared number are preserved. This means that the same secret number can be used repeatedly, on future occasions.

The method can be used in various situations requiring the co-operation of h participants out of N. Two examples were given, showing how the method can be used to (i) authorise a transaction (e.g. signing a cheque) and (ii) achieve mutually authenticated base key exchange.

6. REFERENCES

[1]   Shamir, A., 1979, "How to Share a Secret", Communications of the ACM, 22, November.

[2]   Diffie, W. and Hellman, M.E., 1976, "New Directions in Cryptography", IEEE Transactions on Information Theory, IT-22, November.

[3]   Rivest, R.L., Shamir, A. and Adleman, L., 1978, "A Method for Obtaining Digital Signatures and Public Key Cryptosystems", Communications of the ACM, 21, February.

[4]   Knuth, D.E., 1973, "The Art of Computer Programming", Volume 3, Addison Wesley.

[5]   Odlyzko, A.M., "Discrete logarithm in Finite Fields and their Cryptographic Significance", Advances in Cryptology, Eurocrypt 84 Springer-Verlag.

[6]   Denning, D., 1983, "Cryptography and Data Security", Addison Wesley.

THE GEC ic CARD: A RELIABLE AND SECURE TOKEN

N.A. McDonald and S.J. Sylvester
(GEC Card Technology)

The GEC ic Card is a computer encapsulated in a piece of plastic the size of a credit card. As a smart card, it acts not only as a portable data store but also as a programmable logic unit capable of processing data. A unique feature of the card is that it requires no electrical contacts to communicate with the outside world.

The GEC ic Card has several design features which allow it to be used in areas where data security is important. Its integrated design, with microcircuits embedded in a thin plastic package, makes the card a magnitude harder to forge. A fast authentication algorithm has been designed specifically to protect messages sent to and from the card. The Data Encryption Standard (DES) algorithm has been incorporated in it to satisfy financial organisation requirements.

These secure protocols enable the ic Card to take an intelligent part in electronic transactions where present day banking cards play only a very limited role. The ic Card can respond directly to authorisation requests, without a need for any intervening secure terminal.

1. INTRODUCTION

This paper describes the GEC ic Card and some of the areas in which it can be used. The ic Card is an example of a 'SMART CARD', which today means a token the size of a credit card, with intelligence. Most companies in the field are producing smart cards with surface contacts to allow them to be interfaced to the outside world. GEC Card Technology has taken what it believes to be a better route; a smart card with no contacts. As the various features of the card are described, their contribution to reliability and security will be shown. Several security routines are described in detail.

2. ELEMENTS OF THE IC CARD SYSTEM

2.1 General description:

Like most smart cards, the GEC ic Card has been designed to provide the owner with a conveniently sized token that is both computationally powerful and secure. Thus it contains both microcontroller and memory elements, able to perform calculations and manipulate data independent of any device to which the card may be connected. However, all current smart cards rely upon direct electrical contact to supply the power, clock and data signals required by the card. In this respect, the GEC ic Card is unique; all power and data links between the card and coupler are electrically contactless.

2.2 Contactless interface

2.2.1 Card:

Built into the GEC ic Card is a small coil of wire which develops a voltage across it when the card is in the presence of an inductive radio frequency (r.f.) field. This voltage is rectified and regulated on the card, to provide a steady power supply for the microcontroller and memory. Also built into the card is a reset circuit, designed to activate the card when it is in a field of suitable strength. The r.f. field is also used as a bidirectional data path. Data to the card is sent in serial fashion by modulating the r.f. carrier frequency, and this is decoded in the card. Data is conveyed from the card to the coupler using another form of modulation. The data rate used can be anything from 300 to 9600 baud, with even or odd parity, if desired, and any number of stop bits. These characteristics are fully under the control of the card's software.

2.2.2 Coupler

This device, which in its simplest form is unintelligent, produces the r.f. field for the card. The field strength is sufficient to allow inductive card operation at up to 20mm from the coupler, but falls rapidly after this distance. The unit complies fully with the U.K. Health and Safety Executive and the Department of Trade and Industry standards for frequency and power emission. The coupler also acts as an interface for data flowing between the card and a host system, which is linked to the coupler by a standard (RS232) serial data line. The state of the incoming data from the host modifies the r.f. field, to communicate to the card. The coupler also contains detection circuitry for converting information received from the card into a serial data stream. As its name suggests, the coupler merely acts as the means by which the card interfaces via a bidirectional serial data link to the other system components.

2.3 Microcontroller

The heart of the GEC ic Card is an 8 bit microcontroller. It receives power and incoming data from the contactless interface, and has a memory element where the application program and data are stored. Upon activation of the card, the microcontroller will begin to execute the fixed operating system code stored in part of the memory. Then, under control of the operating system, the application program is executed.

2.4 Memory:

The current ic Card contains 8K bytes of non-volatile RAM memory. The first 1K of memory is taken up by the card operating system which controls the loading of application programs, data transmission, memory access and other functions needed for each ic Card. This area is the same for every card and is secure, execute only memory. The rest of the memory is blank on manufacture. For each specific card application, an application program is written and loaded into the card under the control of the operating system. It is not possible to overwrite the application program unless another program is loaded into the card, and indeed, this loading feature may itself be disabled by an application. The remainder of the memory is completely under the control of the application program, and is generally used as read/write storage.

3. FEATURES OF THE IC CARD SYSTEM

3.1 Contactless interface:

The contactless interface is one of the most important elements of the ic Card system because the electronic circuitry is totally encapsulated within the card and is therefore protected from the outside environment by plastic layers. From a reliability point of view, this has several advantages:-

- The circuitry in a smart card is usually static sensitive. Therefore it is undesirable to have pads on the surface of the card which are in direct electrical contact with the circuit. The insulation properties of the plastic encapsulating the ic Card protect the circuitry from static damage.

- The ic Card is more resistant to abuse by its holder or a thief. The contacts on the card's surface act as an invitation to would-be hackers of fraudsters, whereas it is a degree more difficult to interfere with the ic Card's circuitry.

- There are no contacts to wear out through everyday use, abrasion, chipping or scoring, and therefore the card maintains the same reliability throughout its life.

- The ic Card system can operate in hostile environments where the card could be covered with water, oil, grease or dirt.

Unlike conventional card reading mechanisms the ic Card coupler has no slot and no moving parts. Being totally electronic, it will withstand harsh treatment yet remain very reliable, and so will require little maintenance. As the coupler requires no contact with the card, it can be completely sealed, protecting it from vandalism and the environment. Therefore, like the ic Card, the coupler will operate reliably outdoors, or on a factory shop floor.

The system is more user friendly, as the card holder never loses sight of his ic Card. He does not have to worry how he places his card down as it can be in any orientation, even upside down.

The system can operate with most materials (except metals) separating the ic Card and coupler. This allows the coupler to be placed under counters and inside equipment. If the coupler is mounted under the counter, it frees valuable counter space and is less threatening to the general public as they have only to place their card down on a marked area of the counter surface. It also prevents the general public from damaging the coupler. The coupler only requires a simple low voltage power supply and is small in size. It therefore requires the minimum of redesign for incorporating into OEM equipment. As an example, we have already inserted the coupler into a signature recognition system and also post office letter coding desks.

Part of the ic Card design incorporates a field strength detection circuit allowing the application to be interrupted should the card be prematurely removed from the coupler. This feature gives the card the opportunity to execute a 'graceful shutdown' and to tidy up an incomplete transaction.

The contacless interface is also used for programming the ic Card with the application program. This does not require special programming pulses to be provided by the coupler. Instead the ic Card's operating system contains a loading program capable of receiving a new set of program instructions and storing these in the card's memory. Application program software may only be downloaded from a computer executing an authorised program supplied by GEC Card Technology for a specified batch of ic Cards.

3.2 Microcontroller

The main advantage of a microcontroller over hardwired logic circuitry is that it allows the ic Card to be programmed for any application within its limits of memory and processing power. Therefore the use of the ic Card is only limited by the imagination of the programmer. The ic Card is programmed in assembly language, not a high level language, but this does not make it hard to use. The operating system held in the card's memory contains many essential routines, for example, transmitting and receiving characters, which are easily called from the application program. Once programs have been assembled, they can be sent via an RS232 link from the host to the coupler and hence to the ic Card. Extensive checking is performed by the card's operating system at all times to guard against misuse of the card or its memory, be it fraudulent or unintentional.

An important feature of the microcontroller is that it acts as a gateway to the ic Card's memory. If all the security checks are not satisfied, the microcontroller will not allow access to the memory.

The microcontroller can act as a sieve, allowing only selected data through. It can make efficient use of its data storage by compressing the data received from the outside world. This data can be scrambled to make the memory contents more secure from physical or electronic attack. The microcontroller can do the reverse by expanding data, padding it out, adding checksums or descrambling so it can be easily understood.

Integrating a microcontroller and memory within a plastic card as pieces of unique circuitry makes the card a magnitude harder to forge. This is because its manufacture involves very sophisticated and expensive equipment, as well as expertise in several fields. The capital investment alone acts as a deterrent to all but the very largest criminal organisations.

3.3 Memory:

Memory is the last important element of the ic Card, storing sizeable quantities of program instructions and data. The memory is both non-volatile, and reusable, which lends the ic Card enormous flexibility, and makes the debugging and perfecting of application programs a far simpler and cost effective task. When it is decided that a certain program should remain permanently within the ic Card, software fuses can be blown within the memory which will prevent any further program loading. This would be done to prevent misuse when the cards were issued to the public.

The operating system is hardware protected against reading or writing. The application software is protected by a partition placed in memory by the operating system. One side is made read only, and the application program resides here. On the other side of the partition, data can be read and written freely.

Checksums are used to make sure that the operating system and application program are not corrupted before they are used. If there are errors, the card will report them as its first action after being reset, allowing the device with which the card is in communication to take appropriate action. As RAM is used, each card can be personalised by placing within the operating system area a batch number and a serial number on manufacture. This allows each card to be accounted for and to allow only certain cards to be used with a particular application, which prevents software theft or misuse of the ic Card.

Due to the size of the memory available for the software programmer, several programs can be accommodated in the ic Card at the same time. For example, the ic Card could be used as a notepad, storing personal information and also be used with an EFTPOS (Electronic Funds Transfer at Point of Sale) terminal to check a PIN and authorise a monetary transaction. Allowing the ic Card to have several programs in it makes it more versatile and more economical to use. The memory size has allowed several complex cryptographic routines to be placed in the card at the same time.

4. MARKET AREAS

There are 3 main application areas in which a plastic card with intelligence can be used:

DATA CARRIER
- Intelligent log
- Machine control
- Portable notepad
- Service, and production records
- Medical records
- Customs documentation

CONDITIONAL ACCESS
- Physical and computer access
- Software protection
- Rented services
- Passports

FINANCIAL
- Cheque card
- Credit card
- Electronic token
- Electronic purse
- Pensions
- Allowances

All of these applications require intelligence somewhere in the system, and many require sensitive/secure data to be held on the card. Therefore a card with intelligence is required in order to block illegal attempts to access the card's memory. This intelligence is also used to control and monitor all attempts to use the card. As there can be intelligence on both ends of a transaction, the security of the system is greatly increased by implementation of secure protocols (challenges, encryption, etc) before a transaction can begin. It is possible to use the card in systems where it is the only intelligence in the system, for example monitoring and editing data records. The card can also be used in transactions where secret data known to the user is to be checked (eg a PIN) before a transaction can begin. These systems normally need to be online to a central database of all PIN's as it is impractical to store the list of PIN's in each EFTPOS terminal. In such an application, the ic Card can now perform the check, without revealing the secret data, and so the system can operate off line, saving considerable expense.

It may arise that the financial and other institutions do not agree on a standard procedure for operation with a smart card. It is possible to allocate separate procedures and data areas in

the card's memory for each institution. This allows one card
to operate with a mixture of EFTPOS terminals and financial
institutions.

The flexibility and inherent reliability of the ic Card
system give it a distinct advantage in each of the market areas
mentioned. The low cost of the ic Card coupler makes the
system particularly cost effective in those applications where
the ratio of cards to terminals is relatively low.

5. SECURITY OF THE IC CARD SYSTEM

5.1 *General description:*

If secret or secure information is to be held in the card, it
is essential to have intelligence in the same card to protect
this information. It is not sufficient to have intelligence
elsewhere in the system (coupler/host) since the card issuer and
card user must then rely on the integrity and validity of the card
terminal equipment. The intelligence of the card can also be
used to conduct a transaction which has complete end to end
security between the card and the ultimate host. This has
great advantages where the interface between the card and the
host is not direct (satellite, modem, phone line, exchange,
POS terminal, computer, etc) and where the link could be
subject to active or passive eavesdropping in any of these
devices.

5.2 *Authentication and validation:*

In any communications system, messages are passed between
at least two parties. In many systems, the message content
does not need to be secret, but it is vitally important that
the message is not modified between sender and receiver. Thus
GEC has developed a secure protocol for message authentication
and validation which ensures that:-

1. Any message alteration will be detected. (For instance,
   I intercept a message between my bank and local shop saying
   debit my account by 100 pounds, and credit their account.
   I change this to 10 pounds.)

2. Unauthorised creation of valid messages is virtually
   impossible. (I tell my bank to credit my account with 100
   pounds.)

3. Replay of old valid messages will be rejected. (The shop
   replays a previous message which credited its account.)

4. Messages cannot be rerouted. (I send the message from the
   shop to another bank.)

To ensure all this, both authentication and validation are needed. The GEC authentication system takes a message of length 8 to 256 bytes, and together with a secret key of 64 bits, produces an authenticator (piece of coded text) which is 32 bits long. The algorithm used is of sufficient security and the key sufficiently long, that attack by an exhaustive key search is effectively thwarted. This authenticator acts as an electronic signature for the message, and is sent along with the message to the receiver. It is then checked by the receiver, who is also in possession of the authenticator algorithm and secret key. If the authenticator he produces from the received text does not match the one sent with that text, then he knows that the message has been corrupted in some way. Thus problems 1 and 2 have been solved.

In order to prevent re-routing and replay, a header of 16 bytes is also added to each message. This header contains a random number generated by the sender, which is different for each message, and the sender identification (ID). The header also contains the receiver ID and the random number the receiver generated in its last message (these last two fields are undetermined in the very first header). The authenticator is now produced from the message plus header, and this authenticator, with header and message are transmitted. In the process of validation, three transmissions containing just header and authenticator must be made :-

1. (Card to Host): Ensures the sender has the correct authenticator algorithm and key, and that its ID is a valid one.

2. (Host to Card): Ensures the receiver has the correct authenticator algorithm and key, its ID is valid, and this message is not a replay (returns random number sent in 1).

3. (Card to Host): The sender is not replaying old messages (random no sent in 2 returned).

Once this initial procedure has been successfully carried out, messages can be passed to and fro, with the appropriate header and authenticator.

This system of authentication and validation has been designed abd developed specifically for smart cards, and the GEC ic Card in particular. It is optimised for an 8 bit microcontroller, and a small memory environment. It occupies 0.5 kbytes of memory, and executes at a rate of approximately 16 mS for an 8 byte message block.

5.3 Encryption:

In some communication systems, the messages passed between the two parties are sensitive. Thus it must not be possible for an eavesdropper to gain any knowledge from messages that are issued. This type of system requires encryption of each message. GEC has implemented the Data Encryption Standard (DES) algorithm for message encryption and decryption. This standard was developed and published by the National Bureau of Standards for the protection of computer data, and is currently used in many encryption systems. The system takes a message (plaintext) of 8 bytes in length, and using DES and a secret 56 bit key, produces 8 bytes of cyphertext. The implementation for the GEC ic Card occupies 1 kbyte of memory and encrypts 8 bytes in 400 mS. The message is transmitted in cyphertext, and any alteration to the message will be evident to the receiver, as the decrypted result will be meaningless.

DES is, however, an inefficient method of preventing the replaying and rerouting of messages. This is because each message must be split into blocks of 8 bytes before it can be encrypted, and it is impractical to dedicate part of each block to a header. Thus a system which uses encryption and authentication is preferred. An authenticator is produced for the overall message, which is also given a single header. The combined header, message and authenticator are split into 8 byte blocks, encrypted and transmitted. On reception, the authenticator is checked after decryption, and even if one of the 8 byte blocks of cyphertext had been directly replaced with another legitimate block, this would be detected.

5.4 Personal Identification:

In many applications, it is necessary for an individual to be recognised by a system in order to gain access or authority to perform a task. Thus personal information relating to each authorised individual must be held somewhere. If this information is stored centrally on a database, then a large amount of memory and computational power must be available in order to keep the response time of the system low. An alternative system is to store this information on a plastic token carried by the owner, but in most systems, it is important that this information cannot be read and the system compromised by an unauthorised reader. The information can be stored as plaintext, in an encrypted form with a common or centrally stored key for each card, or it must be a function of other open information such as the account number. The system must therefore either be on line all the time to a central computer (expensive) or risk discovery of the common key or function, which would jeopardise the whole system.

If however, there is intelligence in the card, then all this is unnecessary. On enrolment to the system, certain personal information relating to the user is stored on his card. When access/authority is required, the user must enter this personal information, which is sent to the card. The card compares this with its own stored reference data, and if the two match, authority is given. Other advantages of this system are that the card can monitor its use, and only allow a small number of successive failures before it invalidates itself. It can also modify the stored reference data such as a signature, or a user chosen PIN. Security of the system is also increased, as any discovery of the secret information on the card can at worst allow one card to be used fraudulently, and the rest of the system remains safe.

6. AN EXAMPLE IC CARD APPLICATION: INTAMIC TRANSACTION

6.1 Introduction:

Having developed authentication and encryption for the ic Card, it was decided to implement an independently generated security architecture to illustrate how easy it is to use these routines to establish protocols acceptable to the financial markets. INTAMIC (International Association of Microcircuit Cards) represents the point of view of a large number of banks and financial institutions. They have proposed a set of standard protocols for secure smart card transactions. The architecture allows the card to be used in both offline and online applications, and it ensures that if the security of one card is compromised, the security of the system remains intact. It will be readily appreciated that the proposed system greatly enhances the security of transactions and greatly decreases the opportunity for fraud.

6.2 Financial Architecture:

The architecture has been split into five stages and each stage written as a separate routine for both the ic Card and card issuer's computer (host computer). The system consists of an ic Card and a coupler, an intelligent PIN pad and a link to the host computer. All messages passing between the ic Card and the host pass through the PIN pad. In the online situation, the PIN pad could be part of a terminal in a bank wall which is connected to a distant host computer whereas in the offline case, the PIN pad and coupler could be combined into one EFTPOS terminal. On issue, the ic Card contains an identity number, a PIN, the GEC authenticator, the DES algorithm, and a secret (card) key. The secret key was generated by the host and is a DES function of the card identity number and the host's secret seed key.

6.3 Identification (refer to fig. 1):

The first stage involves the ic Card identifying its card holder. In our implementation the ic Card checks a 4 digit PIN entered on the PIN pad. This allows the routine to be used in both off and online applications. The ic Card will invalidate itself after three consecutive wrong PIN entries. It does not matter if the card is removed between attempts, as it remembers each wrong entry even if it is transferred to another coupler. If the ic Card invalidates itself, it erases the card key and PIN which may only be restored by returning it to the card issuer for reinitialisation. Storing the PIN on the ic Card increases the level of personal identification security and saves the expense of valuable online host computer time.

6.4 Authorisation request (refer to fig. 1):

Once the ic Card is satisfied that the person using it is bona fide, it and the host computer have to agree each other's validity. Since the ic Card starts the whole process of the transaction by being placed on a coupler, it has to prove to the host it is a proper ic Card. In our case the card sends its identity number, which could include an account number. This allows the bank or EFTPOS terminal to check if the card is stolen. The host takes this identity number and, using its seed key and the DES algorithm, it reproduces the card key. Thus the host and the card know this key without it being openly divulged. The host then generates a random message, and sends it to the card. This message is received, and the card uses the authentication algorithm and its card key to produce the authenticator for this message. It then sends the authenticator alone back to the host. Meanwhile, the host has also been calculating this authenticator, and if the one it has calculated matches the one sent by the card, then the host knows that the card has the correctly matching identity number and card key and the correct authenticator algorithm, and therefore must be a valid card. By using a random message to be authenticated, a criminal gains nothing by recording the message sent and the authenticator reply. Replay of this recording will not simulate the presence of an ic Card, as a different random message will have been issued.

6.5 Authorisation request response (refer to fig. 1):

Once the host is satisfies that the card is valid, the host has to prove its validity to the card. The host generates another random message which is also sent to the ic Card. Both the host and the ic Card produce the authenticator for this random message, using the card key, and this authenticator then forms a new key, the transaction key. The host uses the

transaction key to encrypt the card identity number and a date
stamp, and the encrypted result is sent to the card. The ic Card
uses the transaction key and the DES algorithm to decrypt the
message. The messages are sent encrypted so they cannot be read
or tampered with. The card then decodes the received card identity
number; the host must have the correct card key and authenticator
to send the identity number back encrypted correctly. The date
stamp is included to prevent these encrypted messages being copied
and replayed later.

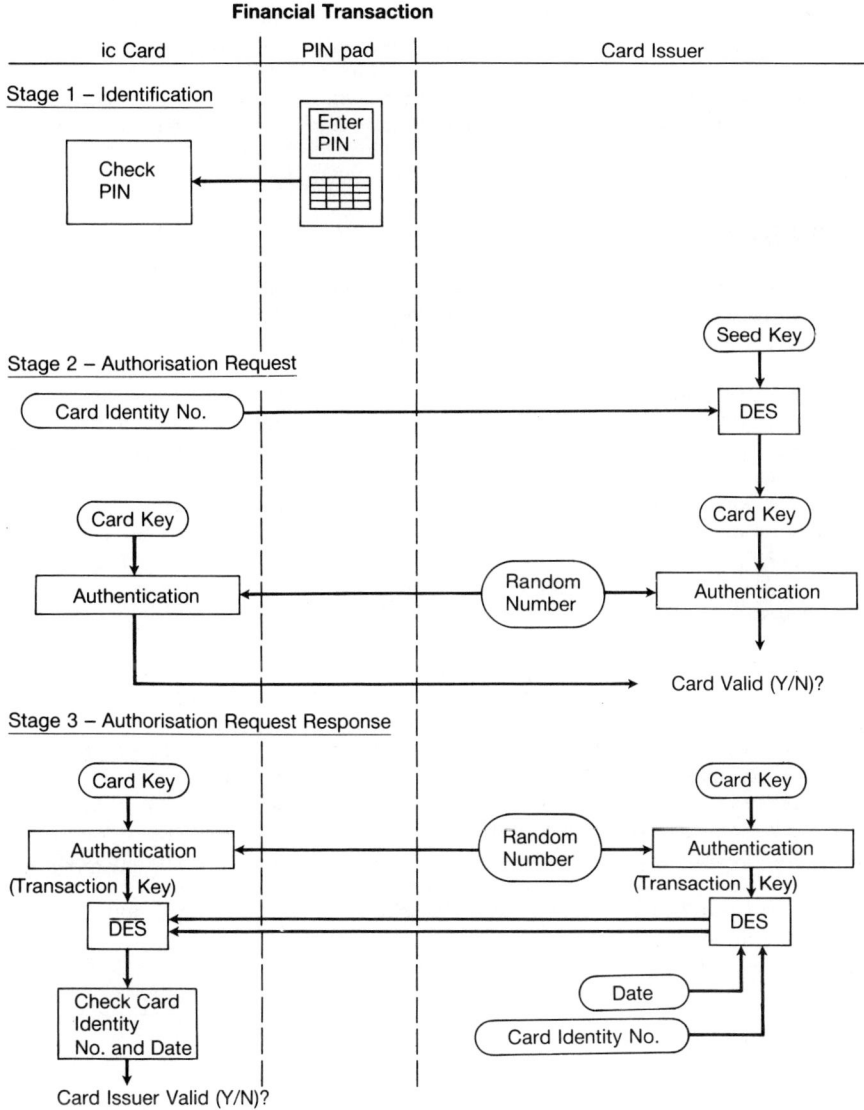

Fig. 1   Financial Transaction

6.6 Transaction request and response (refer to fig. 2):

After the host and card agree, transaction data can be sent. Each time data is to be sent, it is encrypted/decrypted with a new transaction key generated by authenticating a random message sent by the host. This prevents replaying old messages and also makes it extremely hard to find the card key except by key search. A message authentication code (MAC) is also added to the data before it is encrypted. This MAC is simply the result of authenticating the data using the card key. It forms an electronic signature for the message, and allows the card issuer to be replaced by an offline EFTPOS unit. The data and MAC are stored in the EFTPOS unit, and later transmitted to the issuer along with all the other transactions of the day. The MAC ensures that the EFTPOS unit has not tampered with the data before sending it on to the card issuer.

7. SUMMARY

The GEC ic Card is a portable computer, containing microcontroller, memory and interface circuitry, yet no larger in outline than a current credit card.

The most distinctive feature of the GEC ic Card is its contactless interface. This means that all the circuitry can be sealed into the card, and is therefore protected from the environment (dirt, oil, water, static etc.). The link between the card and reader is an inductive r.f. field, and this is used to supply power to the card, and to act as a bidirectional data link. The card can operate with up to 20mm separation from the coupler, allowing convenient location of the coupler (e.g. under a desk, inside equipment).

The card also contains an 8 bit microcontroller, and non-volatile reusable memory used for storing the operating program, application program and data for the card. It can be reprogrammed many times for different applications, under the control of the operating system. GEC has developed authentication and encryption routines for the ic Card, allowing its intelligence to improve the security of the system. The microcontroller also controls the flow of data into the coupler, and decodes the data received from it. This results in an extremely low cost coupler, as it performs no decoding and contains no moving parts.

Financial Transaction

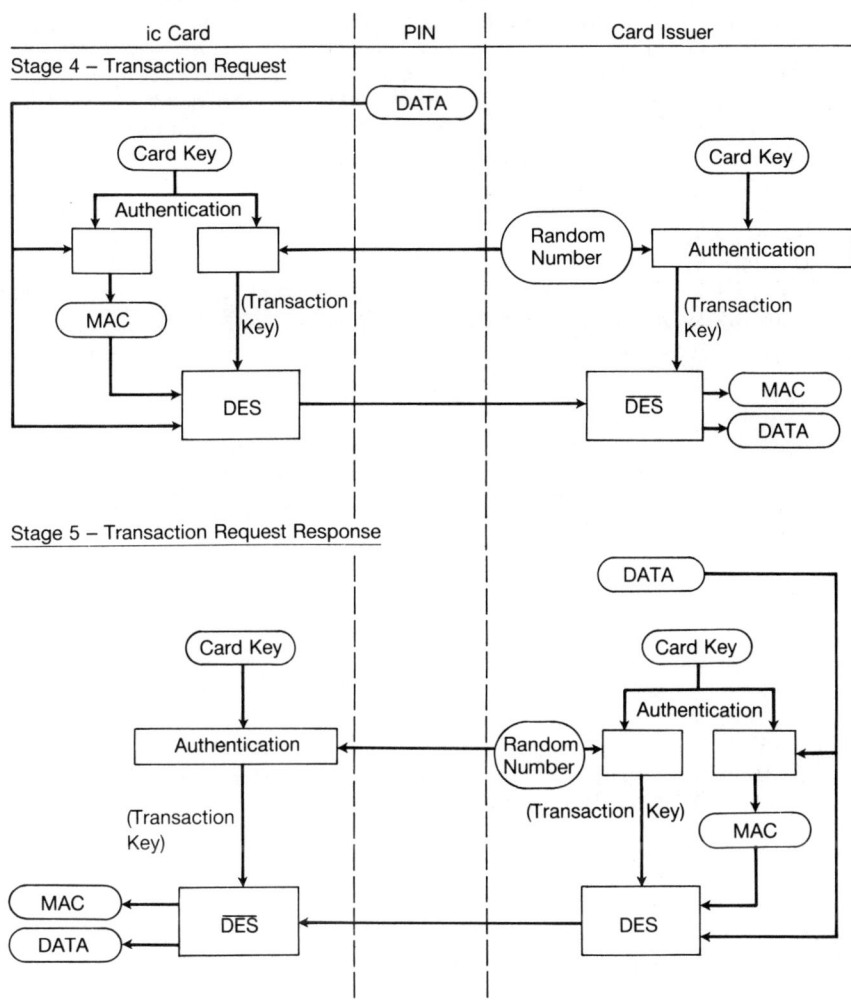

Fig. 2 Financial Transaction

Three main market areas are seen for the ic Card. As a data storage device, the card offers a large amount of reprogrammable memory and the intelligence to use this memory effectively. This is especially useful in systems where there is little or no intelligence in the rest of the system (machine control, notepad). For conditional access, the card is used to store and check personal information, before authority can be granted. The intelligence on the card is used to reduce the complexity of access systems, without reducing its security.
In the financial market, the card can be used to the full, storing open and secret information, and performing complex encryption and authentication routines. Since the GEC ic Card is a truly portable computer, rather than a simple smart card, applications for it are virtually unlimited.

ENCRYPTION USING RANDOM BOOLEAN FUNCTIONS

M. Beale and M.F. Monaghan
*(Department of Electrical Engineering,
University of Manchester)*

1. INTRODUCTION

The use of n-input, one-output Boolean functions in encryption schemes of the stream cipher type is considered. The encryption schemes are not new and, indeed, are general models of large classes of encryption algorithms. The focus here is on certain general properties required of the Boolean functions in such systems, the enumeration of functions with various combinations of these properties, and the randomness properties of the output sequences produced by these functions in the encryption schemes.

2. ENCRYPTION SCHEMES

We consider ways in which n-input, one-output Boolean functions might be employed in systems of the stream cipher type. Perhaps the most obvious initial attempt might be the scheme shown in Figure 1. Here, for each new plaintext bit, the latest n bits of plaintext are mapped into a single ciphertext bit via the Boolean function. The encryption algorithm is simply:

$$c_i = F(p_i, p_{i-1}, \ldots, p_{i-n+1}).$$

It is readily seen that, for this scheme to be decipherable, we require:

$$F(p_i, p_{i-1}, \ldots, p_{i-n+1}) = p_i + G(p_{i-1}, \ldots, p_{i-n+1})$$

where addition is mod 2 and G is some (hopefully nonlinear) function of the previous n-1 plaintext bits. To decipher, the same function G is used:

$$p_i = c_i + G(p_{i-1}, \ldots, p_{i-n+1}).$$

However, it is clear from this relationship that if c_i is received in error, p_i will be erroneous and this will result in an error in all subsequent deciphered bits - i.e. catastrophic error propagation occurs. Since this is generally undesirable, this scheme is not considered further.

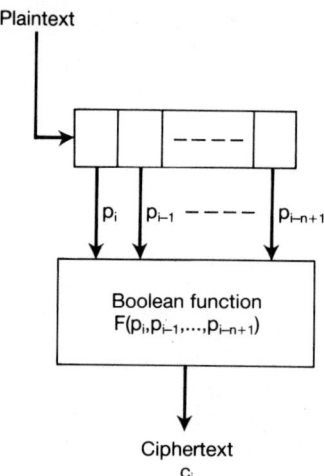

Fig. 1 Simple encryption scheme using a shift-register and Boolean feed forward function

A second scheme is shown in Figure 2. It is well known that although maximal-length, linear feedback shift-register (LFSR) sequences (m-sequences) [1] have many desirable randomness properties, they are also highly predictable, since a knowledge of only 2n bits suffices to predict the entire (2^n-1)-bit m-sequence (via the Berlekamp-Massey algorithm [2]). The stream cipher scheme in Figure 2 aims to circumvent this problem by using some nonlinear Boolean function G(...) of the n-bit LFSR state to 'nonlinearise' the m-sequence. As with all such stream ciphers, no error propagation occurs. The implementation and security of such a scheme, using semiconductor memory for the Boolean function, has been discussed by Rivest [3]. In particular, Rivest has shown that it is an NP-complete problem to determine the value of any bit of the Boolean function output sequence from a knowledge of any previous group of consecutive bits in this sequence, even when the Boolean function is known to the cryptanalyst. While this is certainly encouraging, the assessment of security in this way, via computational complexity, applies only to the <u>generality</u> of the cryptanalyst's

problem; it is easy to think of specific examples of (trivial)
Boolean functions for which prediction of the output sequence
is a relatively easy task. Consequently, if the scheme in
Figure 2 is to be used with any confidence, there are certain
classes of Boolean function which must be excluded.

Examples of functions which would be undesirable in this
scheme are <u>linear</u> functions and <u>degenerate</u> functions (those of
order n which depend on only k < n of their inputs), since
these clearly imply a certain cryptographic weakness. One
desirable property is for ones and zeros to emerge in roughly
equal numbers at the function output. Since all n-bit words
(except all-zeros) occur in equal numbers at the function input,
this can be ensured by requiring the truth-table to be
<u>balanced</u>, with equal numbers of ones and zeros in its output
column (such functions are sometimes described as <u>neutral</u> [4]).
For the scheme in Figure 2 we therefore require Boolean functions
of order n which are balanced, nondegenerate and nonlinear.

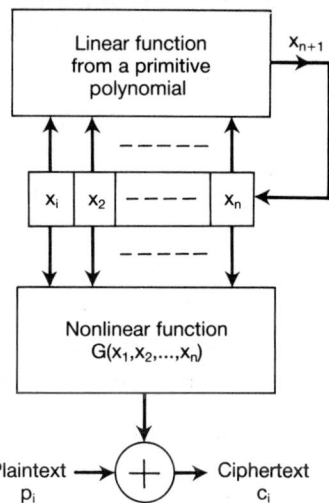

Fig. 2   Stream cipher using a linear-feedback shift-register
and a nonlinear feedforward function.

Now consider the cipher feedback scheme shown in Figure 3.
If the plaintext itself is fairly random, it is reasonable to
suppose that the ciphertext will be also, as long as there is
no significant correlation between the plaintext and the
Boolean function output. In this case, all n-bit words are
expected to occur with equal probabilities at the function
input, so the balance property required for the scheme in
Figure 2 is also appropriate for that in Figure 3. Similarly,
nonlinearity and nondegeneracy would be desirable here also.

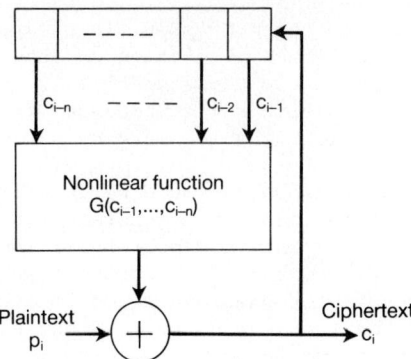

Fig. 3 Cipher feedback system using a shift-register and a non-linear function.

Considering linearity, it is useful to distinguish between <u>strictly linear</u> (SL) functions of order n: those which are purely linear functions of all the k ≤ n inputs on which they depend; and what we call <u>linear in</u> (LI) functions of order n, which are linear in k_1 of their inputs and nonlinear in the remaining k_2 inputs on which they depend ($k_1 + k_2 \leq n$). Clearly, demanding that a function be <u>not-LI</u> is a stronger requirement than <u>not-SL</u> and, to avoid potential weaknesses, the former criterion is of most interest here. Thus, it is desirable for the Boolean functions used in the encryption schemes of Figures 2 and 3 to be <u>not-LI, balanced and nondegenerate</u> and functions with all three of these properties will be referred to as <u>Standard</u> functions, for convenience.

3. ENUMERATION OF BOOLEAN FUNCTIONS

We now consider the number of functions with each of the properties discussed above, separately and in various combinations. Similar enumeration problems have been addressed by Elspas [4], Harrison [5, 6] and others, but the results presented here (with the exception of the trivial result in section 3.1) appear to be new. The Venn diagram in Figure 4 illustrates the partition of Boolean functions into sets with the properties of interest.

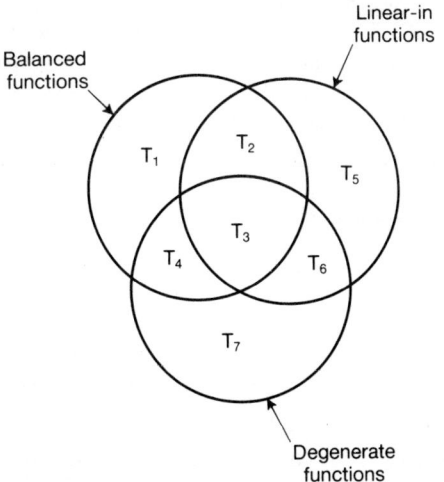

Fig. 4   Venn diagram of sets of functions with various properties (Set T_1 is the desired set of Standard functions)

3.1 Balanced Functions (Set $T_1 \cup T_2 \cup T_3 \cup T_4$ in Figure 4).

The number of balanced functions of order n, B_n, is just the number of ways of placing 2^{n-1} ones in the 2^n positions of the output column of the truth-table, i.e. the central binomial coefficient:

$$B_n = \begin{pmatrix} 2^n \\ 2^{n-1} \end{pmatrix}, \; n \geq 1 \quad (1)$$

(The only functions of order n = 0 are the constants, G = 0 and G = 1, which are not balanced, so $B_0 = 0$).

3.2 Balances, Nondegenerate Functions (Set $T_1 \cup T_2$ in Figure 4).

Some balanced functions of order n are degenerate, depending on k < n of their inputs. However, such functions can be viewed as balanced, nondegenerate functions of order k. Accounting for the number of ways in which each such function can be mapped onto an n-input truth table, it is readily seen that the number of balanced, nondegenerate functions of order n, N_n, can be expressed as:

$$N_n = \begin{pmatrix} 2^n \\ 2^{n-1} \end{pmatrix} - \sum_{k=0}^{n-1} \begin{pmatrix} n \\ k \end{pmatrix} N_k, \; n \geq 1 \quad (2)$$

(Of course, $N_0 = B_0 = 0$ and $N_1 = B_1 = 2$, since both of the balanced functions of order 1, $G = x$ and $G = x + 1$, are nondegenerate). After separating out the term for $k = n - 1$ in the above summation, expanding N_{n-1} using equation (2), and repeating the process for decreasing values of k, this recurrence can be solved to give the following explicit expression for a given order n:

$$N_n = \sum_{k=1}^{n} (-1)^{n-k} \binom{n}{k} \binom{2^k}{2^{k-1}}, \quad n \geq 1 \qquad (3)$$

3.3 Linear-In (LI) Functions (Set $T_2 \cup T_3 \cup T_5 \cup T_6$ in Figure 4)

When considering LI functions, it is convenient to use the following representation for an arbitrary Boolean function of the n inputs $x_1, x_2, \ldots, x_n$:

$$G_n(x_1, x_2, \ldots, x_n) = \Sigma A_{b_1 b_2 \cdots b_n} \cdot (x_1^{b_1} x_2^{b_2} \ldots x_n^{b_n}), \qquad (4)$$

where the sum is taken mod 2 over all 2^n combinations of values for the binary integers $b_1, b_2, \ldots, b_n$. Each coefficient $A_{b_1 b_2 \cdots b_n}$ is either 1 or 0 according to the presence or absence of the corresponding term $x_1^{b_1} x_2^{b_2} \ldots x_n^{b_n}$. The <u>order</u> of a term in this representation is defined as the number of inputs involved in that term or equivalently, the number of 1s in the n-tuple $(b_1, b_2, \ldots, b_n)$ - e.g. $x_1^1 x_2^0 x_3^1 x_4^1 = x_1 x_3 x_4$ is a 3rd order term in a 4th order function.

In terms of this representation, a function which is linear in k inputs can be defined as one for which k of the n inputs ($1 \leq k \leq n$) occur as 1st order terms only. Thus, any such function can be expressed as:

$$G_n(x_1, x_2, \ldots, x_n) = x_1 + x_2 + \ldots + x_k + g_{n-k}(x_{k+1}, \ldots, x_n), \qquad (5)$$

after possible relabelling of inputs. The function $g_{n-k}(\ldots)$ can be any function which is <u>not</u> linear in any of its (n-k) inputs. Denoting the total number of nth order LI functions (those which are linear in one or more inputs) by L_n, the number of functions $g_{n-k}(\ldots)$ in equation (5) is therefore:

$$2^{2^{n-k}} - L_{n-k},$$

for fixed k and n. Allowing for relabelling of the inputs $x_1, x_2, \ldots, x_k$ in equation (5), it follows that L_n can be expressed as:

$$L_n = \sum_{k=1}^{n} \binom{n}{k} \left(2^{2^{n-k}} - L_{n-k}\right)$$

or, equivalently:

$$L_n = \sum_{i=0}^{n-1} \binom{n}{i} \left(2^{2^i} - L_i\right), \quad n \geq 1 \tag{6}$$

with $L_0 = 0$. As before, this recurrence can be solved to yield the explicit formula:

$$L_n = \sum_{i=1}^{n} (-1)^{i+1} \binom{n}{i} 2^{2^{n-i}}, \quad n \geq 1, \tag{7}$$

for the number of LI functions of order n.

It is easily shown [7] that all LI functions are balanced, so the sets labelled T_5 and T_6 in Figure 4 are both empty, and the set of LI functions is just $T_2 \cup T_3$.

3.4 Linear-In, Nondegenerate Functions

Any LI function of order n which is degenerate, depending on only k < n of its inputs, can be viewed as a LI nondegenerate function of order k. Thus, the number of LI nondegenerate functions of order n, F_n, can be expressed as:

$$F_n = L_n - \sum_{k=1}^{n-1} \binom{n}{k} F_k. \tag{8}$$

Solving this recurrence leads to:

$$F_n = \sum_{k=0}^{n-1} (-1)^k \binom{n}{k} L_{n-k} \tag{9}$$

and, using equation (7), we obtain the following explicit result:

$$F_n = \sum_{k=0}^{n-1} \sum_{i=1}^{n-k} (-1)^{i+k+1} \binom{n}{k} \binom{n-k}{i} 2^{2^{n-k-i}}, \quad n \geq 1. \tag{10}$$

3.5 Standard Functions

We have defined Standard functions as those which are not-LI, balanced and nondegenerate. The number of such functions is therefore $\|T_1\|$, the cardinality of the set T_1 in Figure 4, which can be expressed as:

$$\|T_1\| = \|T_1 \cup T_2\| \|T_2\|.$$

Here, $T_1 \cup T_2$ is the set of all balanced, nondegenerate functions and T_2 is the set of all LI nondegenerate functions (since T_5 is null). Thus, the number of Standard functions of order n, S_n, is given by:

$$S_n = N_n - F_n, \tag{11}$$

which can be evaluated for all $n \geq 1$ using the previous results for N_n and F_n in equations (3) and (10).

The number of Standard functions grows very rapidly with the order n, as illustrated by Table I. For large n, S_n is dominated by the term for $k = n$ in equation (3).

n	S_n
2	0
3	32
4	11,800
5	6.007×10^8
6	1.833×10^{18}
7	2.395×10^{37}
8	5.769×10^{75}

Table I The number of Standard functions of order n, S_n

4. PROPERTIES OF STANDARD FUNCTION OUTPUT SEQUENCES

When a Standard function is used in the stream cipher scheme of Figure 2, its n-bit input comprises n consecutive bits from an m-sequence of period 2^n-1 and therefore progresses through all n-bit patterns, except all-zeros, in some pseudo-random order. Since any Standard function is balanced, its output sequence, will therefore contain M_1 ones and M_0 zeros per period of the m-sequence, where $|M_1-M_0| = 1$.

As mentioned in section 2, when a Standard function is used in the cipher feedback scheme of Figure 3, all n-tuples are expected to occur with equal probabilities at the function input, so again, the balance property ensures that the probabilities of ones and zeros in the output sequence are equal. For similar reasons, the transition probabilities between consecutive bits in the output sequence from a Standard function are expected to be equal, and the expected value of the correlation between successive bits is zero.

Now, although Standard functions are, by definition, strictly nonlinear functions of each of their inputs, we are also interested in the degree of linearity associated with their serial output sequences. In particular, we would like these sequences to have a large <u>linear complexity</u> [8] (or equivalent linear span). The linear complexity of the first k bits of a sequence (for all $k \geq 1$), viewed as a function of k, is called its <u>linear complexity profile</u> (LCP). Rueppel [9] has shown that the expected value of the LCP for a truly random sequence is very close to k/2, increasing in a stepwise fashion with k, having a mean step height of 2 and a mean step length of 4 bits along the k-axis. Rueppel also proposed that "a good random sequence" for cryptographic use should closely, but irregularly, approximate this LCP behaviour. In addition, note that a linear complexity of k/2 for a sub-sequence of length k is sufficient to foil an attack based on the Berlekamp-Massey algorithm [2].

We have determined the LCP numerically for a large number of output sequences produced by a large number of Standard functions, when used in both the stream cipher and cipher feedback schemes of Figures 2 and 3. A typical set of results is summarised in Table II. These particular results are for a set of 8 Standard functions of order 5 used in the cipher feedback scheme, with an ASCII-encoded excerpt from 'Hamlet' as the plaintext. However, very similar results were obtained for other choices of plaintext and other Standard functions in both encryption schemes considered [7]. All of the Standard function output sequences investigated were found to satisfy Rueppel's criterion for closely, but irregularly, following the expected LCP of truly random sequences.

STANDARD FUNCTION NO. (ARBITRARY)	MEAN STEP LENGTH	MEAN STEP HEIGHT
0	3.96	1.98
1	4.03	2.02
2	3.79	1.90
3	4.04	2.03
4	4.24	2.13
5	3.92	1.96
6	4.06	2.03
7	4.25	2.13

Tabe II Mean lengths and heights of steps in the linear complexity profiles of standard function output sequences

5. CONCLUSIONS

The use of n-input, one-output Boolean functions in stream cipher and cipher feedback systems has been considered. For both these encryption schemes, it is desirable for the Boolean functions to be balanced (neutral), nondegenerate and not-Linear-In (i.e. strictly nonlinear in each of the n inputs), and functions with all of these properties were referred to as Standard functions. The numbers of Boolean functions with each of these properties, separately and in various combinations, have been determined, and the number of Standard functions was shown to grow very rapidly with the function order n. Further properties of the serial output sequences produced by Standard functions in the two encryption schemes have been investigated and, in particular, the linear complexity profiles of these sequences appear to closely approximate the behaviour of truly random sequences.

Finally, although not presented here, two algorithms for the generation of Standard functions have been devised [7]. One of these generates all Standard functions of a given order, while the other offers significant improvements in efficiency at the expense of omitting a few Standard functions. The number of functions omitted by the latter algorithm is a negligible fraction of the total number of Standard functions, being less than 0.02% for n = 5 and decreasing very rapidly as n increases.

ACKNOWLEDGEMENTS

M. Monaghan acknowledges the support of the U.K. Science and Engineering Research Council. We also express grateful thanks for helpful discussions with Mark Rice of the Electrical Engineering Department, University of Manchester.

REFERENCES

[1] Golomb, S.W., (1982) 'Shift Register Sequences', Revised Edn., Aegean Park Press.

[2] Massey, J.L., (1969) 'Shift Register Synthesis and BCH Decoding', *IEEE Trans. Information Theory*, Vol. IT-15, pp. 122-127.

[3] Rivest, R.L., (1978) 'The Impact of Technology on Cryptography', Proc. IEEE Int. Conf. on Communications, pp. 46.2.1-46.2.4.

[4] Elspas, B., (1960) 'Self-Complementary Symmetry Types of Boolean Functions', IRE Trans. Electronic Computers, Vol. EC-9, pp. 264-266.

[5] Harrison, M.A., (1963) 'The Number of Equivalence Classes of Boolean Functions under Groups Containing Negation', *IEEE Trans. Electronic Computers, Vol. EC-12, pp. 559-561.*

[6] Harrison, M.A., (1964) 'On the Classification of Boolean Functions by the General Linear and Affine Groups", *J. SIAM*, Vol. 12, No. 2, pp. 285-299.

[7] Monaghan, M.F., (1986) 'The Properties and Characteristics of Random Boolean Functions', M.Sc. Thesis, Computer Science Department, University of Manchester.

[8] Key, E.L., (1976) 'An Analysis of the Structure and Complexity of Nonlinear Binary sequence Generators', IEEE Trans. Information Theory, Vol. IT-22, pp. 732-736.

[9] Rueppel, R.A., (1984) 'New Approaches to Stream Ciphers', D.Sc. Dissertion, Swiss Federal Institute of Technology (ETH), Zurich.

SPEECH SECURITY AND PERMANENTS OF (0,1) MATRICES

C. Mitchell
(Hewlett-Packard Laboratories, Bristol)

1. INTRODUCTION

Voice communications still rely to a considerable extent on narrow band channels, such as telephone or radio links. The ease with which conversations over such links can be monitored has led to a continuing wide requirement for means to protect the secrecy of such conversations.

Given that the channel has a narrow bandwidth, the measures that can be taken to protect the secrecy of the voice signal are somewhat limited. This is because, even with expensive and sophisticated modems, bit rates over such channels are normally limited to 2000-3000 bits/second. Thus, if the voice signal is to be encrypted digitally, special low bit rate voice coders must be used. These coders are not only relatively sophisticated and hence relatively costly, but are also highly sensitive to errors.

So if the requirement is for a security system of modest cost and high reliability over poor channels then analogue "scrambling" techniques must be used. This requirement remains an extremely common one, and so analogue voice scramblers remain an important part of the market for security and privacy equipment.

Most analogue speech security systems operate by scrambling the voice signal in either the time domain or the frequency domain, and some operate in both domains. A variety of techniques can be employed to scramble the signal, but we are concerned here with one particular technique for scrambling in the time domain. This technique, known as time element scrambling (TES), is an extremely popular method and can be readily combined with scrambling effects in the frequency domain.

The time element scrambling technique is one of the most effective and easily implemented speech scrambling techniques; speech is divided into segments in the time domain, and then these segments are re-ordered prior to transmission; see, for example, [2]. Properly used, this technique can render the transmitted signal extremely difficult to decipher, and, as a result, this type of technique is widely used in commercially available equipment. However, this technique necessarily introduces a delay into the communications path, which must be minimised for the sake of user convenience.

Thus strategies must be devised for re-ordering the speech segments which minimise the time delay, whilst at the same time maximising the diversity of patterns available in order to maximise the security level. In order to achieve this, a number of different strategies have been produced, and a description and comparison of some of the various different rearrangement methods can be found in [5].

For some of these strategies, the problem of assessing the diversity of rearrangement patterns available reduces to a permutation enumeration problem. For many such systems the enumeration of the possible usable permutations remains an intractable problem.

The purpose of this paper is to consider two such strategies for which the permutation enumeration problem is equivalent to evaluating the permanent of certain (0,1) matrices. Computing the permanent of a (0,1) matrix is known to be a hard problem in the general case, [3], [4]. This paper will describe new work of the author, which, in conjunction with other recent joint work of Beker and the author, [1], means that it is now possible to compute the permanent for a larger number of the relevant matrices than was previously possible.

The new results on permanent evaluation take the form of proving that the permanent of certain (0,1) matrices of dimension n by n is equal to the sum of certain entries in the nth power of another matrix of size independent of n. These results will form the central part of this paper.

Although time element scramblers are still of considerable commercial importance, they do represent just one type of speech security device. For a general introduction to speech security techniques, the interested reader is referred to the recent book of Beker and Piper, [2], which appears to be the only book dedicated to this subject.

2. TWO STRATEGIES FOR TIME ELEMENT SCRAMBLING

2.1 The two techniques

The two techniques described here both represent compromises between pattern diversity and minimal time delay, but have different targetted security levels. The first strategy we consider is that described in [5] as Overlapping Frame Sliding Window Scrambling, which has a somewhat limited security level. The second strategy however, called Disjoint Frame Sliding Window Scrambling in [5], has a level of security approaching the maximum possible from a time element scrambling system.

2.2 Overlapping Frame Sliding Window Scramblers

The first technique involves dividing the clear speech signal into frames of n segments for some pre-selected n, where each segment represents T seconds of speech. For this technique it is necessary to choose a second integer k<n which determines the system delay (in conjunction with the value T chosen for the segment length). In fact the total system delay will equal $(k+1)T$ seconds, and this is a relevant factor in the choice of k. Thus if k=16 and $T=3 \times 10^{-2}$, then the system delay will be 0.51 seconds. It is important to note that n does not affect this delay. Having chosen k we then select permutations from S_n for use in rearranging the speech segments.

We select and use these permutations so that each segment is transmitted within kT seconds of entering the scrambler. This is achieved by limiting the scrambling patterns to those permutations $\pi \in S_n$ satisfying:

$$[\pi(i)]_n \in \{[i-1]_n, [i-2]_n, \ldots, [i-k]_n\} \text{ for every } i \ (1 \leq i \leq n),$$

where $[i]_n$ represents the residue class of i modulo n.

We now describe both formally and by means of an example how these permutations are used. Formally, if we assume that time t=0 occurs at a frame boundary, then the segment transmitted between $t=(s-1)T$ and $t=sT$ is the segment input to the scrambler between $t=(r-1)T$ and $t=rT$, where $1 \leq s-r \leq k$, $r'=\pi(s')$, $[r]_n=[r']_n$ and $[s]_n=[s']_n$.

The way in which these patterns are used is illustrated in Figure 1, where we show a system for which n=8, k=3 and π satisfies $\pi(1)=6$, $\pi(2)=1$, $\pi(3)=8$, $\pi(4)=3$, $\pi(5)=2$, $\pi(6)=5$, $\pi(7)=4$ and $\pi(8)=7$. In the figure we have used different letters to distinguish between different frames. So, for instance, A1 is the first segement of the first frame while B1 is the first segment of the second. Note that the values of n and k used in this example are not realistic in that they are much too small to offer any real security.

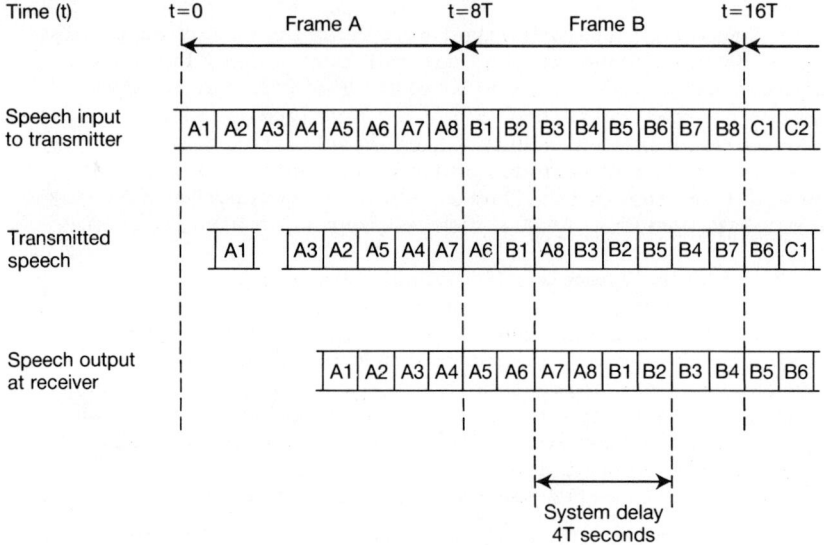

Fig. 1 Overlapping Frame Sliding Window TES

One advantage of this system is that it is not necessary to complete the transmission of the segments from one frame before commencing the transmission of segments from the next frame, thus increasing the diversity of patterns available. However this leads to practical implementation restrictions (discussed in more detail in [2] and [5]); in particular it is normally necessary to force the system to re-use the same segment permutation for a period of time. This in turn limits the security of this scheme.

2.3 Disjoint Frame Sliding Window Scramblers

In the second technique, we again choose a segment length T, and then also select a positive integer h, both of which values affect the system delay. We then select a second positive integer $n \geq h$, which determines the "size" of the permutations used. We then use as our scambling patterns those permutations $\pi \in S_n$ with the property that $|i-\pi(i)| < h$ for all i.

To do the scrambling we first divide the clear speech into frames of n consecutive segments, and a separate permutation is then used to determine how to rearrange the segments within each frame. Suppose that a frame of speech begins at time t=0 and ends at t=nT, and that permutation $\pi \in S_n$ is to be used to

re-order the segments within this frame. As before we label
the segments 1,2,...,n so that segment i was originally spoken
between t=(i-1)T and t=iT. The segments of the frame are then
transmitted between t=hT and t=(n+h)T in such a way that, for
any i between 1 and n, the segment transmitted between
t=(h+i-1)T and t=(h+i)T is π(i). The total system delay is
then 2hT seconds.

As an illustration of this type of system consider Figure 2,
where we give an example having n=8 and h=2. Suppose that
π is used to permute the segments of the first frame, and τ is
used for the second, where π,τ satisfy π(1)=2, π(2)=1, π(3)=3,
π(4)=5, π(5)=4, π(6)=7, π(7)=6, π(8)=8, τ(1)=1, τ(2)=3, τ(3)=2,
τ(4)=5, τ(5)=4, τ(6)=6, τ(7)=8 and τ(8)=7. As before, we label
the segments of the first frame A1, A2, ..., A8 and the
segments of the second frame B1, B2, ..., B8.

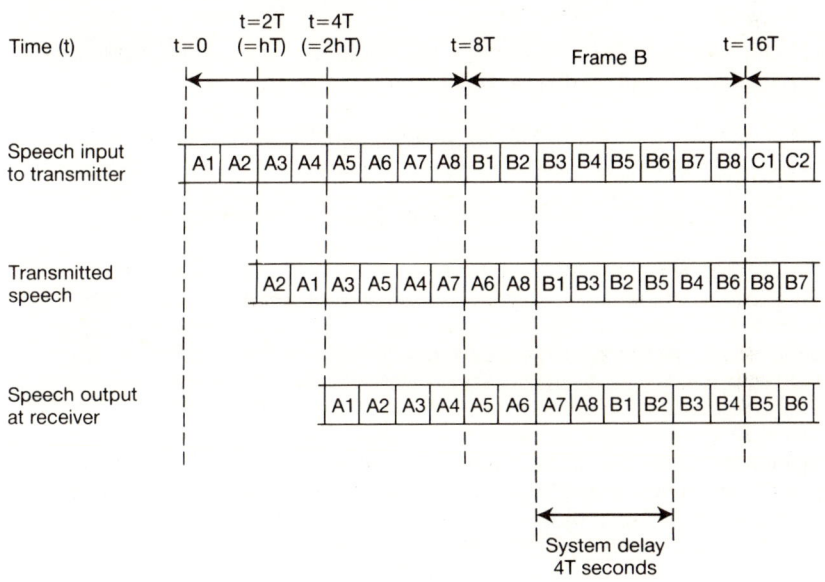

Fig. 2 Disjoint Frame Sliding Window TES

An important advantage of this system over the Overlapping
Frame technique, is that it is now straightforward to arrange
for a different permutation to be used for each frame of speech.

2.4 Permutation selection and enumeration

One problem which is common to both types of scrambler
discussed here is the choice of usable permutations. This is
of great importance because the variety of available scrambling

patterns to a great extent determines the security level of the system. For overlapping frame sliding window scramblers we are restricted to those permutations $\pi \in S_n$ which satisfy:

$$[\pi(i)]_n \in \{ [i-1]_n, [i-2]_n, \ldots, [i-k]_n \} \text{ for every } i.$$

We denote this set of permutations by $A^*(n,k)$, and if we denote the cardinality of this set by $a(n,k)$, i.e. $a(n,k) = |A^*(n,k)|$ then in order to assess the security of such a system we need to evaluate $a(n,k)$. In fact it can be shown that $a(n,k)$ is equal to the permanent of the cyclic (0,1) n by n matrix having (11...100...0) as its first row, where the number of ones in this row is k. Note that the permanent of an n by n matrix (a_{ij}) is

$$\sum_{\pi \in S_n} a_{1\pi(1)} \cdot a_{2\pi(2)} \cdots a_{n\pi(n)}$$

i.e. the definition is exactly the same as the definition of determinant except for the omission of the sign(π) term.

For disjoint frame sliding window scramblers the permutations we are interested in are those $\pi \in S_n$ which satisfy:

$$|\pi(i) - i| < h \text{ for every } i.$$

We call the set of all such permutations $C(n,h)$, and as before we let $c(n,h) = |C(n,h)|$. This enumeration problem also turns out to be equivalent to the evaluation of the permanent of an n by n (0,1) matrix, this time one with a 1 in position (i,j) iff $|i-j| < h$.

We now proceed to give results which enable these permanents to be readily computed for values which might be typical in genuine applications. Certainly, evaluating these permanents for such practical values of n, k and h would not be straightforward without some such result.

3. COUNTING SCRAMBLING PATTERNS AND PERMANENTS OF (0,1) MATRICES

Just as in [1], for the purposes of the theory that follows it is convenient to consider the set

$$A(n,k) = \{\pi \in S_n : [\pi(i)]_n \in \{[i]_n, [i+1]_n, \ldots, [i+k-1]_n\} \text{ for all } i\} \tag{3.1}$$

and it is clear that $|A(n,k)| = a(n,k) = |A^*(n,k)|$.

Before proceeding to specific results we need some notation. Firstly, if $\pi \in S_n$ and $i \in \{1, 2, \ldots, n\}$ then define

$$X_k(\pi, i) = \{\pi(j) : [j]_n \in \{[i]_n, [i+1]_n, \ldots, [i+k-2]_n\} \text{ and}$$

$$[\pi(j)]_n \in \{[j]_n, [j+1]_n, \ldots, [i+k-2]_n\}\}. \quad (3.2)$$

We can now state the following key lemma.

<u>Result 3.1</u> (Lemma 4.1 of [1]) If $\pi \in A(n,k)$ then there exists an integer $r \in \{0, 1, \ldots, k-1\}$ such that:

$$|X_k(\pi, i)| = r \text{ for every } i \in \{1, 2, \ldots, n\}. \quad (3.3)$$

Because of this result, for every $r \in \{0, 1, \ldots, k-1\}$ we define:

$$A(n,k,r) = \{\pi \in A(n,k) : |X_k(\pi, i)| = r \text{ for every } i\}. \quad (3.4)$$

In addition we set $a(n,k,r) = |A(n,k,r)|$. Using this notation, the following result is trivial.

<u>Result 3.2</u> (Lemma 4.2 of [1])

$$a(n,k) = \sum_{r=0}^{k-1} a(n,k,r). \quad (3.5)$$

To complete this introductory material now suppose that k and r are integers satisfying $0 \leq r \leq k-1$, and let $t = {}_{k-1}C_r$. Label the t distinct r-subsets of $\{0, -1, \ldots, -k+2\}$: $R_1, R_2, \ldots, R_t$, and then for every $i \in \{1, 2, \ldots, t\}$ let $S_i = \{j+1 : j \in R_i - \{0\}\}$. We now define the t by t (0,1) matrix $H(k,r) = (h_{ij})$ by:

$$h_{ij} = 1 \text{ iff } S_i \subset R_j.$$

We can now state the following result which gives a direct means of computing $a(n,k,r)$ and hence $a(n,k)$.

<u>Result 3.3</u> (Thereom 4.4 of [1])

$$a(n,k,r) = \text{trace}(H(k,r)^n). \quad (3.6)$$

We now show how a similar result may be achieved for $c(n,h)$ for the situation where $n \geq 2h-1 \geq 3$. This restriction on the values of n and h is necessary for the following theory, and is therefore implicitly assumed for the remainder of this section. In most speech scrambling applications the values of n and h used will satisfy the above inequalities, a typical pair of values being n=16, h=8.

We first need some further definitions. Let $C^*(n,h)$ be the set: $\{\pi^* \in S_n :$ there is $\pi \in C(n,h)$ with $[\pi^*(i)]_n = [\pi(i)+h-1]_n$ for all $i\}$ and clearly $c(n,h) = |C^*(n,h)|$. Then we have:

Lemma 3.4 $|C^*(n,h)| = |D(n,h)|$, where

$$D(n,h) = \{ \tau \in A(n+2h-2, 2h-1) : \tau(n+i) = n+i+h-1 \ (1 \leq i \leq h-1) \text{ and }$$

$$\tau(n+i) = i-h+1 \ (h \leq i \leq 2h-2) \}. \tag{3.7}$$

Proof We establish the lemma by exhibiting a 1-1 correspondence between the elements of $C^*(n,h)$ and $D(n,h)$.

First suppose that $\pi^* \in C^*(n,h)$. Then let $\tau = \Phi(\pi^*)$ be the following element of S_{n+2h-2}:

$$\begin{aligned}
[\tau(i)]_n &= [\pi^*(i)]_n, & h \leq \tau(i) \leq n+h-1, & 1 \leq i \leq n \\
\tau(i) &= i+h-1, & & n+1 \leq i \leq n+h-1 \\
\tau(i) &= i-n-h+1, & & n+h \leq i \leq n+2h-2. \quad (3.8)
\end{aligned}$$

Then Φ is a 1-1 correspondence between $C^*(n,h)$ and $D(n,h)$ and the result follows. □

We now need some further notation. Let $\underline{E}$ be the class of all $(2h-2)$-subsets E of $(-2h+3, -2h+4, \ldots, 2h-2)$ satisfying the property that E contains precisely $h-1$ elements of $\{-2h+3, -2h+4, \ldots, 0\}$. Further, if $E \in \underline{E}$, then let $U(E)$ be the set of all $(2h-2)$-tuples $\underline{c} = (c_1, c_2, \ldots, c_{2h-2})$, where $\{c_1, c_2, \ldots, c_{2h-2}\} = E$ and $c_i \in \{i-2h+2, i-2h+3, \ldots, i\}$ for every $i \in \{1, 2, \ldots, 2h-2\}$.

Then if $E \in \underline{E}$, and if $\underline{c} \in U(E)$, we let $v_n(E) = |P(\underline{c})|$, where $P(\underline{c})$ is defined to be the set of permutations $\pi \in A(n, 2h-1, h-1)$ satisfying:

$$\pi(j) = \begin{cases} c_i & \text{if } \pi(j) < j \\ c_i + n & \text{if } \pi(j) \geq j \end{cases} \text{ where } j = n-2h+i+2, \ 1 \leq i \leq 2h-2.$$

$$(3.9)$$

The fact that $v_n(E)$ is well defined follows immediately from Lemma 5.3 of [1]. We can now state the following result whose proof is implicit in the proof of Theorem 4.4 of [1].

Result 3.5 As before let $R_1, R_2, \ldots, R_t$ be a labelling of the t distinct (h-1)-subsets of $\{0, -1, \ldots, -2h+3\}$ (where $t = {}_{2h-2}C_{h-1}$). In addition let

$$C_i = \{j+2h-2 : j \in \{0,-1,\ldots,-2h+3\}-R_i\}, \quad 1 \leq i \leq t,$$

and let the t by t matrix $W(n) = (w_{ij})$ be defined by

$$w_{ij} = v_n(R_i \cup C_j).$$

Then we have:

$$W(n) = H(2h-1, h-1)^{n-2h+2}. \qquad (3.10)$$

Using this result in conjunction with Lemma 3.4 we now have

Theorem 3.6 If the labelling $R_1, R_2, \ldots, R_t$ is chosen so that $R_m = (0, -1, \ldots, -h+2)$, then

$$c(n,h) = \text{the } (m,m) \text{ entry in } H(2h-1,h-1)^n. \qquad (3.11)$$

Proof First note that, by Lemma 3.4: $c(n,h) = |D(n,h)|$, where $D(n,h)$ is the subset of $A(n+2h-2, 2h-1)$ defined in the statement of the Lemma. Then, using the notation following Lemma 3.4, it is straightforward to see that $|D(n,h)| = v_{n+2h-2}(E)$, where $E = \{-h+2, -h+3, \ldots, 0\} \cup \{1, 2, \ldots, h-1\} = R_m \cup C_m$. Note that to make this latter observation we need to establish that $D(n,h) \subset A(n+2h-2, 2h-1, h-1)$. But this follows by noting that, by definition, $X_{2h-1}(\pi, n+1) = \{n+h, n+h+1, \ldots, n+2h-2\}$ for every $\pi \in D(n,h)$.

Hence $c(n,h) = v_{n+2h-2}(R_m \cup C_m)$. The theorem then follows immediately from Result 3.5. □

REFERENCES

[1] Beker, H.J. and Mitchell, C.J., (1987) Permutations with restricted displacement, *SIAM Journal on Algebraic and Discrete Methods*, **8**, 338-363.

[2] Beker, H.J. and Piper, F.C., (1985) "Secure speech communications", Academic Press, London.

[3] Garey, M.R. and Johnson, D.S., (1979) "Computers and intractability: A guide to the theory of NP completeness", Freeman.

[4] Minc, H., (1984) "Permanents", Cambridge University Press.

[5] Mitchell, C.J. and Piper, F.C., (1985) A classification of time element speech scramblers, *J. Inst. Electronic and Radio Engineers,* **55**, 391-396.

DIGITAL MULTISIGNATURES

C. Boyd
(British Telecom, Ipswich)

1. INTRODUCTION

The idea of digital signature is now well known as a means of replacing written signatures in electronic communications. In many applications a document may need to be signed by more than one party [2]. When a signature depends on more than one person we will call it a multisignature.

One way of achieving a multisignature is by using a so-called 'threshold scheme' [7] which divides knowledge of the signing key between several people. However in this case all the signatories must meet together at the same place and at the same time in order for the key to be re-assembled, which is clearly impractical in many applications.

Another possibility is successive signing by the various parties, when the signature is verified by removing each signature in turn. This has certain disadvantages however. Firstly the time taken for verification is multiplied by the number of signatories. Secondly, in the RSA signature scheme, which is the most popular scheme, reblocking will be necessary when a subsequent signatory has a larger modulus. Thirdly, any verifier will need to have the relevant verification information for each signatory involved.

In this paper we examine ways of adapting the RSA scheme [6] to enable multisignatures to be easily implemented by groups of users such that signature verification will only require a single RSA transformation. The suggested schemes would be particularly applicable for use in companies. Typical applications might be the signing of documents by business partners, or signing of cheques for Electronic Funds Transfer where two or more company representatives may be required to sign any cheque.

In [4] a way of implementing a multisignature scheme using RSA was described. This was essentially a way of overcoming the re-blocking problem mentioned above by assigning an individual's modulus according to company seniority, so that a superior would always have a larger modulus than those under him. This scheme however is only useful when the order of signing is pre-determined (the application envisaged in [4] was the approval of signed documents by a superior). It still suffers from the other drawbacks mentioned above. The idea behind the schemes suggested here is to extend the RSA algorithm to a multiple-key cipher. It is suggested in [1] that for multiple-key ciphers the keys must be inserted simultaneously. We use the multiplicative property of exponentiation to invent a scheme where this is not necessary.

The schemes proposed in this paper are not in fact limited to the RSA algorithm. Any encryption algorithm E with the multiplicative property $E(k1).E(k2) = E(k1.K2)$ will do. For concreteness, however, we will use RSA throughout the paper.

2. A SCHEME FOR DOUBLE SIGNATURES

The scheme described here enables two users to sign, say, a cheque which can be verified by any user. The idea is to extend the RSA scheme by having three keys instead of two: two private keys and one public key. The company chooses a modulus n to be the product of two large primes as in the RSA scheme. The two private keys are then chosen at random in the range 1 to n, subject to the condition that they are coprime to $\emptyset(n)$. Call these keys r and s. The public key t is then chosen so that

$$r.s.t = 1 \bmod \emptyset(n);$$

r and s are now issued to the authorised signatories and t is made public. In order to sign the cheque C the first signatory calculates

$$S1 = C^{**}r \bmod n$$

and sends S1 to the second signatory. The second signatory can now recover C from S1 in order to see what he is to sign by

$$C = S1^{**}(s.t) \bmod n$$

since he knows both s and t. If he is satisfied he now signs S1 to form

$$S2 = S1^{**}s \bmod n$$

and sends S2 to the recipient. Since t is public, the recipient and any member of the public can verify the validity of the cheque by calculating

$$C = S2^{**}t \bmod n.$$

The cheque must have been signed by the two authorised signatories in order to form S2. Note that the order of signing in this scheme does not matter.

Knowledge of S1 is of no use to (and cannot even be read by) an imposter. It seems clear that forging a message for this scheme is the same as forging an RSA signature with secret key r*s, and in this sense the scheme is just as secure as the RSA algorithm. However from a key management viewpoint it is certainly safer to divide the key into two parts and keep them separately. There are many applications where dividing the responsibility for authorisation between two people is required. For example, in the SWIFT system two people must authorise each transaction.

The multiplicative property exploited in this scheme can also be used to attack RSA signatures in certain circumstances, see [5]. For example, since M1**r.M2**r = (M1.M2)**r the signature of M1.M2 can be deduced from those of M1 and M2. Various means are available to avoid these attacks, and they are also applicable in this scheme. One way is to use a one-way hash function h to transform the message prior to signing, so that h(M1.M2) = h(M1).h(M2). This also has the advantage that only one block need be signed however long the message is.

3. EXTENDING THE SCHEME

In certain situations the number of possible signatories may be many. For example in a company any two of a number of authorised signatories may be allowed. At the cost of some extra storage and processing the above scheme may be extended to take account of this. If there are N potential signatories then n random secret keys, k1,k2,...,kN are chosen. The public key t is chosen so that

$$k1.k2. \ldots .kN.t = 1 \bmod \emptyset(n).$$

Each signatory is then issued with all the private keys except one. For example the j-th signatory is given all ki's except kj. Each signatory stores all these keys and also their product. Let kj' = k1...k(j-1)k(j+1)...kn. When the j-th signatory wishes to sign a cheque C he signs it to form

$$S1 = C^{**}kj' \bmod n.$$

and appends his identity. Any other signatory can then complete the signing by looking up the missing key, which also allows him to read the message and then to form

$$S2 = S1^{**}kj \bmod n.$$

The recipient and any member of the public can again verify the signature by one decipherment with t.

4. BLIND MULTISIGNATURES

In certain situations more than two signatories will be required. The above scheme cannot be extended to achieve this. This is because if more than two signatories have secret keys the second signatory (and all others before the last) are unable to read what it is that they are signing. In other words they are only able to create 'blind signatures'.

There are many applications where blind signatures can prove very useful, as discussed in [3] and elsewhere. These include electronic bank notes and secret ballots. We explain here a way that blind multisignatures could be used.

In this scheme the players are a bank and a company. The first problem is to set up the keys. This is done as follows.

The bank chooses a modulus n = p.q, a random private key b, and a random public key t. These are the same for all its customers. The amount debited is defined by the keys b and t chosen by the bank, and there can be various keys published by the bank for different denominations.

The company chooses two random keys k1,k2, coprime to n, and calculates

$$k = k1.k2.$$

The company then sends k to the bank, which returns a number k3 satisfying

$$b.t.k.k3 = 1 \bmod \phi(n).$$

These keys can now be used to form electronic bank notes in the manner described in [3]. The novelty is that the keys k1 and k2.k3 can be destributed to different people in the company. Let us rename these.

$$c1 = k1,$$
$$c2 = k2.k3.$$

If k1 and k2 are chosen to be random primes by the company then the bank has no knowledge of c1 and c2. In order to obtain a single bank note the company chooses a random number r. This number must include some redundancy, say every other bit is 0. Some authorised member of the company (for example from the finance department) calculates r**c1 mod n and sends it to the bank. The bank returns (r**c1)**b to the company and debits the company's account by the appropriate amount. The finance department can then distribute the note to an authorised spender in possession of $c2$.

When the spender wishes to use the note he validates it by forming $((r^{**}c1)^{**}b)^{**}c2 \mod m$. The retailer can verify that it is genuine by recovering r and checking the redundancy condition. The retailer sends the note to the bank to be cleared where it is checked against, and added to, a list of cleared notes.

Although this procedure puts a certain amount of trust in the bank it allows the company to use its money in a way untraceable by the bank. The company has much better control over its money by dividing the responsibility for forming and for spending the bank notes. At the same time if the bank or the retailer allows access to its records of cleared notes, the company's finance department can audit the use of its notes by checking which random numbers were issued to which spender.

5. ANOTHER SCHEME

In this final section we present an alternative scheme to solve the problem of multisignatures with more than two signatories. However, it requires each signatory to sign separately and the results to be combined which may be inconvenient in many applications. In this scheme the company, or any issuing authority, again selects the secret keys at random. Suppose that there are three signatories required. $k1$, $k2$ and $k3$ are selected at random and this time the public key t is selected to satisfy

$$(k1 + k2 + k3).t = 1 \mod \phi(n).$$

Each signatory i takes the message M and signs it by

$$Si = M^{**}ki \mod n.$$

The three signed copies are then multiplied by some central authority to form

$$S = S1*S2*S3 \mod n$$

which is then sent to the recipient. The recipient and any member of the public can verify the signature using t since

$$S^{**}t \mod n = (S1*S2*S3)^{**}t \mod n$$

$$= M^{**}[\,(k1+k2+k3).t\,] \mod n$$

$$= M.$$

In the obvious way this system can be extended to enable any number of signatories to take part.

6. ACKNOWLEDGEMENTS

I would like to thank E.J. Humphreys for valuable suggestions during the preparation of this paper. I also acknowledge the permission of the directors of British Telecom to publish this paper.

7. REFERENCES

[1]   Carroll,J.M.,(1984), "The Resurrection of Multiple-Key Ciphers", Cryptologia, July.

[2]   Chalton, S., (1986), "The Authentification of the Origin and Content of Paperless Transactions, and Questions of Liability in Common Law", Proceedings of Conference on Paperless Trading and the Law in the EEC, Brussels, March.

[3]   Chaum, D., (1982), "Blind Signatures for Untraceable Payments" Proceedings of Crypto, Plenum Press.

[4]   Itakura, K. and Nakamura, K., (1983), "A Public Key Cryptosystem Suitable for Digital Multisignatures", NEC Research and Development, 71, October.

[5]   de Jonge, W. and Chaum, D., (1985), "Attacks on Some RSA Signatures", Crypto, Springer-Verlag.

[6]   Rivest, R., Shamir, A. and Adelman, L., (1978), "A Method for Obtaining Digital Signatures and Public-Key Cryptosystems", Comm. ACM 21, 2, 120-126.

[7]   Shamir, A., (1979), "How to Share a Secret", Comm. ACM 22, 11, 612-613.

SMART CARDS FOR POS-BANKING

A.G. Kersten
(Siemens AG, München, Germany)*

ABSTRACT

In this paper we discusse the security aspects of a practical, economical and secure system for cashless shopping (POS-banking), which is based on intelligent processor-chipcards, so-called smart cards.

1. INTRODUCTION

The aim of this concept is a POS-system which guarantees secure offline-communication. Most present day systems use magnetic-stripe-cards. They have the disadvantage that security can only be achieved by operating in online-mode. But there can never be mutual protection against deception, since only the integrity of the customer and his card can be checked. The customer, however, has nearly no protection. He has no active functions and has to trust the dealer's device and the transfer system. Manipulations such as the alteration of the amount of purchase cannot be excluded.

Nowadays a secure, decentralised communication-system can be created, since there exists a new medium - the intelligent processor-chipcard. The fundamental feature of a smart card is its activity, which enables it to become an adequate partner for a computer, POS-terminal etc. Both parties involved in an interaction have active tools for mutual checks to avoid deception; moreover, the implemented cryptographic methods enable them to protect transaction data against any falsification.

A secure offline-POS-system must satisfy the following security requirements:

. Identification of the customer by the electronic system
___
*Present address: Frauenlobstr. 6, D-6200 Wiesbaden

- mutual authentication of the participants (customer-card and terminal),
- data protection against falsification,
- provability of a transaction.

The use of smart cards is based on their ability to fulfil these basic security requirements.

2. SMART CARDS

In order to guarantee that nobody but the legal cardholder can carry out a transaction with a specific smart card, a secure man-machine-interface is needed. At present, this interface is protected by a PIN (personal identification number). Before an interaction commences the cardholder has to activate his card personally by entering his PIN. The PIN is the individual secret of the cardholder, since he has the possibility to alter it as often as he likes and the customer's bank does not have any knowledge of it. The intelligence of the smart card makes it possible to perform a local check inside the card instead of an external comparison. The cardholder has three attempts for entering the correct PIN. If he fails, the chip-card locks itself and can be reactivated only by the customer's bank. Reactivation of the card can be done just three times and requires a successful PIN-verification.

It seems quite possible that in some years biometrical-identification-methods such as finger-print-verification will be used.

Mutual authentication of the system components is necessary in order to prevent counterfeiting of smart cards and dealer-devices. The basic idea is that the communication is between two smart cards, the customer-card and the "dealer-card" inside the card-acceptor's device. We call this the two-card-system. Only the cards are responsible for secure communication. They verify each others integrity by performing an authentication-algorithm. Another advantage is that the dealer only has to change his dealer-card, whenever a customer uses a card of a different payment system. So the dealer has one card for each system but uses one and the same device for communication with all of them.

The ability of a smart card to perform a cryptographic algorithm can further be used to protect data against falsification. To achieve this the chip computes a so-called message certification code(CER) which depends on every bit of the message and is added to the transmitted message. A CER makes any alteration of data detectable.

Furthermore, the CERs provide a method to make transactions provable and to prevent transaction-simulation. A CER is derived from the message with the help of a secret key which is specific to each smart card and is only known to the card and the corresponding cardholder's bank. Without knowledge of the respective keys the customer's CER_C and the dealer's CER_D cannot be forged by an unauthorised institution. These CERs can be considered as an electronic transfer order and an electronic receipt. They are stored together with the transaction data and make, therefore, a transaction provable.

3. AUTHENTICATION SCHEMES

A smart card has to perform two authentication procedures:

(a) authentication of the communication partner

(b) message authentication and certification.

In order to fulfil these requirements a crypto-algorithm f is implemented in the chip. A modified version of f is the algorithm f_x. Furthermore, each smart card contains two secret keys.

In particular, the customer-card contains the keys

KIC for communication with a dealer-card

K_C for communication with the customer's bank

while the dealer-card contains

K for communication with the customer-cards

K_D for communication with the dealer's bank.

The keys K_C and K_D are used to generate message certification codes, while K and KIC are necessary for mutual authentication of the customer-card and the dealer-card. All keys are stored in the EEPROM of the chip. The use of an intelligent chip makes it possible to prevent external access to the keys.

(a) Authentication of the Communication Partner

For examination of the customer-card the authentication procedure AP1 is used. To "understand" each other the customer-card and the dealer-card have to establish a common key. After transmission of the card identification number (CID) the dealer-card computes the key

$$KIC = f_x(K ; CID),$$

which is the common communication key. The dealer-card generates a random number v_1 and sends it to the customer-card, which has to compute

$$AP1 = f(KIC ; v_1).$$

The dealer-card also computes $f(KIC ; v_1)$. Only if both results coincide, the customer-card is accepted as being authentic.

The authenticity of the dealer-card is proved in a similar way. Both cards choose the common key **KIC** and apply the function **f** to a random number v_2, which was generated by the customer-card and transmitted to the dealer-card. The result is the authentication parameter

$$AP2 = f(KIC ; v_2).$$

The comparison of the two results takes place inside the customer-card.

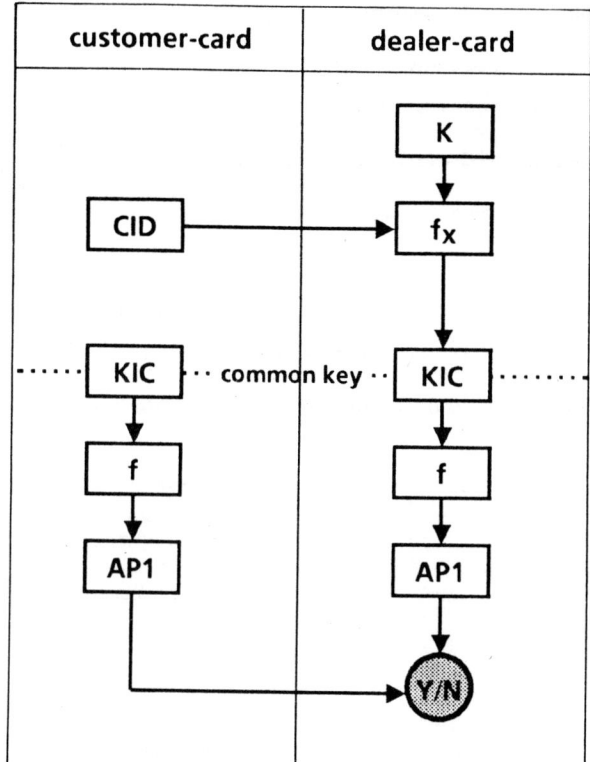

AUTHENTICATION PROCEDURE AP1

(b) Message Certification

For computation of the message certification code **CER**$_C$, which certifies the electronic transfer order, the customer-card uses the key **K**$_C$ which is known only to the customer's bank. The customer-card computes

$$CER_C = f\ (K_C;\ DATA\ 1).$$

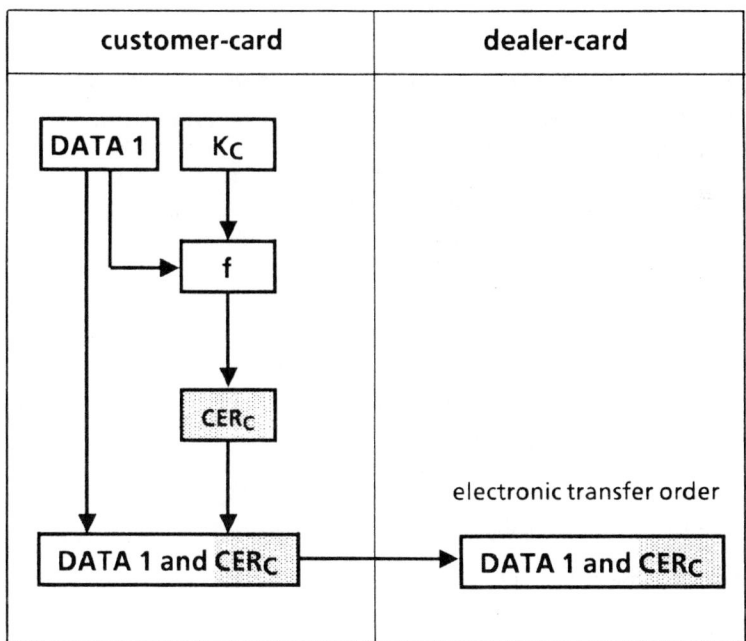

SIGNATURE CER$_C$

Any alteration of transaction data is impossible since the old "signature" does not fit the new data and a new code cannot be computed without knowledge of the key **K**$_C$.

DATA 1 consists of the customer's transaction number, date, amount and CID, and is transmitted to the dealer-card with the message certification code. If the CID and the amount of purchase are correct, DATA 1 and the corresponding CER_C are stored in the card acceptor's device in the RAM or on a floppy-disk. At a convenient time the dealer will transmit this transfer order to his bank. The dealer's and the customer's bank debit the amount of the purchase to the customer's and credit it to the dealer's account by electronic funds transfer.

In order to give the customer a certified receipt, the dealer-card applies its signature key K_D, performs the algorithm f and computes

$$CER_D = f\ (K_D1; DATA\ 2),$$

where DATA 2 consists of the dealer's transaction number, the terminal identification number, date, amount of purchase and the dealer's name.

DATA 2 and the corresponding CER_D are sent to the customer-card, which checks the amount and stores the transaction data including the dealer's signature in the chip's EEPROM. If there is no space left in the transaction memory the card will start to overwrite old information successively.

At special terminals transaction data can be read out of the customer-card after a successful PIN-input.

To check the correctness of the data which is transmitted between the two chipcards a message authentication code (MAC_T) could be used. To do so the customer-card and the dealer-card must establish a common transmission key K_T. This key and the algorithm f are applied to the data for computation of

$$MAC_T = f\ (K_T\ ;\ DATA\ ).$$

4. CRYPTOGRAPHIC DETAILS

Cryptographic methods make it possible to reach a high level of security. The two cryptographic functions f and f_x are deduced from one algorithm - the SICRYPT algorithm, which has been developed especially for chipcard applications. There were several design criteria for SICRYPT.

. The most important requirement was low complexity in order to fit into a smart card chip. Coding this algorithm needs less than 300 bytes, so this requirement is satisfied.
. The algorithm should have a high standard of security. The formal key length is 192 bits and there are 152 effective key bits.

SICRYPT can run in two different modes. It can be used for enciphering and deciphering. As an integral part of the smart card it is used as a one-way function (function f). In this mode deciphering is impossible.

SICRYPT is a block cipher. A 64-bit input block is transformed to a 64-bit output block. The algorithm works in n rounds where each round is represented by a shift of a nonlinear feedback shift register. The number n of rounds is not fixed, it can be chosen by the designer. The magnitude of n is mainly a question of the desired enciphering-rate. The correlation between n and the enciphering-rate is linear. With n = 256 enciphering of a 64-bit block takes about 15 ms.

5. FURTHER APPLICATIONS OF SMART CARDS

Another application of the smart card in the financial sector is its use as an electronic purse. A prepaid amount of money is stored in the card and successively cancelled. This method is implemented in telephone chip-cards.

Of entirely different type are the various access control schemes. Prevention of unauthorised access to buildings, computers, data bases, programs etc. can be achieved by using a smart card as an active identification and authentication tool [2,3,4]. The field of data security provides further applications. Software protection, protection against unauthorised alterations as well as the requirement that certain programs should only run in a specified environment can be satisfied.

Other considerations concern the replacement of documents such as identity cards by smart cards.

REFERENCES

[1] Beutelspacher, A., (1987) Kryptologie. Vieweg-Verlag, Braunschweig/Wiesbaden.

[2] Davies, D.W., and Price, W.L., (1984) Security for Computer Networks. John Wiley & Sons.

[3] Kruse, D.: Sicherheit à la Karte. Chip-Karten identifizieren fälschungssicher. com. Siemens-Magazin für Computer & Communication 21, 4/86, 18-20.

[4] Kruse, D.: Wächter fürs Betriebssystem. Chip-Karte für komfortable Zugangskontrolle zum BS 2000. com. Siemens-Magazin für Computer & Communication 21, 4/86, 20-22.

[5] Svigals, J., (1985) Smart Cards, The Ultimate Personal Computer. Mac Millan Publishing Company, New York.

GEOMETRIC STRUCTURES AS THRESHOLD SCHEMES

A. Beutelspacher[†] and K. Vedder[*]
(Siemens AG, Federal Republic of Germany)

ABSTRACT

Threshold schemes can be used to control the execution of operations which require a quorum. In this paper we exhibit examples of threshold schemes which arise from both Classical and from Finite Geometry. One of them, which is based on subplanes of finite Desarguesian projective planes, we discuss in detail.

1. INTRODUCTION

The usual way to control the execution of an operation which requires a quorum or threshold of t members of a group of s "authorised users" is to hold a meeting at which the members are physically present. Sometimes, however, the authorised users cannot identify each other by inspection; a meeting might not be feasible or the users do not know each other personally (for example, some of them might be computer programs). To achieve a quorum in such a situation so called threshold schemes have been introduced (see, for instance, [1,4,8,11]).

A *t-threshold scheme* consists of $s \geq t$ pieces of information (sometimes called *shadows*) such that the following properties are satisfied:

(i) a secret datum X can be retrieved from any t shadows,
(ii) X cannot be determined from any t-1 or fewer of the shadows.

Some of the schemes which we shall discuss have variants with additional features. The users might consist of different groups (such as human beings and computer programs) and a quorum in each one is required. For instance, the critical operation is not executed as long as only members of one of

---
† current address: Universität Giessen, Federal Republic of Germany
* current address: GAO, Gesellschaft für Automation und Organization, Federal Republic of Germany.

the groups agree on it. We shall also exhibit systems which reflect the fact that in many situations some users have more rights than others.

In terms of geometric language, a t-threshold scheme can be described as follows. In a *geometry* consisting of *points* and blocks one chooses a block B and s points on B in such a way that

(i) any t of the s points determine B uniquely,
(ii) there are 'many' blocks through any t-1 or fewer of the s points.

Thus the shadows in a geometric threshold scheme correspond to points of a (randomly chosen) block which can be retrieved from any t but not from fewer than t of its points. The intuitive way to implement such a scheme is to select any t points of B and store these points secretly. Every time $u \geq t$ points are fed into the system, it tries to construct a block through these u points. If there is no such block or more than one block, the system terminates the process. Otherwise it checks whether the t secretly stored points lie on the unique block it constructed. Only if they do, then the block is equal to B. The following modified implementation has the property that the system has to store only extremely few secret information. We select a set of points S which intersects the block B in a unique point X (or a non-empty set X of points) and store S and X. If u points enter the system, it tries, as before, to construct a block through these points. Only if there is a unique block C, say, which contains the u points, the system computes $C \cap S = X$. This way we need not store any information about the block B, it suffices to make X inaccessible.

What happens if an unauthorised user takes part in the process? Even if there is a unique block C through the points entered we can virtually be certain that this block is different from B and that $C \cap S$ is not the point (or set of points) X. So the existence of only one unauthorised user U makes sure that no group to which U belongs can perform the critical operation.

The precise meaning of 'many' in above description depends of course on the particular scheme. We shall see that we can achieve any level of security by choosing the geometry accordingly. For reasons of integrity it might, however, be useful to keep track of all those attempts to retrieve B which have been foiled.

2. EXAMPLES FROM CLASSICAL GEOMETRY

2.1 Conics. In the Euclidean plane there is a unique conic through any five points no three of which lie on a line. So we can take as B a randomly chosen conic and as S a (randomly chosen) tangent to B at a point X. (If one has the feeling that the number of tangents is too small for a satisfactory security, one can take a secant as S. Then X=B∩S is a set of two points.) Since the number of conics through four points in general position equals $|K|-2$, where K is the coordinatising field of the projective plane in question, we have a 5-threshold scheme.

These examples generalise in the following way. A *rational normal curve* in the d-dimensional projective space is determined by any d+3 of its points. Moreover, there is precisely one rational normal curve through any d+3 points, no d+1 of which are contained in a common hyperplane, (cf. Segre [10] and van der Waerden [12]). For d=2 the rational normal curves are precisely the conics.

2.2 Flats. Let G be an affine or a projective geometry of dimension d. As the block B we take a (t-1)-dimensional subspace (flat) of G. We choose the s shadows to be points on B which are in "general position" (that is, any t of them span B). For S we take a (d-t+1)-dimensional subspace which intersects B in just one point X. (S has the property that every (t-1)-dimensional subspace intersects it in at least one point). This gives a t-threshold scheme for every positive integer t.

Now suppose that we have two types of users, say human users and computer programs. We would like to design our system in such a way that at least i of the t shadows needed to determine the block B have to be human.

To achieve this we take a (t-1)-dimensional flat B and a (t-1-i)-dimensional subflat B* which is contained in B. The points corresponding to programs are chosen to be in general position in B*, while the human users correspond to points in general position in B outside B*. So, no matter how many programs join up to beat the system, they will not manage to succeed as long as fewer than i human users agree. Figure 1 depicts the case t=3 and i=1 (any coalition of three users at least one of which being a human being is granted access to the secret datum X).

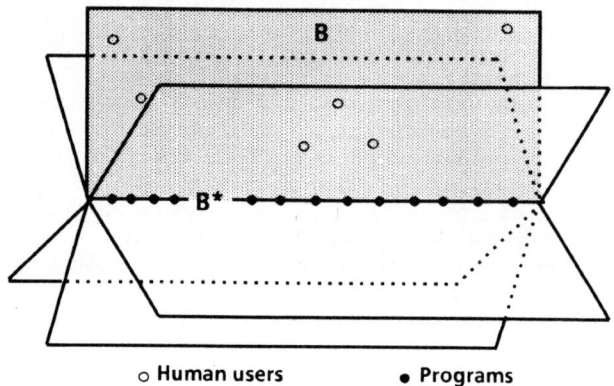

o Human users   • Programs

Fig. 1

In this concept the participation of a computer program is not needed to determine B. Any coalition of t human users can 'overrule' the programs. If the two groups do not trust each other, then the following modified system is more appropriate. We choose a (t_1+t_2-1)-dimensional flat B, where t_j is the number of members of the group G_j which is needed to obtain a quorum within the group (j=1,2). In B we select two disjoint subflats B_j of dimensions t_j-1. They correspond to the groups G_j. So the quorum is only obtained if both groups agree. Figure 2 depicts the case $t_1=t_2=3$.

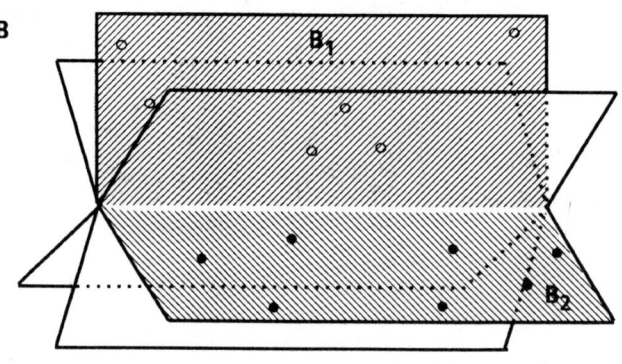

o Members of group 1   • Members of group 2

Fig. 2

If we want to allow for the possibility that one group can overrule the other to a certain extent, then we choose one of the subflats, say B_1, to be of dimension t_1-1+i. In this situation we need between t_1 and $t_1 + i$ members of G_1 and the corresponding number in G_2 to make up the total of $t_1 + t_2$ shadows needed. Note that no shadow should lie in the intersection of the two subflats, which is of dimension $i-1$, to prevent "mistaken identities". These schemes can clearly be extended to more than two groups. Furthermore, we need not check in such a set-up that the threshold is achieved in each of the groups.

If there is a hierarchy of users, then the system should reflect this fact. This can be done by changing the schemes described above in such a way that a user is represented by a subspace instead of a point, where the dimension of the subspace reflects his level in the hierarchy.

Another solution is to design a threshold scheme for every level separately and "join" the different systems. Suppose we have users of two types. The users in one group are represented by a 2-threshold scheme (say by a line ℓ), whereas users in the other group are represented by a 3-threshold scheme (say by a circle C). The line ℓ and the circle C intersect in a point X, at which the line S is a tangent to both of them. If a user enters the system, he has to state to which group he belongs and he is treated accordingly.

3. DESIGNS

While the geometries discussed in the last section can be over the reals or over finite field our next class of examples is properly finite.

A $t-(v,k,\lambda)$ *design* D (or briefly a t-design) consists of a set of points and a set of blocks (we always think of the blocks as sets of points) such that the following properties hold:

(a) D has v points.
(b) Every block of D consists of exactly k points.
(c) Through any t points of D there are exactly λ blocks.

For the theory of designs see the books by Beth, Jungnickel & Lenz [2], Beutelspacher [3] and Hughes & Piper [7].

For our purposes it is of interest that any u points, $0 \le u \le t$, of a $t-(v,k,\lambda)$ design D lie on exactly

$$\lambda_u = \binom{v-u}{t-u} \times \lambda / \binom{k-u}{t-u} \qquad (3.1)$$

points of D. This means that D is a $u-(v,k,\lambda_u)$ design with $\lambda_0=b$ blocks.

A t-design with $\lambda=1$ is also called a Steiner system. Any such design yields a t-threshold scheme which admits a maximum of k shadows. Just choose a block B and s points, $t \leq s < k$, on B. Then B is the unique block through any t or more of these s points, while there are λ_u blocks through any u points for each $u \leq t$. In particular, the λ_{t-1} blocks through a given set of t-1 points partition the remaining points of D. So, if t-1 shadows try to cheat the system by entering just one "extra" point, they determine a unique block no matter which one of the remaining points they select. Hence their probability to have guessed 'correctly' is $1/\lambda_{t-1} = (k-(t-1))/(v-(t-1))$.

There are, however, only a few Steiner systems known for t=4 and 5, while none is known for t>5. In the next section we shall use, in a different way, an infinite class of finite projective planes to construct 4-threshold schemes.

In a t-design with $\lambda>1$ any set of u points, $u \leq t$, lies on $\lambda_u>1$ blocks. More than t points can lie on none, exactly one or more than one block, depending on the points. To construct threshold schemes in t-designs with $\lambda>1$ we need the notion of an "intersection number". An integer $0 \leq \mu \leq k$ is called an intersection number of a $t-(v,k,\lambda)$ design D, if there are two different blocks of D which intersect in precisely μ points. Obviously, if w is an integer which is bigger than the maximal intersection number of D, then there is at most one block through any set of w points of D. If there is a block, and there are 'many' blocks through any w-1 of the points of this block, then this gives a w-threshold scheme.

We shall apply this observation to the class of symmetric designs. These are the $2-(v,k,\lambda)$ designs with the additional property that any two blocks intersect in precisely λ points. Hence every symmetric design with the property that there are many blocks through any λ points of the set of chosen shadows yields a $(\lambda+1)$-threshold scheme. The so-called biplanes are examples of such designs; they have $\lambda=2$.

The number $r=\lambda_1$ of blocks through one point of a $2-(v,k,\lambda)$ design is roughly $v\lambda/k$. By a famous theorem of Wilson [13] there are, for every pair (k,λ), infinitely many values of v such that a 2-design with these parameters exists. In other words, for fixed k and λ, there are 2-designs for an infinite number of r's. Since r measures the difficulty to cheat the system, a designer can choose the level of security as high as he wishes.

4. A 4-THRESHOLD SCHEME

In this section we consider a class of 4-threshold schemes which is constructed from a particular infinite series of finite projective planes. With these schemes we can achieve any level of security and, at the same time, allow any number of shadows required. The scheme utilises the property that there is a unique subplane of a given admissible order through any quadrangle of a Desarguesian plane. In the last part of this section we shall see that projective spaces of dimension d yield (d+2)-threshold schemes in a similar way.

The *finite projective planes* are the $2-(n^2+n+1,n+1,1)$ designs with $n \geq 2$. The integer n is called the *order* of the plane. It follows immediately from the definition and equation (3.1) that a finite projective plane of order n is a symmetric design with $b=v=n^2+n+1$ blocks (called *lines* in this context) and $r=k=n+1$ lines through each point. Obviously, any two distinct lines intersect in a unique point.

If we take as the points the 1-dimensional and as the lines the 2-dimensional subspaces of the 3-dimensional vector space over a finite field $GF(p^a)$, where p is a prime, we obtain a projective plane of order $n = p^a$. These are the so-called *Desarguesian planes*. Since there exists a finite field for every power of a prime, there is such a plane for every prime power. There are infinite classes of non-Desarguesian planes; they do, however, not concern us in this context. Before we introduce the scheme we shall briefly discuss some relevant properties of finite projective planes. The reader is referred to Hughes and Piper [6] for the theory of finite projective planes and to Lidl and Niederreiter [9] for finite fields.

Any set of points which lie on one line are said to be *collinear*. A set of points no three of which lie on a line are called an *arc* a set of four such points a *quadrangle*. It is easily seen that every projective plane contains a quadrangle.

A subplane Π' of a projective plane Π consists of subsets of the sets of points and lines such that Π' is itself a projective plane (we just ignore those points of a line of Π which are not in the relevant subset). By a well-known theorem of Bruck (see [6]), the order m of a subplane of a plane of order n satisfies $m^2=n$ or $m^2+m \leq n$. A Desarguesian plane of order $n=p^r$ contains a subplane for every prime power $m=p^s$, where s is a divisor of r. Conversely, the order of every subplane is of this form. Subplanes of order $m=\sqrt{n}$ are called Baer *subplanes*. They have the important property that every line of Π, which is not a line of the subplane, is a tangent to the subplane (that is, it contains exactly one point of the subplane) and that, dually, every point of Π, which is not a point of the subplane, is on exactly one line of the Baer subplane.

4.1 The Scheme. Desarguesian planes whose orders are proper prime powers yield 4-threshold schemes in a natural way, since there is a unique subplane of a given admissible order through any quadrangle and there are many such subplanes through any three non-collinear points.

Let Π be the Desarguesian plane of order n. We choose a subplane Π' of order m of Π and in this subplane $s \geq 4$ points in such a way that no three of them are collinear. Any four of the s shadows determine the subplane uniquely. The maximal number of shadows we can select depends only on the order m of Π', as the shadows form an arc in the subplane. This number is m+2 or m+1 depending on m being even or odd. Likewise does the security depend on the order of the subplane.

Since we want to store as few information as possible about the subplane itself, we select a point X of Π', and choose a tangent S to Π', at the point X.

There are n+1-(m+1) such tangents, for any line through X, which is not a line of the subplane, is a tangent. So the system only knows X and, possibly, S. Whenever $u \geq 4$ points enter the system, it tries to construct a subplane of a given order through these points and, if there is a unique one, checks whether S is a tangent at X. As an additional feature the system could examine whether any three of the u points are collinear.

Whether we keep S secret depends on the particular implementation. If the subplane is a Baer subplane, then the probability that three shadows manage to break the system is in either case in the order of 1/n. Only if m is relatively small in comparison with n it makes sense to store S secretly.

4.2 Attacks. The projective plane Π contains n^2+n+1 points of which n+1 lie on the line S. So the probability that one or two users guess X correctly is less than $1/n^2$, if S is stored secretly, and $1/(n+1)$ otherwise. We shall henceforth assume that the system can only be activated by feeding it four points.

We will now consider the situation that three shadows join to beat the system. Let them correspond to the points, P, Q and R, and let f, g and h be the lines of this "triangle" (see Figure 3).

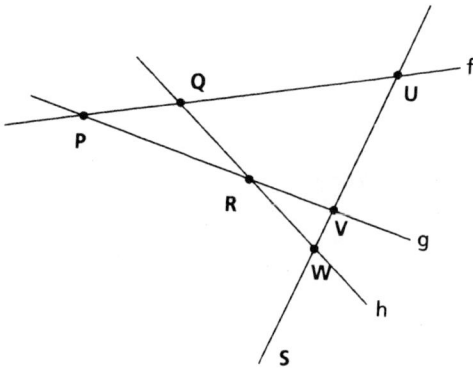

Fig. 3

We firstly consider the case that they try to "create" a fourth shadow without having any knowledge of S.

To judge their chance we need to know the total number of subplanes through the three points. Every point not on f, g or h forms a quadrangle with the points P,Q and R. This implies that two subplanes, which contain these three points, are distinct if and only if all their common points lie on f, g or h. So the subplanes through P,Q and R partition the set of those points of Π which are not on f, g or h. As these three lines are incident with $3n$ points of Π and $3m$ points of a subplane of order m, the total number N of subplanes through P,Q and R is

$$N = \frac{n^2+n+1-3m}{m^2+m+1-3m} = \frac{(n-1)^2}{(m-1)^2}. \tag{4.1}$$

Hence the knowledge of three non-collinear points of the subplane gives the probability prob to guess the "correct" subplane as

$$\text{prob} = \frac{1}{N} = \frac{(m-1)^2}{(n-1)^2} \leq \frac{1}{n+2\sqrt{n+1}}, \tag{4.2}$$

where the upper bound is attained in the case of a Baer subplane. We note that, if Π' is not a Baer subplane, there are planes which have no point in common with S.

This is also the probability that the three shadows in conjunction with the created fourth one determine the secret datum X, if X is not one of the points U,V or W. For in this case X forms a quadrangle with P,Q and R.

If, however, X is collinear with two shadows, then there is more than just one subplane containing P,Q,R and X to which S is a tangent at X. Let X be collinear with P and Q, say. The subplanes which contain, P,Q,R and X=U have three points on the line f and hence, since Π is Desarguesian, all their points on f in common. They mutually intersect exactly in their points on f and and the point R and partition the remaining points of those lines through R which intersect f in one of the common points. Hence their number is (n+1)/(m-1). Using equation (4.1), we have shown that the probability to guess a subplane to which S is a tangent at X and thus obtain the secret datum X is

$$\text{prob} = \frac{m-1}{n-1} < \frac{1}{\sqrt{(n+2\sqrt{n}+1)}} < \frac{1}{\sqrt{n}}. \qquad (4.3)$$

If the number of shadows is m+2, then each of the lines of the subplane Π', through one of the shadows contains another shadow and each point of Π' is on one of these lines. In most cases, however, there will not be a need for such a huge number of shadows. It is easily seen that the s(s-1)/2 lines which contain two shadows cover at most

$$s+(s-1)(m-1)+\frac{(s-1)(s-2)}{2}(m-s) = \frac{1}{2}s(s-1)(m-s-2)+1 \qquad (4.4)$$

points of Π'. This means that in all relevant implementations there is a sufficient number of points of the subplane which are not collinear with two shadows.

If the three shadows know the line S, then they could make the sensible, though not necessarily correct, assumption that X is none of the points U,V,W. The points they can definitively exclude are those of a subplane which contains the points P,Q,R and the line S. For S is not a line of the 'correct' subplane. There is exactly one such subplane, since two subplanes of the same order which have three collinear points (U,V and W in this case) and a quadrangle in common are equal. Hence they can beforehand exclude at least m-2 points of S. So their probability to guess a correct subplane is

$$\text{prob} = \frac{1}{n-m+1}. \qquad (4.5)$$

Obviously, if they do not want to feed the point on S to the system, they just compute a point which forms a quadrangle with the points P,Q and R in the unique subplane through these three points and the point on S.

Comparing (4.2) with (4.5) we see that, if Π' is a Baer subplane and thus $m=\sqrt{n}$, then the two expressions are of the same magnitude. If, however m is relatively small compared with n (in most cases there will not be a need for a large number of shadows), then it might be advisable to store S secretly. For instance, for m=4 (which allows a maximum of six shadows) equation (4.2) gives a probability of approximately $1/n^2$.

4.3 Implementation. We briefly discuss the coordination of Π over the field GF(n), to be able to judge the magnitude of the calculations needed in our algorithm.

The points and lines of Π are the 1-dimensional subspaces and hyperplanes, respectively, of the 3-dimensional vector space over the field GF(n). So we can represent both points and lines by homogeneous coordinates, that are non-zero 3-tuples with entries in GF(n). A point $<x,y,z>$ lies on a line $[a,b,c]$ if and only if $xa + yb + zc = 0$. Recall that two 3-tuples represent the same point or line if and only if one is a scalar multiple of the other. Hence we may write

$\{<1,y,z>,<0,1,z>,<0,0,1> \mid y,z \in GF(n)\}$ for the set of points and

$\{[a,b,1],[a,1,0],[1,0,0] \mid a,b \in GF(n)\}$ for the set of lines.

If $P=<x,y,z>$ and $Q=<x',y',x'>$ are two points, then $P=Q$ if and only if $x=x', y=y'$ and $z=z'$. If $P \neq Q$, then we obtain the unique line PQ through P and Q by using the diagram in the following figure. If it is not known whether the two points are distinct, then this need only be checked at the branches marked with an asterisk.

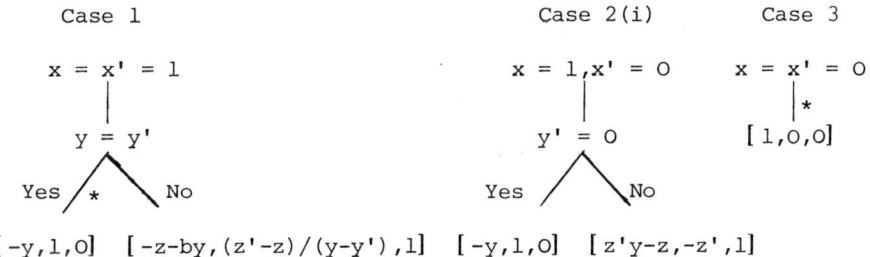

Fig. 4

The missing Case 2(ii) is the same as 2(i) with the rôles of P and Q reversed. Furthermore, at most two of the shadows correspond to points the first coordinate of which equals 0. So one should check Case 1 before the remaining cases.

The algorithm consists of three steps. When constructing a line through two points according to the above diagram, it will automatically abort the whole programme if the two points are equal.

STEP 1. The system (randomly) selects four of the u points entered, say P_1, P_2, P_3 and P_4. To examine whether these points form a quadrangle it carries out the following four operations.

Construction of the line P_1P_2.
Check that neither P_3 nor P_4 are points of the line P_1P_2.
Construction of the line P_3P_4.
Check that neither P_1 nor P_2 are points of the line P_3P_4.

STEP 1'. The system examines all the points entered whether they form an arc. After having satisfactorily completed Step 1 and checked the first $2i$ of the points the system proceeds as follows.

If the point P_{2i+1} is on one of the i lines $P_1P_2, P_3P_4, \ldots, P_{2i-1}P_{2i}$, then the programme is terminated. Otherwise it constructs consecutively the lines $P_{2i+1}P_j$ for $j = 2i, \ldots, 3$. (Note that the point P_{2i+1} is distinct from the points $P_1, P_2, \ldots, P_{2i}$ and that, therefore, operation * in Figure 4 need not be executed.) In each case it controls that none of the points $P_1, P_2, \ldots, P_{j-2}$ (if j is even) or $P_1, P_2, \ldots, P_{j-1}$ (if j is odd) are collinear.

To see whether the points $P_1, \ldots, P_{2i+1}, P_{2i+2}$ form an arc, it checks that P_{2i+2} is on none of the i lines $P_1P_2, P_3P_4, \ldots, P_{2i-1}P_{2i}$, constructs the line $P_{2i+1}P_{2i+2}$ and controls that none of the points $P_1, \ldots, P_{2i}$ is on the new line.

We remark that the system has to memorise only the lines $P_1P_2, \ldots, P_{2i-1}P_{2i}$, of which there are less than $u/2$.

STEP 2. The algorithm determines the plane through the points P_1, P_2, P_3 and P_4 by performing a coordinate transformation. In

addition it could check that the remaining u-4 points lie in
this plane.

STEP 3. In this final step the system determines the
intersection of the plane with the line S. Only if this is the
point X the secret datum is revealed.

4.4 *Higher Dimensions*. In a similar way we can construct
t-threshold schemes for $t \geq 4$ by using Baer subspaces of the finite
projective spaces $P = PG(d,n)$ of dimension d and order n (for
definitions see [2],[3] or [7]).

It is well-known that for $d \geq 3$ every projective space can be
constructed as follows. Let V be the vector space of dimension
d+1 over the finite field with n elements. Then the points of
P are the 1-dimensional subspaces of V, the lines of P are the
2-dimensional subspaces of V, etc, while the hyperplanes of P
are the d-dimensional subspaces of V. In other words, every
projective space of dimension at least 3 is Desarguesian. We
call a subspace of P of the same dimension as P an order
$\sqrt{n}$ a *Baer subspace*.

The construction of (d+2)-threshold schemes is based on
the following lemma.

LEMMA. Let P be the projective space of dimension d and order
n. Then there is precisely one Baer subspace of P through any
d + 2 points of P no d + 1 of which being in a common hyperplane.

Proof. We proceed by induction on d. The projective spaces
of dimension d = 2 are the Desarguesian planes we already dealt
with. So let $d \geq 3$ and assume that the result holds for d-1.
Let $P_1, \ldots, P_{d+2}$ be d + 2 points of P no d + 1 of which lie in
a common hyperplane. Let H be the hyperplane generated by
$P_1, \ldots, P_d$ and define Q to be the point of intersection of the
line $P_{d+1} P_{d+2}$ with H.

It is easy to see that the points $P_1, \ldots, P_d, Q$ are d + 1
points of H having the property that no d of them lie in a
common hyperplane of H. It follows by induction that there is
a unique Baer subspace B* of H through them.

Moreover, it can be checked by direct calculations that any
two points X, Y of P-H with XY∩H in B* lie in exactly one of
the Baer subspaces of P which contain B*. Hence the points
P_{d+1}, P_{d+2} are in a unique Baer subspace of P through B*. This
proves the assertion. □

Using this lemma, (d+2) - threshold schemes can be constructed for every $d \geq 2$ in a similar way as for Desarguesian planes.

REFERENCES

[1] Blakley, G.R., (1979) Safeguarding cryptographic keys. Proc. NCC **48**, AFIPS Press, Montvale, N.J., 317-319.

[2] Beth, T., Jungnickel, D. and Lenz, H., (1987) Design Theory. B.I.-Wissenschaftsverlag, Mannheim - Wien - Zurich, 1985 and Cambridge University Press, Cambridge.

[3] Beutelspacher, A., (1982) Einführung in die endliche Geometrie I. Blockpläne. B.I.-Wissenschaftsverlag, Mannheim - Wien - Zürich.

[4] Chaum, D., (1979) Computer Systems established, maintained and trusted by mutually suspicious groups. Memorandum No. UCB/ERL M79/10, University of California, Berkeley, CA.

[5] Denning, D.E.R., (1983) Cryptography and Data Security. Addison-Wesley, Reading, Mass.

[6] Hughes, D.R. and Piper, F.C., (1973) Projective Planes. Springer-Verlag, Berlin-Heidelberg-New York.

[7] Hughes, D.R. and Piper, F.C., (1985) Design Theory, Cambridge University Press, Cambridge.

[8] Kothari, S.C., (1985) Generalized Linear Threshold Schemes. Advances in Cryptology (Proceedings of CRYPTO 84), Lecture Notes in Computer Science **196**, Springer, 231-241.

[9] Lidl, R. and Niederreiter, H., Finite Fields, Encyclopedia of Mathematics and its Applications, Vol. 20,

[10] Segre, B., (1961) Lectures on modern geometry. Cremonese, Roma.

[11] Shamir, A., (1979) How to share a secret. Comm. ACM Vol. 22(1),612-613.

[12] van der Waerden, B., Einfuhrung in die algebraische Geometrie.

[13] Wilson, R., (1975) An existence theory for pairwise balanced designs III. J. Combinat. Theory(A)**18**, 71-79.

FAST MULTIPLICATIVE INVERSE IN MODULAR ARITHMETIC

J. Gordon
(Cybermation, St. Albans)

OVERVIEW

A common number-theoretic requirement is to determine the multiplicative inverse of one integer modulo another. Public Key Cryptography has given rise to such a need. For example the Rivest, Shamir and Adleman (RSA) Public Key Cryptosystem [1] requires just such a determination every time a new set of keys is generated, and the numbers involved are of the order of magnitude (say) 2^{512} (= 10^{154} approx).

The traditional technique for finding a multiplicative modular inverse is Euclid's Algorithm [2] which in this instance requires many time-consuming multiplications and divisions of very large numbers.

Although this algorithm has been around for thousands of years surprisingly enough it is still possible to make improvements.

Here we introduce a new, very fast and very simple algorithm in which these operations are replaced by left and right shifts.

INTRODUCTION

The problem:

GIVEN: integers X, M with X < M,

FIND: hcf(X,M) and A such that AX = hcf(X,M) mod M

is commonly solved by a procedure which is really an extension of Euclid's Algorithm [2].

The most common case of interest is where hcf(X,M)=1 and we are asked to find A such that AX = 1 mod M.

A typical implementation of Euclid's algorithm consists of two intertwined parts. The first part takes two numbers which are initialised to the values M and to X, and then repeatedly exploits the fact that the HCF of these two numbers is not affected when the larger is replaced by the larger modulo the smaller. Eventually one of these numbers becomes zero and the other becomes the HCF. The second intertwined part of the algorithm is concerned with finding the inverse.

The whole procedure is so simple that it is easier to list (in say PASCAL) then to describe:

```
procedure Euclid(var HCF,INV: integer;X,M:integer);
var U,V,Q,temp:integer;
begin
   HCF:=M; INV:=0; V:=1; U:=X;      {initialise}
   repeat
     Q:=HCF div U;       {* see below}
     temp:=HCF - Q*U;    {* see below}
     HCF:=U;
     U:=temp;
     temp:=INV - Q*V;    {* see below}
     INV:=V;
     V:=temp;
   until U=0;
   if INV<0 then INV:=INV + M;
end;
```

A simple example is the following, (M=152, X=47).

	HCF	Q	INV
	152		0
	47	3	1
	11	4	-3
	3	3	13
	2	1	-42
HCF=	1	2	55 = INV
	0		-152

INV=55, 47x55 = 1 mod 152

In this example, we write down 152 and 47 (M and X) in the left column, and the first quotient Q (=3) in the middle column. We then subtract 3x47 from 152 and write the result (=11) below 47. We iterate till zero appears. The row above this contains the hcf.

FAST MULTIPLICATIVE INVERSES

Meanwhile the right column is seeded with 0 and 1 and we iterate the operation of forming a new row from Q times the row above subtracted from the row before that. The inverse is picked off as shown. If the inverse is negative we add M.

Incidentally, while finding the hcf is intuitive, finding the inverse seems to need more validation (see appendix).

In this algorithm most of the computational effort is expended evaluating the lines:

Q=HCF div U,

temp:=HCF - Q*U,

  and

temp:=INV-Q*V

which involve a full long-division generating both quotient Q and remainder temp, and the multiplications to form the products Q*V and Q*U.

Knuth [2] describes a much faster algorithm due to Stein [3] and improved by Penk [2] which avoids multiplications and divisions, and instead uses shifts. This algorithm is less intuitive and more complicated than the original algorithm and continually updates 9 variables U1, U2, U3, V1, V2, V3, T1, T2 and T3.

It is based on the observations that:

(1) hcf(x,y) = hcf(x/2,y) if x is even
(2) hcf(x,y) = 2hcf(x/2,y/2) if x and y both even
(3) hcf(x,y) = hcf((x-y)/2,y) if x and y both odd

Rather than use Knuth's description we give here a PASCAL implementation for direct comparison with the original algorithm.

(It is not necessary to understand this algorithm to follow the drift of the paper).

```
procedure bineuclid(var HCF,INV:integer:X,M:integer);
var u1,u2,u3,v1,v2,v3,t1,t2,t3,k,u,v:integer;

begin

  k:=0;          {beginning of initilisation}

  while even(x) and even(m) do
  begin
    x:=x div 2;
    m:=m div 2;
    k:=k+1;
  end;

  u1:=1;    u2:=0;      u3:=x;
  v1:=m;    v2:=1-x;    v3:=m;

  if  odd(x) then
  begin
     t1:=0; t2:=-1; t3:=-m;
  end
  else
  begin
     t1:=1; t2=0;    t3:=x;
  end;                         {end of initialise}

  repeat   {main loop}

    while even(t3) do
    begin
      t3:=t3 div 2;
      if even (t1) and even(t2) then
      begin
        t1:=t1 div 2;
        t2:=t2 div 2;
      end
      else
      begin
         t1:=(t1+m) div 2;
         t2:=(t2-x) div 2;
      end
    end;
```

```
    if (t3>=0) then
    begin
        u1:=t1; u2:=t2; u3:=t3;
    end
    else
    begin
        v1:=m-t1; v2:=-x-t2; v3:=-t3;
    end;

    t1:=u1-v1; t2:=u2-v2; t3:=u3-v3;

    if (t1<0) then
    begin
        t1:=t1+m;
        t2:=t2-x;
    end;

until t3=0;  {end of main loop}

HCF:=u3 shl k;  {u3 leftshifted k places}
INV:=u1;
end;
```

Example

We provide the same example (M=152 and X=47) as before to give the flavour of this algorithm.

k=0

U1	U2	U3	V1	V2	V3	T1	T2	T3
1	0	47	152	-46	152	0	-1	-152
1	0	47	152	-46	152	76	-24	-76
1	0	47	152	-46	152	38	-12	-38
1	0	47	152	-46	152	19	-6	-19
1	0	47	133	-41	19	20	-6	28
1	0	47	133	-41	19	10	-3	14
1	0	47	133	-41	19	81	-25	7
81	-25	7	133	-41	19	100	-31	-12
81	-25	7	133	-41	19	126	-39	-6
81	-25	7	133	-41	19	139	-43	-3
81	-25	7	13	-4	3	68	-21	4
81	-25	7	13	-4	3	110	-34	2
81	-25	7	13	-4	3	55	-17	1
55	-17	1	13	-4	3	42	-13	-2
55	-17	1	13	-4	3	97	-30	-1
55	-17	1	55*	-17	1	0	0	0

* INV=55

The extra complexity of this algorithm should be clear from the program listing and from the example.

New Algorithm

The new algorithm retains the speed advantage of the binary algorithm with the simplicity and structure of the original algorithm.

The improvement of the new algorithm results from the observation that Q in the original algorithm does not need to be the quotient HCF div U, but can be any positive integer up to this value.

Our choice for Q is just a power of two so that multiplication is just leftshift. In fact the effective Q we will use in the largest power of two less than or equal to HCF div U, and Q*U can be obtained merely by leftshifting U. At no time do we multiply or divide.

The reason for setting Q to HCF div U in the original algorithm was presumably to minimise the number of passes through the loop.

The alternative choice for Q used here gives only a minor increase in the number of passes but enormously speeds up each pass.

The algorithm to be described has been in constant use for a long period and is reliable and extremely fast.

In the improved algorithm, Q does not explicitly appear, being replaced by the number of leftshifts, which is in effect the (base 2) logarithm of Q.

The improved algorithm is given by:

```
procedure New-Euclid(var HCF,INV:integer;X,M:integer);
var U,V,temp,shifts:integer; EnterLoop:boolean;
begin
    HCF:=M; INV:=0; V:=1; U:=X;  {initialise}

    repeat    {main loop}
        shifts:=-1; EnterLoop:=false;
        if U>HCF then temp:=0 else
        begin
            EnterLoop:=true; temp:=U;
            while (temp<=HCF) do  {see below}
            begin
                shifts:=shifts+1;
                leftshift(temp,1);
            end;
            rightshift(temp,1);
        end;

        temp:=HCF-temp; HCF:=U; U:=temp;
        temp:=INV; INV:=V;

        if EnterLoop then
        begin
            leftshift(V,shifts);
            temp:=temp-V;
        end;
        V:=temp;

    until (U=0) or (U=HCF); {end of main loop}
    if INV<0 then INV:=M+INV;
end;
```

NB: "Leftshift(X,k)" leftshifts X thru k bits, similarly "Rightshift(X,k)"

Example

M=152   X=47

HCF	shifts	INV
152		0
47	1	1
58		-2
47	0	1
11	2	-3
3	1	13
5		-29
3	0	13
2	0	-42
HCF= 1	1	55 =INV
0		-152

INV=55   47x55 = 1 mod 152

In this example each new term is obtained from two rows earlier, sometimes after subtracting a shifted version of the term one row earlier.

In a real application assembly language is used and the "integers" are multi-word structures to handle very large numbers.

The test "if U>HCF then ..." above does not require a subtraction. A comparison of two very large non-negative integers may be economically carried out starting from the most significant end and comparing the first word in which they differ.

Finally for completeness, a short validity proof of the whole algorithm is given in the appendix, and can be ignored if desired. This proof covers both the improved and the original algorithms.

Appendix

Proof of Both Versions of Euclid's Algorithm

Problem:

 Given X, M, with M>X, find A such that

  A.X = 1 mod M

(Or more generally given X, M, with M>X, find A,B such that A.X = B.M + hcf(X,m)).

FAST MULTIPLICATIVE INVERSES

We shall derive and prove both the original Euclid's algorithm and the fast version in the following constructive, inductive proof.

Proof (by induction):

The equations:

(1) $A_0 X = B_0 M + U_0 - k_0 U_1$

(2) $U_2 = U_0 - k_0 U_1$

and

(3) $A_1 X = B_1 M + U_1 - k_1 U_2$

are trivially satisfied with the assignments below.

Assignments (4):

$k_0 = 0$,

and choose k_1 so that $0 < k_1 X < M$,

and choose

$A_0 = 1$, $A_1 = -k_1$,

$B_0 = 0$, $B_1 = 1$,

$U_0 = X$ and

$U_1 = M$.

Now suppose an extended sequence of equations is satisfied up to and including:

(5) $A_{n-2} X = B_{n-2} M + U_{n-2} - k_{n-2} U_{n-1}$

(6) $U_n = U_{n-2} - k_{n-2} U_{n-1}$

and

(7) $A_{n-1} X = B_{n-1} M + U_{n-1} - k_{n-1} U_n$

where

k_{n-2} is chosen so that $0 < k_{n-2}U_{n-1} < U_{n-2}$
and k_{n-1} is chosen so that $0 < k_{n-1}U_n < U_{n-1}$.

NB any value in the range will do for k_{n-1} (and similarly for k_{n-2}), and in particular $k_{n-1} = U_{n-2}$ div U_{n-1} satisfies the conventional Euclid's algorithm while leftshifting U_{n-1} until the result exceeds U_{n-2} and then backing off satisfies the improved algorithm.

Put $U_{n+1} = U_{n-1} - k_{n-1}U_n$ and choose k_n so that

$$k_n U_{n+1} < U_n.$$

By subtracting k_n times (7) from (5) we get:

$$(A_{n-2} - k_n A_{n-1})X$$
$$= (B_{n-2} - k_n B_{n-1})M$$
$$+ (U_{n-2} - k_{n-2}U_{n-1})$$
$$- k_n(U_{n-1} - k_{n-1}U_n)$$

and if we put

$$A_n = A_{n-2} - k_n A_{n-1}$$
$$U_{n+1} = U_n - k_{n-1}U_n$$

and $B_n = B_{n-2} - k_n B_{n-1}$

and recalling that (6)

$$U_n = U_{n-2} - k_{n-2}U_{n-1}$$

we get

$$A_n X = B_n M + U_n - k_n U_{n+1}$$

and thus the sequence may be continued until for some n

$$U_{n+1} = U_{n-1} - k_n U_n = 0.$$

This must inevitably happen since by careful choice of the k's successive values of

$$U_{n+1} = U_{n-1} - k_n U_n$$

are monotonically decreasing.

At this time we have

$$A_n X = B_n M + U_n.$$

Now since if $k_{n-1} > 0$, then $\text{hcf}(U_{n-2}, U_{n-1})$ also divides $U_{n-2} - k_{n-1}U_{n-1}$ it follows that the process we have used, namely starting with

$$U_0 = Xm \text{ and } U_1 = M$$

and forming the sequence

$$U_n = U_{n-2} - kU_{n-1}$$

where k is chosen to make U_n non-negative must terminate with $U_n = \text{hcf}(X, M)$ and $U_{n+1} = 0$. Therefore we have solved the original problem with $A = A_n$, $B = B_n$.

REFERENCES

[1] Rivest, R., Shamir, A. and Adleman, L., (1978) "A Method for Obtaining Digital Signatures and Public Key Cryptosystems", Comms. ACM, 21, 2, 120-126.

[2] Knuth, D.E., (1981) "The Art of Computer Programming - Vol. 2 Seminumerical Algorithms', 2nd Ed., Addison-Wesley, Pages 319, 321, 339 (exercise 35) and 599 (solution).

[3] Stein, J., (1967) *J. Comp. Phys*, **1**, 397-405 (referred to in [2] above).

STANDARDS FOR DATA SECURITY

W.L. Price
(National Physical Laboratory, Teddington)

ABSTRACT

Developments over the last 13 years in the field of data security standards are reviewed, with particular reference to recent events. The standards fall naturally into several classes - encipherment algorithms, modes of use for encipherment algorithms, enhancement of communication protocols, message authentication and key management. There is a strong body of opinion that considers that algorithms should not be the subject of standardisation, but there is general agreement that the other classes are essential for the proper conduct of secure communication and transaction processing systems.

1. INTRODUCTION

In this paper we shall review the state of development of standards for data security, paying particular attention to encipherment and its applications, especially those related to data communication, including electronic funds transfer. Progress has been made in this respect during the last 13 years, though there have been some recent significant changes in policy regarding standards for data encipherment.

We meet standards in many ways every day of our lives; they specify the screw threads that hold together equipment, they specify the sizes of the clothes we wear, they determine criteria for transport safety, etc., etc. What is required of a standard in general is threefold - to specify what a product does, how well it should do it and to what extent it is expected to be interoperable with other related products .

The need for standards for data security arises from a desire to establish common methods and protocols for data protection, thus making possible the secure exchange of messages and files between systems that may possibly belong to totally different organisations. Development of the concept of Open Systems Interconnection (OSI) [1] by the International Standards Organisation (ISO) is due to the perceived need for standards which will allow convenient connection of diverse systems without having to go to the lengths of developing a special gateway between every pair of different systems; this concept facilitates information exchange and finds expression in the development of a framework for communication protocols. Thus we see that facilities for freer exchange of information are becoming available. Within these facilities there is an undoubted need for provision of security and for the means of ensuring that security functions are compatible between different systems. Greatest awareness of the need for security has been evident in the banking community. We shall see that some security standards have been developed specifically by representatives of the banking world.

Traditionally, message protection has been considered to be in the province of military and diplomatic agencies where the relevant techniques are not public knowledge as a matter of policy; recently it has been recognised that the 'civil' and commercial sectors need to provide protection against interference with their communications and data processing activities. This paper will concern itself exclusively with the civil and commercial domains.

Interference with data communication can be categorised into two main classes - disclosure and unauthorised alteration of data; customary terms for the protective qualities needed to combat these threats are respectively 'privacy' and 'integrity'. Privacy can be achieved by encipherment of data, whilst integrity can be achieved by application of encipherment techniques. It is not usually possible to prevent unauthorised alteration of data, but measures can be provided which will detect unauthorised alteration and permit the required remedial action to be taken.

2. STANDARDISATION OF ENCIPHERMENT ALGORITHMS

The best known algorithm for symmetric encipherment in the public domain is undoubtedly the Data Encryption Standard (DES); this began life in the mid-1970's as a US Federal Information Processing Standard [2] and has later been adopted as a US National Standard [3]. Within ISO, TC97/SC20 has been preparing to publish the DES as an international standard. However, ISO Council recently took a decision not to proceed with publication of this standard. The reasons for this decision

are concerned with the degree of over-dependence on the DES that
was becoming apparent. The algorithm has been used extremely
widely, especially in the banking community, leading to the
creation of a very attractive target for any criminal cryptanalyst.
A break of DES security would have cataclysmic results for
international and domestic banking. No-one has yet given any
indication that the DES has been broken and the US government has
recently indicated a change of mind concerning it. Under the
US government Commercial COMSEC Endorsement Program (CCEP)
[4] it was the intention to discontinue endorsement of new DES
equipment after 1988; new algorithms, not published and available
only within the US, would replace it. However, the US banks have
indicated that they need the DES algorithm, if only for their
international business and the government has now said that
equipment which includes the algorithm will be endorsed for the
purposes of the banks beyond 1988. For federal and internal
commercial applications, the new algorithms mentioned above are
expected to supplant the DES.

Even more recently TC97 is being advised to discontinue all
work on standards for encipherment algorithms. This affects
preparations for publication of a standard for the RSA public
key cryptosystem, an algorithm that is being increasingly widely
used by the banks, especially for management of symmetric keys
and for digital signatures, applications for which it is well
suited.

To replace specific standards for data encipherment, ISO is
likely to create a register of encipherment algorithms. It is
hoped that a number of alternative algorithms will be presented
on this, some published, some unpublished. Published algorithms
will carry a specific reference to a base document which gives
a definition. Unpublished algorithms will be presented simply
by a statement of their 'external appearance', i.e. block size,
key domain, available implementations, speeds of operation.
etc. By offering a range of available algorithms, it is
expected that over-dependence on one algorithm will be
discouraged. For compatibility there must then be agreement
between communicating parties on the choice of algorithm.

It seems now that public key algorithms will also appear on
the register. At present only the RSA algorithm is being used
in practical systems, but it is possible that other candidate
algorithms of this type will appear.

3. STANDARDS FOR MODES OF OPERATION

The disquiet that has affected the work on preparation of
standards for data encipherment has not influenced work on the
related subject of modes of operation to the same extent.

Modes of operation are required in order to make the application of block cipher algorithms secure, otherwise an intruder could interfere with a block stream without necessarily being detected. Modes of operation work by making successive units of cipher text dependent on the preceding text, thereby masking any structure in the cipher text and preventing undetected interference in the form of re-orderings, replications, deletions, etc.

Four modes of operation are specified for the DES, being defined in US federal and national standards [5,6]. From these sources ISO has developed a standard for 64-bit block cipher modes of operation. The ISO document is therefore not specific to the DES and will accommodate any 64-bit block cipher. This may be followed later by an even more general document relating to n-bit block ciphers.

Whether modes of operation will be required for public key cryptosystems is not yet certain. Since the block size of the RSA algorithm is likely to be much larger than that of the DES, much more information can be accommodated in one block and therefore the need for ensuring inter-block dependence in a stream of blocks may not be as great. On the other hand, for very long messages, some means must be found for linking adjacent blocks in a secure manner. Work is proceeding on this subject.

4. STANDARDS FOR SECURE COMMUNICATION

The massive international effort that is being put into development of standards in the Open Systems Interconnection context can only be of the greatest benefit to organisations making use of data communication. System compatibility can be ensured by reliance on the standards already published and to be published. OSI provides a framework in which individual communication protocols can be defined and in which compatibility between associated protocols can be maintained. The very 'open-ness' of the concept demands particular attention to security.

OSI is essentially an architecture into which communication protocols can be fitted, at all levels from the physical layer (defining the characteristics of the communications medium) to the application layer (serving the user process). In all, seven layers have been defined and security measures could potentially be fitted into every one of them. To install security measures in every layer would be very wasteful of resource, both in terms of capital and of running costs; indeed, it is almost certainly not necessary, from the point of view of achieving adequate security, to locate security functions at all layers.

In order to provide guidance to users as to the preferred locations for security functions, an addendum to the OSI definition document has been in preparation. This addendum has been issued as a Draft Proposal and been voted upon once; at the time of writing a second Draft Proposal has been prepared, taking into account the suggestions made to ISO by the national member bodies, and this will be submitted to a further vote in due course. Since the OSI concept is one of an architectural framework, the publication of the security addendum will not enable users directly to provide protocol security enhancements immediately; however, the appearance of the addendum will undoubtedly encourage work to proceed on specific protocol security enhancements and some of this work is already in hand.

Standards for secure protocols exist in the US for OSI layers 1 and 2 (physical and link). Federal Telecommunications Standard 1026 [7] gives a compact definition of encipherment implementation at the physical layer. An US national standard [8] defines implementations at the physical and link layers.

5. SECURITY-RELATED STANDARDS IN THE BANKING DOMAIN

We have already indicated our view that there is a high level of awareness of the requirement for data security in the operations carried out by and on behalf of banks. Modern banking depends very heavily on various forms of electronic funds transfer, ranging from the CHAPS system in the City of London to automatic teller machine networks and the newly emerging point of sale operations. The security of these systems and operations is of vital concern to the various banks.

The first security-related standards for banking came from the American National Standards Institute (ANSI) and related respectively to management of personal identification numbers (PINs) [9] and to message authentication [10]; the latter standard has been re-issued twice since initial publication, the latest version being specific to wholesale banking (transactions directly between banks). More recently we have a very comprehensive standard [11] describing techniques for the management of keys in the wholesale financial context. Very recently a standard for message authentication in the retail context has been issued [12] and a draft standard for key management in the retail context is at an advanced stage.

At ISO the responsible technical committee is TC68 and several draft standards are in progress of development. Draft International Standard (DIS) 8370 relates to the techniques of message authentication, drawing heavily on the

ANSI standards for this purpose. DIS 8371 specifies three possible algorithms that may be used for message authentication and DIS 8372 describes key management.

Related work, though not specifically on a security topic, is being carried out in ISO TC97/SC17 on identity tokens. This relates to standards for smart cards, which are being widely promoted as transaction tokens, and covers topics including physical and electrical requirements, together with the necessary protocol definitions needed for communication with the card. Work is also going on within TC68 to define some of the banking procedures that will relate to the smart card.

6. STANDARDS FOR PHYSICAL SECURITY

It is a fundamental principle of the design of secure systems that encipherment and similar measures are worse than useless unless they are backed up by adequate physical security. Thus it is futile to encipher messages and not to prevent disclosure of the encipherment keys. Security measures installed in these circumstances are worse than useless because they create a false impression of a secure system.

It is often necessary to provide a physically secure environment within which sensitive parameters can safely be stored. Recommendations for the characteristics of such an environment can be found in the US Federal Telecommunications Standard 1027 [13], which is concerned with general security requirements for equipment using the DES; these requirements include methods of protecting the device against various intrusions and interferences and also of handling keys in a secure manner.

A document giving recommendations for physical security of equipment is expected to be published by the British Standards Institution in due course. This is based on a text developed by British Telecom from the US federal standard mentioned above with substantial additional material.

7. WHAT NEXT?

Having spent some time on developing standards for data encipherment that are not, after all, to be published, the international community working on standards in this area will turn its energies to making certain that the register of encipherment algorithms is a success. There is no doubt that the banks are calling for definitive statements of security procedures and recommendations of preferred methods.

The level of concern and awareness in the commercial world in general seems to be at a much lower level than that of the banks. Either commerce in general does not have any sensitive traffic or data storage that needs protection, or else this sector considers that adequate security measures have already been taken. With technology of increasing sophistication becoming available to the criminal world, this view can be considered dangerous.

Much remains to be done to ensure that the right standards are produced to describe the approved ways in which encipherment can be applied in general and, in particular, in communication protocols. Protection of data in storage has not yet received much attention in the standards field, but this is an important sector which must not be ignored.

REFERENCES

[1] International Standards Organisation. (1984) Information Processing Systems, Open Systems Interconnection, Basic Reference Model. International Standard 7498.

[2] National Bureau of Standards. (1977) Data Encryption Standard. Federal Information Processing Standard Publication 46.

[3] American National Standards Institute. (1981) Data Encryption Algorithm. American National Standard X3.92.

[4] Newman, D.B. and Pickholtz, R.L., (1986) Cryptography in the private sector. IEEE Communications Magazine, 24, 8, pp. 7-10.

[5] National Bureau of Standards. (1980) DES Modes of Operation. Federal Information Processing Standard Publication 81.

[6] American National Standards Institute. (1983) Modes of Operation for the Data Encryption Algorithm. American National Standard X3.106.

[7] Federal Telecommunications Standards Committee. (1983) Telecommunications: Interoperability and Security Requirements for the Use of the Data Encryption Standard in the Physical Layer of Data Communications. Federal Telecommunications Standard 1026.

[8] American National Standards Institute. (1983) Information Systems - Data Link Encryption. American National Standard X3.105.

[9] American National Standards Institute. (1982) Personal Identification Number (PIN) Management and Security. American National Standard X9.8.

[10] American National Standards Institute. (1984) Financial Institute Message Authentication (Wholesale). American National Standard X9.9, (revised).

[11] American National Standards Institute. (1985) Financial Institution Key Management (Wholesale). American National Standard X9.17.

[12] American National Standards Institute. (1986) Financial Institution Message Authentication (Retail). American National Standard X9.19.

[13] Federal Telecommunications Standards Committee. (1982) Telecommunications: General Security Requirements for Equipment Using the Data Encryption Standard. Federal Telecommunications Standard 1027.

CORRELATION ANALYSIS OF CASCADED SEQUENCES

D. Gollmann
(University of Karlsruhe)

ABSTRACT

We examine the autocorrelation function of cascaded sequences and show that cascaded sequences fulfil a modified version of Golomb's postulates. Furthermore we examine the cross correlation between internal signals and the output of cascades of clock controlled shift registers.

1. INTRODUCTION

Clock controlled shift registers have received some attention in cryptography as they have reasonably long periods and high linear complexity. Most papers on this subject deal with circuits built from two registers where the output of the first register controls the clock of the second. It is also quite common to use registers with primitive feedback polynomials (see [7], [10], [11]). Results have also been reported for cascades of clock controlled shift registers (see [2], [6]). We are in particular interested in cascades of cyclic shift registers where all registers are of the same length. The properties of these pseudo random generators do not depend on properties of the individual registers but can be derived from the structure of the cascade.

Correlation analysis has two applications in the examination of cascaded sequences. Autocorrelation is used in Golomb's definition of pseudo random sequences [5]. It thus can be adopted as a quality measure for pseudo random sequences. Cross correlation attacks have been successfully applied on some classes of pseudo random generators by Siegenthaler [9]. It might be possible that the initial state of some register in the cascade has sufficient influence on the overall behaviour so that it might be inferred from the output. It is, however, not possible to apply Siegenthaler's attack directly as the output of our cascade is the XOR of the outputs of the individual registers.

2. CASCADES OF CLOCK CONTROLLED SHIFT REGISTERS

A clock controlled shift register is a feedback shift register with an input to its clock. Input 1 switches the register to its next state, input 0 leaves it unchanged. We add this clock input to the output of the register (modulo 2) to obtain the input to the next register in a cascade or the output respectively. All the clock inputs are computed before stepping the registers. Fig. 1 gives an example of such a cascade.

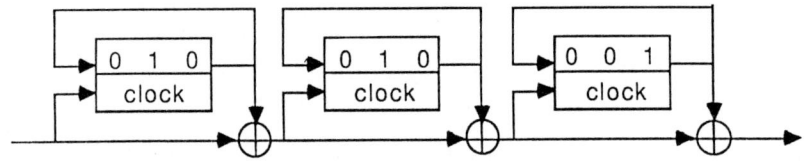

Fig. 1 A cascade of clock controlled shift registers

When we apply the input 1111 to the cascade in Fig. 1 we get the following sequence of states

```
      0 1 0     0 1 0     0 0 1
      0 0 1     0 0 1     1 0 0
      1 0 0     0 0 1     0 1 0
      0 1 0     1 0 0     0 1 0
```

Note that the third register can step although the second does not. We restrict ourselves to cascades of cyclic registers, all registers shall be of the same length p, $p \geq 3$ prime. Let n be the number of registers. No register shall contain only 0's or only 1's. The input to the cascades is the sequence 1 1 1 ... . The following properties hold for such cascades.

Property 1: The output sequence has period p^n [2].

Property 2: The linear complexity of the output sequence is not less than $d(p^n-1)/(p-1)$ where d is the degree of an irreducible factor of the cyclotomic polynomial $1+x+x^2+\ldots+x^{p-1}$. When this polynomial is irreducible we get the lower bound p^n-1. p^n is the trivial upper bound of the linear complexity [3].

Property 3: $\lim_{n\to\infty} \text{prob}_n(w) = 1/2^{|w|}$ (2.1)

for all binary strings w. $\text{prob}_n(w)$ is the probability of string w in the output of a given cascade of length n. The rate of convergence depends on the length of w [2].

3. AUTOCORRELATION

In this paper we will consider sequences of cascades of clock controlled shift registers. Such a sequence $(\text{CASC}_n)_{n=1}^\infty$ will be obtained as follows. CASC_1 consists of a single register with a fixed initial state. If CASC_n has already been constructed we get CASC_{n+1} by appending another register to CASC_n and fixing the initial state of that register. Let $a_n(i)$ denote the output of CASC_n at time i. $A_n(\tau)$ is the autocorrelation function of the p^n-periodic sequence $(a_n(i))_{i=1}^\infty$.
Define $\alpha_n(i) := (-1)^{a_n(\tau)}$.

To compute $A_n(\tau)$ we relate the time instances i to strings w. A pair $(a_n(i), a_n(i+\tau))$ corresponds uniquely to the string $a_n(i)a_n(i+1)\ldots a_n(i+\tau)$ of length $\tau+1$. Thus we get for a given τ

$$A_n(\tau) = (1/p^n) \sum_{i=1}^{p^n} \alpha_n(i)(i+\tau) = \qquad (3.1)$$

$$= \sum_{w, |w|=\tau-1} \text{prob}_n(0w0) - \text{prob}_n(0w1) + \text{prob}_n(1w1) - \text{prob}_n(1w0)$$

and further

$$|A_n(\tau)| \le \sum_{w, |w|=\tau-1} |\text{prob}_n(0w0) - 2^{-\tau-1}| + |2^{-\tau-1} - \text{prob}_n(0w1)| + |\text{prob}_n(1w1) - 2^{-\tau-1}| + |2^{-\tau-1} - \text{prob}_n(1w0)|$$

Applying (2.1) we conclude the proof of

Theorem 1

$$\lim_{n\to\infty} |A_n(\tau)| = 0 \quad \text{for all } \tau > 0 \qquad (3.2)$$

As we make use of (2.1) this proof does not give uniform convergence.

4. MODIFYING GOLOMB'S POSTULATES

Golomb's criterion for the autocorrelation function $A(\tau)$ of a periodic pseudo random sequence is

$$A(\tau) = \begin{cases} 1 & \tau \equiv 0 \text{(modulo period)} \\ c & \text{else} \end{cases} \quad (4.1)$$

(see [5]). This property does not hold in general for cascades of clock controlled shift registers. However, recent results suggest that the above criterion is too strict.

Rueppel has investigated the expected linear complexity of periodic sequences. (2^n-1)-periodic sequences for Mersenne primes n have expected linear complexity $2^n - 5/2 + 1/2^{n-1}$ [8], [4], whereas Bromfield has established an upper bound less than 2^{n-1} for the linear complexity of balanced sequences fulfilling the above criterion [1].

Theorem 1 indicates a possible modification of the autocorrelation criterion. Instead of considering a single pseudo random sequence one could start from a sequence of generators (or a sequence of classes of generators) and instead of demanding strict equality in (4.1) one could demand convergence towards the ideal value. We can extend this modification also to Golomb's

Postulate 1: The number of 1 s and the number of 0 s in a period of the sequence differ at most by 1.

and

Postulate 2: In every period $1/2^i$ of the runs have length i, as long as there are at least two runs of length i. For each of these lengths there is an equal number of gaps (0-runs) and blocks (1-runs).

and replace them by

Postulate 1* $\lim_{n \to \infty} \text{prob}_n(0) = \lim_{n \to \infty} \text{prob}_n(1) = 1/2$ (4.2)

and

Postulate 2* $\lim_{n\to\infty} \text{runs}_n(i)/\text{runs}_n = 1/2^i$, (4.3)

$$\lim_{n\to\infty} \text{gaps}_n(i)/\text{blocks}_n(i) = 1$$

Here runs_n, $\text{runs}_n(i)$, $\text{gaps}_n(i)$, $\text{blocks}_n(i)$ count the number of runs, runs of length i, gaps of length i, and blocks of length i respectively. These definitions were proposed by Fabris in a private communication.

Theorem 2: Postulate 1* and Postulate 2* are fulfilled by the sequence (CASC_n).

Proof: (4.1) follows immediately from (2.1).
To prove (4.2) we first show

$$\lim_{n\to\infty} \text{runs}_n/p^n = 1/2. \qquad (4.4)$$

The number of runs is obviously equal to the frequency of the pairs 01 and 10 in the output. We get

$$\lim_{n\to\infty} \text{runs}_n/p^n = \lim_{n\to\infty}(\text{prob}_n(01)+\text{prob}_n(10))=1/2$$

This leads to

$$\lim_{n\to\infty} \text{gaps}_n(i)/\text{runs}_n(i) = \lim_{n\to\infty}(\text{gaps}_n(i)/p^n)/(\text{runs}_n(i)/p^n) =$$

$$2 \cdot \lim_{n\to\infty} \text{prob}_n(10^i1) = 1/2^{i+1} \qquad (4.5)$$

In the same way we get

$$\lim_{n\to\infty} \text{blocks}_n(i)/\text{runs}_n(i) = 1/2^{i+1} \qquad (4.6)$$

and we combine these two results to conclude the proof.

5. CROSS CORRELATION

We again consider the sequence (CASC_n) of the cascades of clock controlled shift registers. $a_n(i)$ and $\alpha_n(i)$ are defined as before, $b_{n,k}(i)$ shall denote the sum of the outputs of the last k registers of $CASC_n$, thus we have

$$a_n(i) = a_k(i) \oplus b_{n,n-k}(i). \tag{5.1}$$

We define $\beta_{n,k}(i) := (-1)^{b_{n,k}(\tau)}$. $C_{k,n}(\tau)$ is the cross correlation function between $(a_k(i))_{i=1}^{\infty}$ and $(a_n(i))_{i=1}^{\infty}$. $a_k(i)$ is an internal signal in $CASC_n$. We get

$$C_{k,n}(\tau) = 1/p^n \sum_{i=1}^{p^n} a_n(i) \, a_k(i+\tau) = \tag{5.2}$$

$$1/p^n \sum_{i=1}^{p^k} \sum_{j=0}^{p^{n-k}-1} a_k(i+jp^k) \beta_{n,n-k}(i+jp^k) a_k(i+\tau+jp^k) =$$

$$1/p^n \sum_{i=1}^{p^k} a_k(i) a_k(i+\tau) \sum_{j=0}^{p^{n-k}-1} \beta_{n,n-k}(i+jp^k)$$

Because of Property 1, $\beta_{n,n-k}(i+jp^k)$ runs through all possible states of the last n-k registers. Thus

$$B_{n,n-k} := \sum_{j=1}^{p^{n-k}} \beta_{n,n-k}(i+jp^k) \tag{5.3}$$

is independent of i.

Lemma 1: $|B_{n,k}| \leq (p-2)^k$ for all $n \geq 1$, $1 \leq k \leq n$.

Proof: $|B_{n,k}| = ||\{j | b_{n,k}(jp^{n-k}) = 0\}| - |\{j | b_{n,k}(jp^{n-k}) = 1\}||$

$$\tag{5.4}$$

We proceed by induction on k.
$B_{n,1} \leq (p-2)$ as there is at least one 1 and one 0 in the last register.
Assume the proposition has been shown for some k. Let z_k denote the number of 0 s in $(b_{n,k}(jp^{n-k}))$, $j=1,\ldots,p^k$, and z the number of 0 s in register n-k.

From $|B_{n,k}| = |p^k - 2z_k|$ we can derive

$$|B_{n,k+1}| = |(p^k - z_k)(p-z) + z_k z - (p^k - z_k)z - z_k(p-z)| =$$
$$= |(p^k - 2z_k)(p-z) - (p^k - 2z_k)z| =$$
$$= |(p^k - 2z_k)(p-2z)| = (p-2z)|B_{n,k}| \leq (p-2)^{k+1}$$

(5.5)

Thereby we get

Theorem 3: $|C_{k,n}(\tau)| \leq (p-2)^{n-k}/p^n | \sum_{i=1}^{p^k} \alpha_k(i) \alpha_k(i+\tau)| =$

$$= ((p-2)/p))^{n-k} |A_k(\tau)|$$

(5.6)

Thus we have for all k

Corollary 1: $\lim_{n \to \infty} C_{k,n}(\tau) = 0$ for all $\tau > 0$. (5.7)

Convergence is uniform in τ.
To give two examples of possible correlation attacks we examine attacks on the first and on the last register of a cascade. An attack on the first register could proceed as follows. The initial state of the first register is fixed and the cross correlation between its output and the output of the cascade is computed. If the correct initial state has been selected this is the cross correlation $C_{1,n}$ as given above. Otherwise we have to replace $A_k(\tau)$ in Theorem 3 by the cross correlation between the output of the selected initial state and the output of the correct initial state. In both cases the absolute values of the cross correlation functions are bounded by $((p-2)/p))^{n-1}$. Thus the cryptographer is in a position to control the feasibility of a cross correlation attack by choosing the length of the cascade. In an attack on the last register the initial state of this register will be fixed. If we assume that the input to the last register is a pseudo random sequence there is no way of distinguishing the correct initial state. As clock controlled shift registers are invertible we can construct for a given initial state and a given output sequence an input sequence that generates this output. Therefore one has to make use of certain non-random properties in the input to the last register. However, in Theorem 1 and Theorem 2 we have shown that cascaded sequences "converge" towards perfect pseudo random sequences.

5. CONCLUSION

The output of a given cascade of clock controlled shift registers does not fulfil Golomb's postulates. However, a modified version of these postulates holds for sequences of cascade connections. Finally we can show that the cross correlation between the output of a cascade and the output of its first k registers can be forced arbitrarily close to zero by increasing the length of the cascade.

REFERENCES

[1] Bromfield, A.J., (1986) "Some Properties of Binary Codes", Ph.D.Thesis, Westfield College, University of London.

[2] Gollmann, D., (1985) Pseudo Random Properties of Cascade Connections of Clock Controlled Shift Registers, Springer Lecture Notes in Computer Science, 209, 93-98.

[3] Gollmann, D., (1985) Linear Recursion of Cascaded Sequences, Contributions to General Algebra 3, 173-179 Hölder-Pichler-Tempsky & Teubner, Vienna.

[4] Gollmann, D., (1986) Linear Complexity of Sequences with period p^n, (Abstract), Eurocrypt 86, Technical University of Linköping.

[5] Golomb, S.W., (1967) "Shift Register Sequences", Holden-Day, San Francisco.

[6] Kjeldsen, K., Andresen, E., (1980) Some Randomness Properties of Cascaded Sequences, IEEE Trans. Inf. Theory, 26, 227-232.

[7] Nyffeler, P., (1975) "Binäre Automaten und ihre linearen Rekursionen", Thesis, Universität Bern.

[8] Rueppel, R.A., (1984) "New Approaches to Stream Ciphers", Thesis, ETH Zürich.

[9] Siegenthaler, T., (1985) Decrypting a Class of Stream Ciphers Using Ciphertext Only, IEEE Trans. Comp. 34, 81-85.

[10] Smeets, B.J.M., (1986) A Note on Sequences Generated by Clock Controlled Shift Registers, Springer Lecture Notes in Computer Science, 219, 142-148.

[11] Smeets, B.J.M., (1985) On the Autocorrelation Function of Some Sequences Generated by Clock Controlled Shift Registers, Proc. of the Joint Swedish-Soviet International Workshop on Information Theory, publ. by the Technical Universities of Linköping and Lund.

DEAN B. ELLIS LIBRARY
ARKANSAS STATE UNIVERSITY